Greek Sculpture

Also from Westphalia Press

westphaliapress.org

Select Passages from Ancient Writers Illustrative of the History of Greek Sculpture

---

With a Translation and Notes by H. Stuart Jones, M.A.

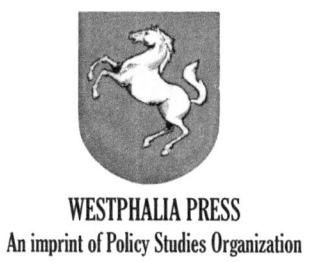

WESTPHALIA PRESS
An imprint of Policy Studies Organization

Westphalia Press
An imprint of Policy Studies Organization
1527 New Hampshire Ave., NW
Washington, D.C. 20036
info@ipsonet.org

ISBN-13: 978-1-63391-696-8
ISBN-10: 1-63391-696-0

Cover design by Jeffrey Barnes:
jbarnesbook.design

Daniel Gutierrez-Sandoval, Executive Director
PSO and Westphalia Press

Updated material and comments on this edition
can be found at the Westphalia Press website:
www.westphaliapress.org

GREEK SCULPTURE

SELECT

PASSAGES FROM ANCIENT WRITERS

ILLUSTRATIVE OF THE HISTORY OF

GREEK SCULPTURE

EDITED

WITH A TRANSLATION AND NOTES

BY

H. STUART JONES, M.A.

FELLOW OF TRINITY COLLEGE, OXFORD; LATE CRAVEN UNIVERSITY FELLOW
FORMERLY STUDENT OF THE BRITISH SCHOOL AT ATHENS

London
MACMILLAN AND CO.
AND NEW YORK
1895

Oxford

HORACE HART, PRINTER TO THE UNIVERSITY

TO

PROFESSOR PERCY GARDNER

PREFACE

THE History of Greek Sculpture, 600–323 B.C., forms one of the subjects of examination in the classical school at Oxford. The only collection of ancient authorities on this subject available for study is that of Overbeck (*Die antiken Schrift-quellen zur Geschichte der bildenden Künste bei den Griechen*, Leipzig, 1868). Since this work aims at completeness, it contains some thousands of passages which are not necessary for such study of Greek sculpture as is required of University students, while, on the other hand, it provides neither translation nor commentary. I have, therefore, at the request of Professor Gardner, selected such passages as appeared from their intrinsic interest or difficulty to require special study by those offering the subject for examination, adding some few to which attention has been called since the publication of Overbeck's work. As a rule, the inscriptions of artists (which may be read in Löwy's *In-schriften griechischer Bildhauer*) have not been included, except in a few cases where the matter or form of the inscription seemed to make this desirable; to those which are merely signatures reference is made in the discussions of date which follow each heading where necessary. In order to save space many passages have been omitted in which the text presents no difficulty of translation and has no descriptive interest: a list of the works mentioned in such passages is appended to the account of each sculptor.

Since this book is not intended to fill the place of systematic histories of sculpture, such as those of Overbeck and Collignon, notes are not given where a reference to those works can be supplied, and references to periodical and current literature are in general not given except where the book or article quoted has appeared within the last two years, or where it seems worthy of consultation in addition to the text-books. It has not been thought necessary to devote much space to questions of textual criticism; the passages are quoted from the standard texts of each author with but few divergences.

The author desires to express his sincere thanks to Professor Gardner for his constant help and encouragement, and for the thorough revision to which the proof-sheets were submitted by him as they issued from the press.

CONTENTS

PART I.

THE BEGINNINGS OF GREEK SCULPTURE.

Nos. 1–41.

PART II.

ARCHAIC AND TRANSITIONAL SCULPTURE.

Nos. 42-95.

PART III.

THE AGE OF PHEIDIAS AND POLYKLEITOS.

Nos. 96–181.

PART IV.

SCULPTURE IN THE FOURTH CENTURY.

Nos. 182–260.

APPENDIX I.

THE SCHOOLS OF PERGAMON AND RHODES.

Nos. 261–267.

APPENDIX II.

DAMOPHON OF MESSENE.

Nos. 268–271   235

INTRODUCTION

§ 1. HISTORICAL SKETCH.

THE earliest works of Greek literature dealing with the subject of Sculpture were the practical treatises of artists whose aim was to lay down a canon of proportions applicable to the human figure. Of these the first was the 'Canon' of POLYKLEITOS (mentioned by Galen, No. 163), which dates from the latter half of the fifth century, and took the form of a commentary on the 'doryphoros' of the same master. If we may judge by the only quotation preserved (v. No. 163 note), it attempted a mathematical demonstration of the proportions which produce beauty in the human frame. Polykleitos had many followers in the branch of literature which he founded[1], amongst whom we may select for remark EUPHRANOR (No. 230), and MENAICHMOS, an artist briefly referred to by Plin. *N. H.* xxxiv. 80 in the words ' Menaechmi uitulus genu premitur replicata ceruice ; ipse Menaechmus scripsit de sua arte.' His date cannot be fixed with certainty, but he may probably be assigned to the fourth century B. C.

The history and criticism of sculpture became objects of a new interest in the days of the early Peripatetics and their many-sided literary activity. ARISTOTLE himself

---

[1] Vitruu. VII. *Praef.* 14, gives a list of writers who 'praecepta symmetriarum conscripserunt.'

is the author of some interesting criticisms of painting[1],
and in *Eth.* vi. 1141 *a*, 10, mentions Pheidias and Polykleitos as the masters of their respective crafts—sculpture
in marble in the first case, bronze-casting in the second.
His successors in the Peripatetic school seem to have
collected biographical material for the history of sculpture. Quasi-genealogical tables showing the succession
in schools of philosophy were drawn up, and it would
seem that artistic pedigrees were traced in the same
manner. It is probable that DURIS of Samos, a pupil
of Theophrastos, was among the first to take up these
studies; we find him quoted by Pliny as the authority
for an anecdote told of Lysippos. The collection of
anecdotes and ἀποφθέγματα was a favourite occupation
with the Peripatetics; it has left marked traces in the
conventional history of Painting as seen in Pliny's thirty-
fifth book. No doubt, too, the numerous writers περὶ
εὑρημάτων to whom this period of learned activity gave
birth, contributed somewhat to the history of Art.

The most important works, however, for our purpose
were still those of men who were themselves sculptors.
XENOKRATES, a member of the school of Lysippos
(v. Part IV, § 2 *ad fin.*), is mentioned by Pliny as an
authority both on sculpture and painting, and may with
much probability be identified with the artist of the
same name known to us from inscriptions found at
Oropos and Elateia (Löwy 135 *a b c*). If this be correct,
he was an Athenian by birth, the son of Ergophilos; his
'floruit' must be placed about the middle of the third
century B.C. Pliny couples with his name that of
ANTIGONOS, one of the sculptors employed by Attalos I
of Pergamon on the memorials of his victories over the

---

[1] *Poet.* 1448 *a*, 5, 1450 *a*, 26; *Pol.* v (viii). 1340 *a*, 35.

Gauls (No. 261). From a notice relating to the Nemesis of Agorakritos at Rhamnus (No. 137 note) we learn that he was a native of Karystos; and Wilamowitz therefore identifies him with Antigonos of Karystos, the author of lives of the philosophers and of a παραδόξων συναγωγή. We may with much probability attribute to one or other of these writers the series of criticisms tabulated in § 2, which clearly proceed from an admirer of Lysippos, and take no account of early sculpture. Beside criticism of style, however, these writers certainly gave a statistical account of the works of the great artists; they wrote of painting as well as of sculpture, and Diogenes Laertios (vii. 188) speaks of a picture whose existence is unknown to Xenokrates and *even* to Antigonos.

The work of Antigonos called forth a reply from the pen of POLEMON of Ilion, a widely-travelled man, who wrote numerous guide-books to the places which he visited. He flourished in the reign of Ptolemy Epiphanes (204–181 B.C.), and is probably to be identified with the person of the same name and origin who obtained προξενία from the Delphians in 176 B.C. (Dittenberger, *Syll.* 198). The title of one of his works is given as τὰ πρὸς 'Αδαῖον καὶ 'Αντίγονον, the first named author being a Mitylenaean by birth, who wrote περὶ ἀγαλματοποιῶν. We seem to hear an echo of the controversy in the passage of Zenobius (*O. S.* 836) referred to above, where the statement of Antigonos as to the inscription on the Nemesis of Rhamnus is met by a counter argument introduced by the words οὐ θαυμαστὸν δέ[1]. To each of the great artistic centres of Greece—Olympia[2], Delphi,

---

[1] For other possible cases cf. Urlichs, *Ueber griechische Kunst-schriftsteller*, pp. 34 ff.

[2] This is assumed by Preller, who assigns Fr. 21-23 to the work.

the Athenian Akropolis—Polemon devoted a special
work. He busied himself with the collection of inscriptions bearing on the subjects of his study, and
hence earned the sobriquet of ὁ στηλοκόπας. Other
περιηγηταί were HELIODOROS of Athens, whose work
de Atheniensium anathematis is mentioned by Pliny, and
HEGESANDROS of Delphi, from whom the notice preserved
in No. 31 is quoted by Athenaios. ALKETAS also wrote
an account of the offerings at Delphi (v. No. 196 note).

The next phenomenon of importance in the history of
art-criticism is that of the comparative method employed
by the literary critics. It would seem that especially
at Pergamon, where the royal house accumulated art-
treasures of all periods—it became the fashion to draw
up chronological tables of the great authors, to each of
whom a brief criticism—often a catchword—was assigned;
and we find unmistakable traces of an arrangement of
sculptors and painters in parallel series [1]. Robert has
endeavoured to show that the Canon of ten sculptors
given by Quintilian (§ 4) was drawn up at Pergamon as
the counterpart of the famous Canon of the Ten Orators,
but it seems clear that that Canon is itself of later origin
than was formerly supposed [2], and that we are only
justified in attributing to the Pergamenes the formation
of a list or Canon of sculptors of indefinite number
arranged chronologically, with a fixed scale of apprecia-
tions. The great importance of their work lies in the fact
rightly pointed out by Robert, that they put an end to

---

[1] See § 4, Nos. 87, 125, and the collection of passages in Brzoska,
De Canone decem oratorum, pp. 81 ff.

[2] See the authors quoted by Susemihl, Geschichte der griechischen
Litteratur in der Alexandrinerzeit, ii. 485, note 110, and 675,
additional note on chap. xx, pp. 521–523.

the exclusive primacy of Lysippos, and brought earlier sculpture and with it Pheidias in to the place of honour which they merited. To this school of critics belong CICERO (106–43 B.C.), DIONYSIOS of HALIKARNASSOS (temp. Augustus), and above all QUINTILIAN (35–95 A.D.).

The last century before Christ produced one more book written by an artist which was of importance. This was the work in five volumes by PASITELES dealing with ' nobilia' or 'mirabilia opera in toto orbe,' as the title is given by Pliny. The author was a Greek sculptor born in Magna Graecia, who became a Roman citizen in 87 B.C., and is twice spoken of by Pliny as a contemporary of Pompey the Great (106–48 B.C.).

With Pasiteles closes the series of professional writers on art ; henceforward we have to deal with the encyclopaedic writers of the Roman period, who draw their information from the copious stores of Greek learning. The first of these is VARRO (116–27 B.C.), quoted by Pliny as a cardinal authority, in the sphere of whose all-embracing activity art was naturally included, although we have no direct testimony to the existence of a special ' History of Art' amongst his works. No doubt biographies of the great sculptors found a place in the gallery of ' Imagines' which he formed.

We may pass rapidly over the Augustan period, briefly mentioning the geographical work of STRABO and the treatise of VITRUVIUS on architecture, both of which furnish information relating to our subject, and, after noticing the work of C. Licinius MUCIANUS 'ter consul' (for the last time in 72 A.D.), who was relegated by Nero to an honourable banishment as proconsul of Asia, and wrote a popular account of his province and

its sights which seems to have been tinged by a taste
for the marvellous, proceed at once to deal with the elder
PLINY (23–79 A.D.), our capital authority for the history
of sculpture and sculptors. It is characteristic of his
great work[1], the *Natural History* in thirty-seven books,
published in 77 A.D. and dedicated to Titus, the Imperator
and co-regent, that sculpture and painting find a place
as branches of mineralogy—since the last five books treat
of metals, minerals, rocks and precious stones, with their
uses in medicine, daily life, and art.

The sections important for our purpose are the following :—

(1) xxxiv. 15–48. On the art of bronze-casting, portrait
statues, famous colossi, &c.

(2) xxxiv. 49–93. A history of bronze-casters. Pliny
opens with a chronological table of the masters of the
art (v. infr. § 4), followed by special notices of Pheidias,
Polykleitos, Myron, Pythagoras, Lysippos and his school,
—with a series of criticisms collected infr. § 2—to which
are appended short notes on Telephanes, Praxiteles, and
Kalamis. This takes us to § 71, after which we have an
alphabetical list of artists and their works extending from
§§ 72–83, followed by notes on the Pergamene artists and
Boethos (§ 84). Pliny then gives three short alphabetical
lists, comprising

(*a*) Aequalitate celebrati artifices sed nullis operum
suorum praecipui (§ 85).

(*b*) Qui eiusdem generis opera fecerunt (§§ 86–90).
Amongst the subjects enumerated the term 'philosophi'
frequently appears ; this seems to refer not to statues
of famous philosophers, but to portraits of civilians in
the garb of daily life.

---

[1] His History of his own Times in thirty-one books is lost.

(c) (Qui fecerunt) athletas et armatos et uenatores sacrificantesque (§ 91).

Miscellaneous notes (§§ 92, 93) complete the account of bronze-casting.

(3) xxxiv. 140, 141. On the use of iron in sculpture.

(4) xxxvi. 9–43. On sculpture in marble. After a historical section, beginning with the earliest sculptors, and dealing chiefly with Pheidias and his pupils, Praxiteles, Skopas, and their contemporaries (§§ 9–31) and some miscellaneous notes (§ 32), Pliny enumerates briefly some of the most famous works of sculpture preserved at Rome, notably in the 'monumenta' of Asinius Pollio, the 'porticus Octauiae,' the 'horti Seruiliani,' and the Palace of the Caesars on the Palatine (§§ 33–38). A group of miscellaneous notes (§§ 39–43) brings the section to a close.

The question as to the sources whence Pliny drew his information is a difficult one to answer. He tells us in his Preface (§ 17) that the *Natural History* embodies the results of a reading which extended to 2000 volumes, and that 100 'exquisiti auctores' were employed in its composition. The Preface is followed by a series of Indices, giving for each book a table of contents and a list of 'auctores,' in which Latin authors are first enumerated, then Greek. Two facts seem to be clearly established by the study which Brunn and others have devoted to these Indices :—

(i.) The Roman authors are mentioned in the order in which they were used.

(ii.) The Greek authors are often grouped according to their subjects ; in such cases only one was (generally speaking) directly or at least constantly used by Pliny, who places his name either first or last on the list.

The second principle has an important application in the present case. In the Index to Book XXXIV we find a list of Greek authorities on sculpture [1] terminating with the name of Pasiteles—the others are Menaichmos, Xenokrates, Antigonos, Duris, and Heliodoros—while in those of Books XXXIII and XXXV the name of Pasiteles heads the list of Greek writers on art and in the Index to Book XXXVI the same author figures early in the list and seems to be the only source of information on sculpture. We are therefore entitled to assume that Pasiteles was the chief authority—the 'exquisitus auctor'—among the Greeks consulted by Pliny in these sections. But it does not follow that he did not also consult the other authors above-named; Duris is quoted by name in No. 241, and the criticisms which seem to proceed from Xenokrates or Antigonos may be immediately derived from those authors. Among the Roman authors the name of Varro, which appears in the Indices of Books XXXIII–XXXVII, may clearly be recognized as that of the chief authority on art. Indeed, Mucianus is the only other writer named in the Indices who can have contributed much information on the subject of sculpture. But there can be no doubt that a large element in the sections under discussion consists of information drawn from miscellaneous sources and from Pliny's own observation. This is especially true of the notices of works preserved at Rome, with regard to which Pliny notices any changes in the place of exhibition made by the Emperors down to Vespasian. There is no adequate ground for the supposition that catalogues of the principal collections in Rome were

---

[1] Sculpture is rendered by 'toreutice,' on which use see Nos. 119, 160 and notes.

made by Vespasian's order and were among the authorities
used by Pliny.

The younger Pliny has left us an amusing account of
his father's studious habits (*Ep.* iii. 5). From sunrise to
sunset he amassed notes and filled commonplace books
—'nihil enim legit quod non excerperet.' Even in his
bath 'audiebat aliquid aut dictabat'; and on his jour-
neys he was constantly accompanied by a shorthand
writer. The question has been debated whether in the
sections on sculpture we have a collection of such scat-
tered notes as the younger Pliny describes, arranged as
far as possible under heads—or whether Pliny copies as
far as possible from a single source with occasional
insertions. The latter view is maintained by Oeh-
michen, who tries to show from the construction of
the alphabetical lists and other signs that Pliny copied
from an alphabetic dictionary of artists, written by Pasiteles and translated by Varro, making numerous additions
referring to his own times. But this is more than doubtful, since Pliny himself tells us that the title of Pasiteles'
work was 'quinque uolumina nobilium operum in toto
orbe,' which cannot have been a dictionary of artists,
nor is the rule that the order KX, ΠΦ, ΘT is preserved
in the Latin lists without exceptions. Analogies to
both the methods of composition mentioned above may
be drawn from other parts of Pliny's work, and it is
probably safer to assume that the chronological table
and alphabetical lists are both the handiwork of Pliny,
while the notices of individual artists are to be referred
to his miscellaneous sources, of whom Varro and Pasiteles are no doubt the chief. On the criticisms of the
great bronze-casters see § 2.

Among the Greek writers of the following generation

the names of PLUTARCH (circ. 46–120 A.D.) and his
somewhat younger contemporary, the rhetorician DION
CHRYSOSTOM(·)S of Prusa, deserve mention, since both
display an interest in art and furnish information of
value, although the accuracy of the last-named is
doubtful.

The second century A.D. supplies one authority of
capital importance. This is PAUSANIAS, a native of
Asia Minor, who wrote a περιήγησις Ἑλλάδος in ten
books, of which the fifth at least was completed in
173 A.D. The honesty of Pausanias is a matter of hot
dispute, and his detractors seek to prove that, although
he speaks as an eye-witness, his work is in fact a com-
pilation from earlier sources, amongst which the work of
Polemon (v. supr.) is supposed to hold the chief place as
an authority on works of art. This view is not, however,
confirmed by a comparison of the fragments of Polemon
with the work of Pausanias, and the tendency of recent
criticism[1] has been to absolve Pausanias from the charge
of dishonesty, and to regard his account of his travels
as generally credible, though not to exclude the use
of literary sources in the work of composition. It is
specially noticeable that the objects of interest which he
describes belong *either* to the period previous to 150 B.C.
or to his own time. Whatever conclusions may be
drawn from this fact, there can be no question as to
the value of Pausanias' descriptions so far as they go,
although the affectations and archaisms of the language
in which they are clothed render them unattractive.
The style and tone of Herodotos are imitated throughout.
Pausanias is the latest author who deals professedly with

---

[1] See especially Gurlitt, *Ueber Pausanias* (1890); Heberdey, *Die
Reisen des Pausanias* (1894).

art-criticism, but much valuable information is to be gleaned from the *littérateurs* and compilers of his generation and that which succeeded it. LUCIAN (born 125 A.D.) was keenly interested in sculpture of all periods, and has left us some just and striking criticisms, of which No. 67 is a good specimen. Two of his numerous writings may be singled out for mention. The first is the Εἰκόνες, in which an ideal beauty ('Panthea') is constructed by a synthetic process, four masterpieces of sculpture and a like number of pictures being called into requisition. The first-named are—the Knidian Aphrodite of Praxiteles, the Aphrodite ἐν Κήποις of Alkamenes, the 'Sosandra' of Kalamis, and the Lemnian Athene of Pheidias, and the special points of beauty in each are noted. In the Φιλοψευδής, a satire on the appetite for the marvellous, the scenery of the ghost-story is laid in a house filled with works by the great masters—the diskobolos of Myron, the Harmodios and Aristogeiton of Kritios and Nesiotes, the diadumenos of Polykleitos, and a realistic portrait by Demetrios.

Before we leave the writers of the Second Sophistic, we must mention among other sources ATHENAIOS, whose Δειπνοσοφιστής seems to have been published later than the death of Commodus (192 A.D.); DIOGENES LAERTIUS, whose lives of the philosophers contain biographical details of some importance; and KALLISTRATOS, who took up a branch of literature of which the two Philostrati were the masters, the application of rhetoric to the description of works of art;—whether real or imaginary, may be and has been disputed. Reference is made to his descriptions of statues on pp. 161, 172.

To the period of the Second Sophistic belong also the writings of those among the early fathers of the Christian

Church, who for apologetic or controversial purposes touch on the subject of Greek art. Their statements must, however, be received with caution, as neither TATIAN, who devotes a section of some length in his treatise 'contra Graecos' to the enumeration of criminal or disreputable characters to whom statues had been raised; nor ATHENAGORAS, who in his 'Libellus pro Christianis' deals with the principal 'idols' and their makers, were critical as to their sources of information. Nor is the testimony of CLEMENT of Alexandria above suspicion.

The classical literature of Greece expired with the ancient religion, and among the last writers of declining Paganism we may briefly mention the rhetoricians LIBANIOS and HIMERIOS, who occasionally notice works of art. Meanwhile lexicographers were storing the mutilated remains of ancient learning, derived ultimately from the Alexandrine cities, and recast by such commentators as Didymos in the Augustan age and Symmachos somewhat later. Some fragments of these compilations have reached us in the annotated texts of the poets, and notably in the Scholia Vetera on Aristophanes.

In the voluminous literature of Byzantium only one name need detain us—that of NIKETAS AKOMINATOS of Chonai in Phrygia, who seems to have been genuinely interested in the art-treasures removed from Greece to Constantinople. Both in his historical writings and in his special treatise 'On the Statues at Constantinople,' he has left us descriptions turgid in style and possibly not too accurate, but yet of distinct value. He lived circ. 1150–1210 A.D. His somewhat older contemporary, John TZETZES, was a thoroughly uncritical and inaccurate writer, whose interest is merely in anecdote; no passage from his writings is included in this selection.

No mention has been made in this summary of the Anthology as a source of information on sculpture. Among the epigrams of all periods which find a place in it many have reference to works of art, but few of these are of any value, since the greater number are not descriptive but purely 'epideictic' in character. Two epigrammatists alone deserve to be named, and both belong to the Hellenistic period. These are POSEIDIPPOS (not to be identified with the comedian), whose 'floruit' may be placed circ. 250 B.C., and ANTIPATER of Sidon, of whom Cicero (*De Or*. iii. 194) speaks as recently deceased in 91 B.C.

§ 2. THE CRITICISMS OF THE GREAT BRONZE-CASTERS.

Plin. *N. H.* xxxiv. 54 sqq. (PHIDIAS) primus artem toreuticen aperuisse atque demonstrasse merito iudicatur. (POLYCLITUS) consummasse hanc scientiam iudicatur et toreuticen sic erudisse ut Phidias aperuisse; proprium eius est uno crure ut insistere ut signa excogitasse, quadrata tamen esse ea ait Uarro et paene ad exemplum. (MYRON) primus multiplicasse ueritatem uidetur, numerosior in arte quam Polyclitus et in symmetria diligentior; et ipse tamen corporum tenus curiosus animi sensus non expressisse, capillum quoque et pubem non emendatius fecisse quam rudis antiquitas instituisset. (PYTHAGORAS) primus neruos et uenas expressit capillumque diligentius. (LYSIPPUS) statuariae arti plurimum traditur contulisse capillum exprimendo, capita minora faciendo quam antiqui, corpora graciliora sic-

cioraque, per quae proceritas signorum maior uideretur.
Non habet Latinum nomen symmetria quam diligentissime custodiuit noua intactaque ratione quadratas
ueterum staturas permutando.

Diog. Laert. viii. 46 Πυθαγόραν, πρῶτον δοκοῦντα ῥυθμοῦ
καὶ συμμετρίας ἐστοχάσθαι.

The above criticisms, abstracted from Pliny's account
of the great bronze-casters, and from Diogenes Laertius,
unmistakably form a connected series. They corre-
spond to a parallel series of criticisms on the great
painters — especially Apollodoros, Zeuxis, Parrhasios,
Euphranor, Aristeides, Apelles (v. *O. S.* 1641, 1647,
1724, 1802, 1779, 1900)—which are couched in the
same technical language. Catchwords of criticism
such as the use 'hic primus ...' (borrowed, no doubt,
from the literature περὶ εὑρημάτων of the Hellenistic and
later periods), and the phrase 'plurimum arti contulit'
recur in both series, and the technical and professional
character of the criticisms themselves shows them to
proceed from an artist or a school. The mention of
Varro seems to show that Pliny derived them directly
from him[1]. But we must go beyond Varro in the
search for their origin. Furtwängler notes that the
critic had two main points in view:

(1) ῥυθμός and συμμετρία. Both are mentioned in the
fragmentary note on Pythagoras preserved only by
Diogenes. 'Symmetria' which 'non habet Latinum
nomen' is prominent in Pliny, and 'numerosior' seems
to be a translation of εὐρυθμώτερος.

---

[1] That Varro is quoted, as it were, incidentally does not prove
that he was the authority *only* for the sentence containing his
name. Furtwängler compares a similar quotation from Cato in
xvii. 86.

(2) Naturalism in details, such as sinews, veins, and especially hair.

These are precisely what we should expect from an artist of the school of Lysippos; and accordingly it is not surprising to find that the series leads up to Lysippos as the goal of progress in sculpture. From this standpoint Pheidias was the first to 'reveal' the art (cp. 'artis fores apertas,' xxxv. 61 of the painter Apollodoros); Polykleitos expounded it more fully, but left somewhat to be desired in the proportions of his squarely built figures; Myron is placed above Polykleitos, because there was more variety in his attitudes and therefore in his proportions; Pythagoras succeeded where Myron had failed, in the treatment of hair and similar details, while Lysippos surpassed his predecessors in all points. A Greek artist, then, subsequent to Lysippos but influenced by his school, must be the author of the criticisms. Robert held that Xenokrates (v. supr.) fulfilled the conditions; but some indications appear to point rather to Antigonos of Karystos. It is to be noted that Pliny and Diogenes Laertius, both of whom preserve portions of the criticism on Pythagoras, also distinguish *two* artists of the name. Now Diogenes certainly read the work of Antigonos, which he quotes, ii. 15 ($= O. S.$ 435), and ix. 49 ($= O. S.$ 466). Moreover, it may perhaps be inferred from the fact that Pausanias knows only one Pythagoras, that Polemon corrected the error in his polemic against Antigonos. In xxxv. 68 Pliny quotes 'Antigonus et Xenocrates qui de pictura scripsere' for a statement regarding Parrhasios—a form of expression which in such a writer as Pliny might well be the equivalent of 'Antigonos, *quoting* Xenokrates.' It seems highly probable that the same pair of authors are to be recognized in the 'artifices qui compositis uoluminibus condidere haec' of No. 180. 'Alii,' in the same passage, may perhaps refer to Polemon.

§ 3. THE CANON OF SCULPTORS.

Quint. xii. 10. 7 Similis in statuariis differentia. Nam duriora et Tuscanicis proxima CALLON atque HEGESIAS, iam minus rigida CALAMIS, molliora adhuc supra dictis MYRON fecit. Diligentia ac decor in POLYCLITO supra ceteros, cui quamquam a plerisque tribuitur palma, tamen, ne nihil detrahatur, deesse pondus putant. Nam ut humanae formae decorem addiderit supra uerum, ita non expleuisse deorum auctoritatem uidetur. Quin aetatem quoque grauiorem dicitur refugisse nihil ausus ultra leues genas. At quae POLYCLITO defuerunt, PHIDIAE atque ALCAMENI dantur. PHIDIAS tamen dis quam hominibus effingendis melior artifex creditur, in ebore uere longe citra aemulum, uel si nihil

The same variety reigns among sculptors. For the works of KALLON and HEGESIAS are stiff, and closely resemble Etruscan sculptures, those of KALAMIS are less rigid, and those of MYRON yet more supple. In accurate workmanship and in grace POLYKLEITOS is unsurpassed; although, however, many authorities award him the palm, yet— lest he should be accounted perfect—it is thought that he lacks dignity. For while he imparted to the human form a grace beyond nature, he failed, as it seems, to express adequately the majesty of the gods. Moreover it is said that he shrank from the treatment of mature age and attempted nothing save beardless cheeks. But the qualities lacking in POLYKLEITOS

nisi Mineruam Athenis aut Olympium in Elide Iouem fecisset, cuius pulchritudo adiecisse aliquid etiam receptae religioni uidetur: adeo maiestas operis deum aequauit. Ad ueritatem LYSIPPUM ac PRAXITELEN accessisse optime adfirmant: nam DEMETRIUS tanquam nimius in ea reprehenditur et fuit similitudinis quam pulchritudinis amantior.

are assigned to PHEIDIAS and ALKAMENES. PHEIDIAS, however, is thought to have displayed higher art in his statues of gods than in those of mortals: in ivory indeed he would be without a rival, had he only made the Athena at Athens or the Olympian Zeus in Elis, whose beauty seems to have added somewhat to the received religion; so adequate to the divine nature is the grandeur of his work. It is asserted that LYSIPPOS and PRAXITELES most successfully aimed at truth to nature, while DEMETRIOS is blamed for excess in this respect; he attached more value to precise resemblance than to beauty.

Cic. Brut. 18. 70 Quis enim eorum qui haec minora animaduertunt, non intelligit CANACHI signa rigidiora esse quam ut imitentur ueritatem; CALAMIDIS dura illa quidem, sed tamen molliora quam CANACHI; nondum MYRONIS satis ad

Who is there among those who pay attention to these minor arts who does not feel that the statues of KANACHOS are too rigid to be true to nature? Those of KALAMIS are stiff, it is true, but more supple than those of KANACHOS; those

c

ueritatem adducta, iam tamen quae non dubites pulchra dicere: pulchriora etiam POLYCLITI et iam plane perfecta, ut mihi quidem uideri solent?

of MYRON have not attained complete fidelity to nature, but they may without hesitation be pronounced beautiful: while those of POLYKLEITOS are yet more beautiful and indeed, in my own opinion, quite perfect?

Strab. viii. 372 τὰ Πολυκλείτου ξόανα τῇ μὲν τέχνῃ κάλλιστα τῶν πάντων, πολυτελείᾳ δὲ καὶ μεγέθει τῶν Φειδίου λειπόμενα.

The statues of Polykleitos are artistically speaking the most beautiful of all, but in magnificence and sublimity they are surpassed by those of Pheidias.

On the school from which these criticisms proceed v. supr. § 1. Although Quintilian selects ten names, which form a parallel series to that of the Ten Orators (he enumerates *eleven* painters in § 3), we are not to suppose that a classical Canon of Ten Sculptors had been formed. Cicero adds Kanachos, Dionysios of Halikarnassos (No. 87), Kallimachos, Lucian (No. 67), Kritios and Nesiotes, all in passages which betray the influence of the same school of criticism. For the parallel series of painters see Quint. xii. 10. 3. A comparison of the two series will show that the criticisms are of a wholly different order to those tabulated in § 2. They do not bear on technical points, but embody a broad appreciation of style, and are often illustrated by a catchword ('pondus' 'decor,' 'diligentia,' 'ueritas,' 'μέγεθος,' in the Canon of Sculptors; 'cura,' 'ratio,' 'facilitas,' 'gratia,' in that of painters may be mentioned). Pheidias and Polykleitos take the place of Lysippos as the masters of their art, while even earlier sculptors, who are passed over in silence by the professional critics, obtain due recognition.

§ 4. PLINY'S CHRONOLOGICAL TABLE

(xxxiv. 49 sqq.).

B.C.

448　PHIDIAS Atheniensis ... floruit ... Olympiade LXXXIII, circiter CCC urbis nostrae annum, quo eodem tempore aemuli eius fuere ALCAMENES, CRITIAS, NESIOTES, HEGIAS,

432　et deinde Olympiade LXXXVII HAGELADES, CALLON, GORGIAS Lacon,

420　rursus LXXXX POLYCLITUS, PHRADMON, MYRON, PYTHAGORAS, SCOPAS, PERELLUS. Ex his POLYCLITUS discipulos habuit Argium ASOPODORUM, ALEXIM, ARISTIDEM, PHRYNONEM, ATHENODORUM, DEMEAN Clitorium, MYRON LYCIUM.

400　LXXXXV Olympiade floruere NAUCYDES, DINOMENES, CANACHUS, PATROCLUS,

372　CII POLYCLES, CEPHISODOTUS, LEOCHARES, HYPATODORUS,

364　CIIII PRAXITELES, EUPHRANOR,

352　CVII AETION, THERIMACHUS.

328　CXIII LYSIPPUS fuit, cum et Alexander Magnus, item LYSISTRATUS frater eius, STHENNIS, EUPHRON, EUCLES, SOSTRATUS, ION, SILANION—in hoc mirabile quod nullo doctore nobilis fuit, ipse discipulum habuit ZEUXIADEN—

296　CXXI EUTYCHIDES, EUTHYCRATES, LAIPPUS, CEPHISODOTUS, TIMARCHOS, PYROMACHUS.

156　Cessauit deinde ars, ac rursus Olympiade CLVI reuixit, &c.

The above list is printed as Pliny gives it, although it is not free from mistakes in orthography. Kritios appears as Critias, Patrokles as Patroclus, Daippos as Laippus (owing to a confusion of Δ and Λ in the Greek source). The table is set forth by Pliny in fulfilment of a promise made by him in xxxiv. 7. He desires to confute those who speak of bronzes of the best period as 'Corinthia' and proceeds 'Corinthus capta est Olym-

piadis CLVIII anno tertio, nostrae urbis DCVIII, cum
ante saecula fictores nobiles esse desissent, quorum isti
omnia signa hodie Corinthia appellant. Quapropter ad
coarguendos eos ponemus artificum aetates. Nam urbis
nostrae annos ex supra dicta comparatione Olympiadum
colligere facile erit.' 'Nam' in the last sentence is
elliptical, and implies 'I give Olympiads only, for ...' We
may therefore be prepared to find that Pliny's table is
his own construction, but also that it is derived ultimately
from Greek sources. A parallel series of dates forms the
skeleton of Pliny's account of painting in xxxv. 60 sqq.—
indeed the note '(Ol.) CVII. Aetion Therimachus' appears
to have been erroneously transferred from xxxv. 78 where
it recurs in the history of painting, to which it properly
belongs—and we are justified in inferring that the Greek
authority followed by Pliny placed the earliest bronze-
casters of importance in Ol. 83, the earliest painters in
Ol. 90, since in xxxv. 54 Pliny prefaces the history of
painting by the words 'Non constat sibi in hac parte
Graecorum diligentia multas post Olympiadas celebrando
pictores quam statuarios ac toreutas, primumque Olympiade LXXX, cum et Phidiam ipsum initio pictorem fuisse
tradatur,' &c., while in xxxvi. 15 he says (of sculpture
in marble) 'non omittendum hanc artem tanto uetustiorem fuisse quam picturam aut statuariam, quarum
utraque cum Phidia coepit octogensima tertia Olympiade' (the words refer to No. 25, q. v.). The words with
which Pliny closes the list ('cessauit deinde ars,' &c.)
imply nothing as to period to which his authority for
the dates belonged, although they may be held to prove
the importance of the works of Antigonos and Xenokrates, which would no doubt carry the history of
sculpture down to the point at which Pliny marks its

decline. It is possible that Apollodoros of Pergamon was the chronological authority, but perhaps unlikely that he would have entirely passed over Pergamene art, while he gave the dates of his own contemporaries, many of whom are mentioned under Ol. 156. But the list is full of serious errors, and the most rational explanation of its origin appears to be that Pliny excerpted the dates of a few important artists and grouped their 'aemuli' and 'discipuli' with them. Thus we have the fixed date Ol. 83 = PHEIDIAS—determined perhaps by the 'floruit' of Perikles or the completion of the Olympian Zeus—with whom are grouped on the one hand his *teacher* Hegias, and the contemporaries of the latter, Kritios and Nesiotes, on the other his *pupil* and rival, Alkamenes. Again Ol. 87 = AGELADAS—a date fixed by the erroneous impression as to the plague commemorated by No. 43. Kallon follows him as his contemporary. The next date, Ol. 90, is clearly that of POLYKLEITOS, fixed by the burning of the Heraion Ol. 89. 2, with whom were grouped amongst others Myron and Pythagoras, because they followed him in the series of criticisms discussed in § 2, and no independent date could be found for them. We cannot in all cases trace the origin of the dates and combinations, but Pliny himself tells us that that of LYSIPPOS was fixed by the 'floruit' of Alexander, and the equation Ol. 121 = EUTYCHIDES is doubtless based on the foundation of Antioch (Ol. 120). (Cp. No. 254.) It is therefore safer to regard *one* date only in each group as due to Pliny's source, while the rest must be received with caution as the result (in most cases) of his own uncritical combinations.

LIST OF ABBREVIATIONS

C. I. A. = Corpus Inscriptionum Atticarum (Berlin, 1873—).

I. G. S. = Inscriptiones Graeciae Septentrionalis (Berlin, 1892—).

Löwy = Löwy, Inschriften griechischer Bildhauer (Leipzig, 1885).

Dittenberger, *Syll.* = Dittenberger, Sylloge Inscriptionum Graecarum (Leipzig, 1883).

Brunn, *K. G.*² = Brunn, Geschichte der griechischen Künstler (ed. ii, Stuttgart, 1889).

Brunn-Bruckmann = Brunn-Bruckmann, Denkmäler griechischer und römischer Sculptur (Munich, 1888—).

Coll. = Collignon, Histoire de la Sculpture Grecque (vol. i, Paris, 1892).

F. W. = Friedrichs-Wolters, Bausteine zur Geschichte der griechischen Plastik (Berlin, 1885).

Furtw., *Meisterwerke* = Furtwängler, Meisterwerke der griechischen Plastik (Berlin, 1894).

Num. Comm. = Imhoof-Blumer and Gardner, A Numismatic Commentary on Pausanias (London, 1887).

Gerhard, *A. V.* = Gerhard, Auserlesene griechische Vasenbilder (Berlin, 1840–1858).

Helbig, *Führer* = Helbig, Führer durch die öffentlichen Sammlungen klassischer Alterthümer Roms (Leipzig, 1891).

*Ov.*⁴ = Overbeck, Geschichte der griechischen Plastik (ed. iv, vol. i, Leipzig, 1892; vol. ii, Leipzig, 1893).

Overbeck, *Kunstmyth.* = Overbeck, Griechische Kunstmythologie (Leipzig, 1871—).

O. S. = Overbeck, Schriftquellen zur Geschichte der bildenden Künste bei den Griechen (Leipzig, 1868).

J. H. S. = Journal of Hellenic Studies (London, 1880—).

Class. Rev. = Classical Review (London, 1887—).

M. d. I. = Monumenti inediti pubblicati dall' Instituto di Corrispondenza Archeologica (Rome, 1829-1885).

A. d. I. = Annali dell' Instituto di Corrispondenza Archeologica (Rome, 1829-1885).

Jahrb. = Jahrbuch des kaiserlich deutschen archäologischen Instituts (Berlin, 1886—).

Ath. Mitth. = Mittheilungen des deutschen archäologischen Instituts in Athen (Athens, 1876 —).

Röm. Mitth. = Mittheilungen des kaiserlich deutschen archäologischen Instituts, römische Abtheilung (Rome, 1886—).

Antike Denkmäler = Antike Denkmäler, herausgegeben vom kaiserlich deutschen archäologischen Institut (Berlin, 1887—).

A. Z. = Archäologische Zeitung (Berlin, 1843–1885).

Rev. Arch. = Revue Archéologique (Paris, 1860—).

Gaz. Arch. = Gazette Archéologique (Paris, 1875—).

'Εφ. 'Αρχ. = 'Εφημερὶς 'Αρχαιολογική (Athens, 1883—).

Δελτ. 'Αρχ. = Δελτίον 'Αρχαιολογικόν (Athens, 1885—).

PART I

THE BEGINNINGS OF GREEK SCULPTURE

Nos. 1–41.

§ 1. THE DAIDALIDAI.

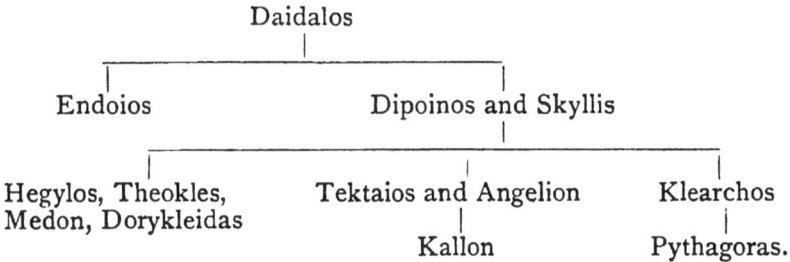

The above scheme is presupposed by a group of notices in Pausanias relating to the several artists (v. infr. Nos. 1–21). It was in all probability framed in order to claim the honour of the cradle of sculpture for Athens, as represented by Daidalos, a mythical figure of Attic legend. He was the ἐπώνυμος of the deme Δαιδαλίδαι, and the γένος of the same name (to which Sokrates belonged), and was inserted in the royal pedigree as grandson of Erechtheus. He is also connected by legend with Crete and Sicily, but it is unlikely that there was an historical Cretan artist of the name, as Kuhnert supposes.

1. DAIDALOS.

1. Diod. iv. 76 Δαίδαλος μὲν ἦν τὸ γένος 'Αθηναῖος, εἷς τῶν 'Ερεχθειδῶν ὀνομαζόμενος· ἦν γὰρ υἱὸς Μητίονος τοῦ Εὐπαλάμου τοῦ 'Ερεχθέως ...κατὰ δὲ τὴν τῶν ἀγαλμάτων κατασκευὴν τοσοῦτο τῶν ἁπάντων ἀνθρώπων διήνεγκεν, ὥστε τοὺς μεταγενεσ-

Daidalos was an Athenian by birth and was called one of the Erechtheidai: for he was the son of Metion the son of Eupalamos the son of Erechtheus...And in the sculptor's art he so far excelled all other men that in after times the fable was

τέρους μυθολογῆσαι περὶ αὐτοῦ
διότι τὰ κατασκευαζόμενα τῶν
ἀγαλμάτων ὁμοιότατα τοῖς
ἐμψύχοις ὑπάρχει· βλέπειν
τε γὰρ αὐτὰ καὶ περιπατεῖν,
καὶ καθόλου τηρεῖν τὴν τοῦ
ὅλου σώματος διάθεσιν, ὥστε
δοκεῖν εἶναι τὸ κατασκευασθὲν
ἔμψυχον ζῷον. πρῶτος δὲ
ὀμματώσας καὶ διαβεβηκότα
τὰ σκέλη ποιήσας, ἔτι δὲ τὰς
χεῖρας διατεταμένας ποιῶν,
εἰκότως ἐθαυμάζετο παρὰ τοῖς
ἀνθρώποις· οἱ γὰρ πρὸ τούτου
τεχνῖται κατεσκεύαζον τὰ
ἀγάλματα τοῖς μὲν ὄμμασι
μεμυκότα, τὰς δὲ χεῖρας ἔχοντα
καθειμένας καὶ ταῖς πλευραῖς
κεκολλημένας.

told of him that the statues
which he made were like
living beings ; for they saw
and walked, and, in a
word, exercised every
bodily function, so that
his handiwork seemed to
be a living being. And
being the first to give them
open eyes, and parted legs,
and outstretched arms, he
justly won the admiration
of men : for before his time
artists made statues with
closed eyes and hands
hanging down and cleav-
ing to their sides.

The foregoing account of Daidalos is repeated with slight
variations by many ancient authors. The name seems to cover
the transition from the primitive ξόανον, with limbs imperfectly,
if at all, indicated, to the type seen in the so-called early ' Apollo '
figures.

2. Paus. ix. 40. 3 Δαι-
δάλου δὲ τῶν ἔργων δύο μὲν
ταῦτά ἐστιν ἐν Βοιωτίᾳ,
Ἡρακλῆς τε ἐν Θήβαις καὶ
παρὰ Λεβαδεῦσιν ὁ Τροφώ-
νιος· τοσαῦτα δὲ ἕτερα ξόανα
ἐν Κρήτῃ, Βριτόμαρτις ἐν
Ὀλοῦντι καὶ Ἀθηνᾶ παρὰ
Κνωσίοις. παρὰ τούτοις δὲ καὶ

Of the works of Daidalos
two are in Boeotia, namely
Herakles at Thebes and
Trophonios at Lebadeia,
and there are also two
statues of wood in Crete,
Britomartis at Olus and
Athena at Knossos. The
Knossians also possess the

ὁ τῆς Ἀριάδνης χορός, οὗ καὶ Ὅμηρος ἐν Ἰλιάδι μνήμην ἐποιήσατο, ἐπειργασμένος ἐστὶν ἐπὶ λευκοῦ λίθου. καὶ Δηλίοις Ἀφροδίτης ἐστὶν οὐ μέγα ξόανον, λελυμασμένον τὴν δεξιὰν χεῖρα ὑπὸ τοῦ χρόνου· κάτεισι δὲ ἀντὶ ποδῶν ἐς τετράγωνον σχῆμα. πείθομαι τοῦτο Ἀριάδνην λαβεῖν παρὰ Δαιδάλου, καὶ ἡνίκα ἠκολούθησε τῷ Θησεῖ, τὸ ἄγαλμα ἐπεκομίζετο οἴκοθεν· ἀφαιρεθέντα δὲ αὐτῆς τὸν Θησέα οὕτω φασὶν οἱ Δήλιοι τὸ ξόανον τῆς θεοῦ ἀναθεῖνα τῷ Ἀπόλλωνι τῷ Δηλίῳ.

dance of Ariadne, which is mentioned by Homer in the Iliad, a relief in white marble. And the Delians have a small wooden image of Aphrodite, which has lost its right hand through lapse of time, and terminates below in a square block instead of feet. I believe that Ariadne received it from Daidalos, and that when she followed Theseus she carried away the image from her home : and the Delians relate that when Theseus was parted from her he dedicated the image of the goddess to the Delian Apollo.

The above list comprises various images of high antiquity, regarded with great reverence from their long association with the cults to which they belonged, and linked by tradition with Daidalos as the earliest of known sculptors. It is possible that the first-named is represented on silver coins of Thebes of the fifth century (*B. M. Cat.* xii. 1–8, *Num. Comm.* p. 111). The coin represents Herakles advancing with club and bow ; the artist has, however, translated the figure into the style of his own time. The ' dance of Ariadne ' is mentioned in Σ 590 ff. :—

ἐν δὲ χορὸν ποίκιλλε περικλυτὸς Ἀμφιγυήεις
[τῷ ἴκελον, οἷόν ποτ' ἐνὶ Κνωσσῷ εὐρείῃ
Δαίδαλος ἤσκησεν καλλιπλοκάμῳ Ἀριάδνῃ.]

There too did the famous halting god fashion a dance, [like unto that which once in broad Knossos Daidalos devised for Ariadne of the lovely locks.]

The last two lines are an interpolation, probably of the sixth century (Kuhnert, *Dädalos*, pp. 205 ff.). The work was a plastic representation of a dance in honour of the Cretan *goddess* Ariadne, for which we may compare the votive bronzes found at Olympia (Furtw., *Bronzefunde*, p. 24 f.; cp. Helbig, *Das Homerische Epos*, fig. 67). Note that with this exception the works of Daidalos enumerated by Paus. are all ξόανα, i.e. *wooden* images.

3. Paus. ii. 4. 5 τὸ δὲ ἱερὸν τῆς Ἀθηνᾶς τῆς Χαλινίτιδος πρὸς τῷ θεάτρῳ σφίσιν ἐστίν, καὶ πλησίον ξόανον γυμνὸν Ἡρακλέους· Δαιδάλου δὲ αὐτὸ φασὶν εἶναι τέχνην. Δαίδαλος δὲ ὅποσα εἰργάσατο, ἀτοπώτερα μέν ἐστιν ἔτι τὴν ὄψιν, ἐπιπρέπει δὲ ὅμως τι καὶ ἔνθεον τούτοις.

At Corinth.

The temple of Athena Chalinitis is beside the theatre, and near it is a nude wooden image of Herakles, which they assert to be a work of Daidalos. But the works of Daidalos are stranger still to look upon, although there is a kind of divinity resting even upon them.

4. Skylax, p. 39, 4 Fabr. ἐπὶ δὲ τῷ ἀκρωτηρίῳ τῆς ἄκρας ἔπεστι βωμὸς μεγαλοπρεπὴς Ποσειδῶνος. Ἐν δὲ τῷ βωμῷ εἰσὶ γεγλυμμένοι ἄνδρες, γυναῖκες, λέοντες, δελφῖνες· Δαίδαλον δέ φασι ποιῆσαι.

At Soloeis in Sicily.

On the edge of the promontory stands a magnificent altar of Poseidon. On the altar are carved figures of men, women, lions, and dolphins. It is said to be the work of Daidalos.

5. Paus. i. 27. 1 κεῖται δὲ ἐν τῷ ναῷ τῆς Πολιάδος ... δίφρος ὀκλαδίας, Δαιδάλου ... ποίημα.

At Athens; the temple is the Erechtheion.

In the temple of Athena Polias is treasured a folding seat, the work of Daidalos.

6. Plat. Hipp. mai. 282

A ὥσπερ καὶ τὸν Δαίδαλόν
φασιν οἱ ἀνδριαντοποιοί, νῦν
εἰ γενόμενος τοιαῦτ᾽ ἐργάζοιτο
οἷα ἦν ἀφ᾽ ὧν τοὔνομ᾽ ἔσχε,
καταγέλαστον ἂν εἶναι.

As the sculptors say that
Daidalos, were he now to
be born and to make
statues such as those by
which he won his fame,
would be laughed to scorn.

Other plastic works ascribed to Daidalos :—
HERAKLES at Pisa (Apollod. ii. 6, 3).
HERAKLES on the borders of Messenia and Arkadia (Paus.
viii. 35, 2).
ARTEMIS at Monogissa in Karia (Steph. Byz. s. v.).
Offerings of the Argives in the Heraion (Paus. ix. 40. 4).
A figure brought from Omphake to Gela in Sicily (id. *ib.*).

2. ENDOIOS.

7. Paus. i. 26. 4 Ἔνδοιος
μὲν ἦν γένος μὲν ᾿Αθηναῖος,
Δαιδάλου δὲ μαθητής, ὃς καὶ
φεύγοντι Δαιδάλῳ διὰ τὸν
Τάλω θάνατον ἐπηκολού-
θησεν ἐς Κρήτην· τούτου
καθήμενόν ἐστιν ᾿Αθηνᾶς
ἄγαλμα, ἐπίγραμμα ἔχον, ὡς
Καλλίας μὲν ἀναθείη, ποιήσειε
δὲ Ἔνδοιος.

Endoios was an Athenian
by birth, and a pupil of
Daidalos, whom he followed
to Crete when he was exiled
on account of the murder
of Talos ; by him is a
seated statue of Athena,
with an inscription to the
effect that Kallias dedicated
and Endoios made it.

Although tradition claimed Endoios as a native of Athens, it
is probable that he was really an Ionian, since we find him at work
at Ephesos and Erythrai, at a time when the stream of influence
ran from East to West, and he uses the Ionic alphabet in an inscription found on the Akropolis (Δελτ. ᾿Αρχ. 1888, f. 208). The statue
here mentioned may with some probability be identified with the
seated figure of Athena from the Akropolis, published in Lebas-
Reinach, *Voyage Archéologique*, Pl. II, 1 and elsewhere (v. *op. cit.*
p. 51). Kallias, the dedicator, was the son of Phainippos, and one
of the richest men in Athens. He was a violent opponent of the
Peisistratids, and was victorious at Olympia in Ol. 57 = 552 B. C.

8. Athenag. Libell. pro
Christ. 17, p. 19, 8 Schw. τὸ
μὲν γὰρ ἐν Ἐφέσῳ τῆς Ἀρτέμιδος (εἴδωλον) . . . Ἔνδοιος
εἰργάσατο, μαθητὴς Δαιδάλου.

For the image of Artemis
at Ephesos was the work
of Endoios, a pupil of
Daidalos.

Pliny (*N. H.* xvi. 214) informs us that this statue was commonly
held to be of ebony, but that Mucianus, who was proconsul of Asia
and published an account of its sights, found it to be of vine-wood.

9. Paus. viii. 46. 4 τῆς
Ἀθηνᾶς τὸ ἄγαλμα τῆς Ἀλέας
. . . ἐλέφαντος διὰ παντὸς
πεποιημένον, τέχνη δὲ Ἐνδοίου.

The image of Athena
Alea, made entirely of
ivory, the work of Endoios.

This work stood in the temple of Athena Alea at Tegea, until it
was brought by Augustus to Rome and dedicated in his Forum.

10. Paus. vii. 5. 9 ἔστι
δὲ ἐν Ἐρυθραῖς καὶ Ἀθηνᾶς
Πολιάδος ναὸς καὶ ἄγαλμα ξύλου μεγέθει μέγα καθήμενόν
τε ἐπὶ θρόνου καὶ ἠλακάτην ἐν
ἑκατέρᾳ τῶν χειρῶν ἔχει, καὶ
ἐπὶ τῆς κεφαλῆς πόλον. τοῦτο
Ἐνδοίου τέχνην καὶ ἄλλοις
ἐτεκμαιρόμεθα εἶναι . . . καὶ
οὐχ ἥκιστα ἐπὶ ταῖς Χάρισί τε
καὶ Ὥραις, αἳ πρὶν ἐσελθεῖν
ἑστήκασιν ἐν ὑπαίθρῳ λίθου
λευκοῦ.

At Erythrai there is also
a temple of Athena Polias,
and a colossal wooden
image, seated upon a throne,
holding in each hand a
spindle, and having a circular crown on its head. This
I conjectured to be a work
of Endoios from various
tokens, notably its resemblance to the Graces and
Seasons which stand before
the entrance in the open air
and are of white marble.

3. DIPOINOS AND SKYLLIS.

11. Plin. *N. H.* xxxvi. 9
Marmore sculpendo primi

The first to win fame as
sculptors in marble were

omnium inclaruerunt Di-
poenus et Scyllis geniti
in Creta insula etiamnum
Medis imperantibus prius-
que quam Cyrus in Persis
regnare inciperet, hoc est
Olympiade circiter L. Hi
Sicyonem se contulere,
quae diu fuit officinarum
omnium talium patria. Deorum simulacra publice loca-
uerunt iis Sicyonii, quae
prius quam absoluerentur
artifices iniuriam questi
abiere in Aetolos. Protinus
Sicyonem fames inuasit
ac sterilitas moerorque
dirus. Remedium petentibus
Apollo Pythius respondit,
' si Dipoenus et Scyllis deorum simulacra perfecissent,'
quod magnis mercedibus
obsequiisque impetratum
est. Fuere autem simulacra
ea Apollinis Dianaé Her-
culis Mineruae (quod e
caelo postea tactum est).

Dipoinos and Skyllis, who
were born in Crete while the
empire of the Medes still
lasted, and before Cyrus
became king in Persia, i. e.
about the fiftieth Olym-
piad (= 580 B.C.). They
repaired to Sikyon, which
long remained the home of
all such crafts. The Sikyo-
nians contracted with them
for statues of the gods, but
before they were completed
the artists complained that
they were ill used and
departed to Aetolia. Im-
mediately Sikyon was at-
tacked by famine, barren-
ness and dire calamity.
When they asked relief, the
Pythian Apollo answered
that it should come ' when
Dipoinos and Skyllis should
finish the statues of the
gods,' a favour which cost
them dearly in rewards and
attentions. These statues
represented Apollo, Arte-
mis, Herakles, and Athena
(which last was afterwards
struck by lightning).

The date is only approximate, since Cyrus became king in 560
B.C. The calculation may be based on a fact recorded by the

Armenian historian Moses of Chorene, who states that Ardashir
(=Cyrus) captured from Croesus (in 546 B.C.) three statues of gilt
bronze representing Artemis, Herakles, and Apollo, of which the
Herakles at least was a work of Dipoinos and Skyllis. The four
statues named by Pliny have been supposed to have formed a group
representing the capture of the Delphic tripod by Herakles, but
were more probably temple-statues. Pliny states that Ambrakia,
Argos, and Kleonai were 'full of the works of Dipoinos,' and that
Parian marble (λυχνίτης) was the material employed.

12. Paus. ii. 15. 1 (At
Kleonai) ἐστὶν ἱερὸν ᾿Αθη-
νᾶς, τὸ δὲ ἄγαλμα Σκύλλιδος
τέχνη καὶ Διποίνου· μαθητὰς
δὲ εἶναι Δαιδάλου σφᾶς, οἱ
δὲ καὶ γυναῖκα ἐκ Γόρτυνος
ἐθέλουσι λαβεῖν Δαίδαλον, καὶ
τὸν Δίποινον καὶ Σκύλλιν ἐκ
τῆς γυναικός οἱ ταύτης γενέσθαι.

(At Kleonai) there is
a temple of Athena, and
the image is the work
of Skyllis and Dipoinos.
Some hold them to have
been pupils of Daidalos,
while others will have it
that Daidalos married a
woman of Gortyn, and that
Dipoinos and Skyllis were
his sons by this wife.

μαθητὰς δὲ εἶναι] οἱ μέν is understood, as in No. 26.

13. Paus. ii. 22. 5 (At
Argos) Διοσκούρων ναός,
ἀγάλματα δὲ αὐτοί τε καὶ
οἱ παῖδές εἰσιν, ᾿Αναξις καὶ
Μνασίνους, σὺν δέ σφισιν αἱ
μητέρες ῾Ιλάειρά τε καὶ Φοίβη,
τέχνη μὲν Διποίνου καὶ Σκύλλιδος, ξύλου δὲ ἐβένου· τοῖς
δὲ ἵπποις τὰ μὲν πολλὰ ἐβέ-
νου καὶ τούτοις, ὀλίγα δὲ καὶ
ἐλέφαντος πεποίηται.

(At Argos) is a temple of
the Dioskouroi, and statues
of themselves and their
sons, Anaxis and Mnasi-
nous, as well as the mothers
of these, Hilaeira and
Phoibe, the work of Di-
poinos and Skyllis, made
of ebony. Their horses
too are sculptured mainly
in ebony, but partly also
in ivory.

14. Clem. Al. Protr. iv.
42 Σκύλλις καὶ Δίποινος
. . . κατεσκευασάτην . . . τὸν
ἐν Τίρυνθι Ἡρακλέους ἀν-
δριάντα καὶ τὸ τῆς Μουνιχίας
Ἀρτέμιδος ξόανον ἐν Σικυῶνι.

Skyllis and Dipoinos made the statue of Herakles at Tiryns, and the wooden image of Artemis Munichia at Sikyon.

4. THE SPARTAN SCULPTORS AT OLYMPIA.

(HEGYLOS, THEOKLES, MEDON, DORYKLEIDAS.)

15. Paus. v. 17. 2 τὰς
δὲ Ἑσπερίδας πέντε ἀριθμὸν
Θεοκλῆς ἐποίησε, Λακεδαι-
μόνιος μὲν καὶ οὗτος, πατρὸς
Ἡγύλου· φοιτῆσαι δὲ καὶ
αὐτὸς παρὰ Σκύλλιν καὶ
Δίποινον λέγεται.

The Hesperids (in the Heraion at Olympia), five in number, were made by Theokles, also a Spartan, the son of Hegylos: he too is said to have been a pupil of Dipoinos and Skyllis.

16. Paus. vi. 19. 8 (The treasury of the Epidamnians) ἔχει μὲν πόλον ἀνεχό-
μενον ὑπὸ Ἄτλαντος· ἔχει δὲ
Ἡρακλέα καὶ δένδρον τὸ παρὰ
Ἑσπερίσι, τὴν μηλέαν, καὶ
περιειλιγμένον τῇ μηλέᾳ τὸν
δράκοντα· κέδρου μὲν καὶ ταῦτα,
Θεοκλέους δὲ ἔργα τοῦ Ἡγύ-
λου· ποιῆσαι δὲ αὐτὸν ὁμοῦ τῷ
παιδί φησι τὰ ἐπὶ τοῦ πόλου
γράμματα.

(The treasury of the Epidamnians) contains the heavenly sphere supported by Atlas, and also Herakles and the apple-tree of the Hesperids, with the serpent coiled about it. These too are of cedar-wood, the work of Theokles, the son of Hegylos, who is stated by the inscription on the sphere to have assisted his son in the making.

17. Paus. vi. 19. 12 Με-
γαρεῖς δὲ οἱ πρὸς τῇ Ἀττικῇ
θησαυρόν τε ᾠκοδομήσαντο,

The Megarians who live on the border of Attica built themselves a treasury,

καὶ ἀναθήματα ἀνέθεσαν ἐς τὸν θησαυρόν, κέδρου ζῴδια χρυσῷ διηνθισμένα, τὴν πρὸς Ἀχελῷον Ἡρακλέους μάχην. Ζεὺς δὲ ἐνταῦθα καὶ ἡ Δηιάνειρα καὶ Ἀχελῷος καὶ Ἡρακλῆς ἐστίν, Ἄρης τε τῷ Ἀχελῴῳ βοηθῶν, εἱστήκει δὲ καὶ Ἀθηνᾶς ἄγαλμα, ἅτε οὖσα τῷ Ἡρακλεῖ σύμμαχος· αὕτη παρὰ τὰς Ἑσπερίδας ἀνάκειται νῦν τὰς ἐν τῷ Ἡραίῳ. 13. τοῦ θησαυροῦ δὲ ἐπείργασται τῷ ἀετῷ ὁ γιγάντων καὶ θεῶν πόλεμος. . . . τὰ δὴ ἀναθήματα ἐκ παλαιοῦ σφᾶς ἔχειν εἰκός, ἅ γε ὁ Λακεδαιμόνιος Μέδων αὐτοῖς Διποίνου καὶ Σκύλλιδος μαθητὴς ἐποίησε.

and dedicated offerings therein, figures of cedar-wood inlaid with gold, representing the fight of Herakles against Acheloos. There is Zeus and Deianeira and Acheloos and Herakles, and Ares assisting Acheloos. There was also at one time a statue of Athena as the ally of Herakles; but it now stands beside the Hesperids in the temple of Hera. On the pediment of the treasury is wrought the battle of the gods and giants. The Megarians would seem to have possessed these offerings from great antiquity, since they were made for them by Medon, the Spartan, a pupil of Dipoinos and Skyllis.

The language of Pausanias is not explicit as to the inclusion of the pediment-sculptures among the works of Medon. Fragments of them were discovered at Olympia (see F. W. 294, 5).

Μέδων αὐτοῖς] MSS. Δόντας. The name seems an impossible one, and should no doubt be corrected in accordance with the next No. Brunn makes the contrary change, reading μὲν Δόντα for Μέδοντος in No. 18.

18. Paus. v. 17. 1 τῆς Ἥρας δὲ .. ἐν τῷ ναῷ .. Θέμιδος ἅτε μητρὸς τῶν Ὡρῶν

In the temple of Hera there stands an image of Themis as mother of the

ἄγαλμα ἕστηκε Δορυκλείδου τέχνη, γένος μὲν Λακεδαιμονίου, μαθητοῦ δὲ Διποίνου καὶ Σκύλλιδος . . . τὴν δὲ ᾿Αθηνᾶν κράνος ἐπικειμένην καὶ δόρυ καὶ ἀσπίδα ἔχουσαν Λακεδαιμονίου λέγουσιν ἔργον εἶναι Μέδοντος, τοῦτον δὲ ἀδελφόν τε εἶναι Δορυκλείδου, καὶ παρὰ ἀνδράσι διδαχθῆναι τοῖς αὐτοῖς. . . . . τὰ μὲν δὴ κατειλεγμένα ἐστὶν ἐλέφαντος καὶ χρυσοῦ.

Seasons. It is the work of Dorykleidas, a Spartan by birth, and a pupil of Dipoinos and Skyllis. The Athena wearing a helmet and holding spear and shield, is said to be the work of Medon, who, as is alleged, was the brother of Dorykleidas, and was a pupil of the same masters. The above-named works are of gold and ivory.

The Heraion, which was the oldest temple at Olympia, contained other works of archaic sculpture besides those above mentioned. The Seasons, to which allusion is made in the above passage, were the work of Smilis (v. infr. No. 23). The Athena of Medon is that mentioned in No. 17. On the disposition of these works in the Heraion, see Wernicke, *Jahrb.*, 1894, p. 105 ff., who believes that the temple was converted into a kind of museum at the time of Nero's visit to Olympia.

5. TEKTAIOS AND ANGELION.

19. Paus. ii. 32. 5 μαθητὴς δὲ ὁ Κάλλων ἦν Τεκταίου καὶ ᾿Αγγελίωνος, οἳ Δηλίοις ἐποίησαν τὸ ἄγαλμα τοῦ ᾿Απόλλωνος· ὁ δὲ ᾿Αγγελίων καὶ Τεκταῖος παρὰ Διποίνῳ καὶ Σκύλλιδι ἐδιδάχθησαν.

Kallon was a pupil of Tektaios and Angelion, who made the image of Apollo for the Delians, and Angelion and Tektaios learnt their art from Dipoinos and Skyllis.

20. Plut. de Mus. 14 ἡ ἐν Δήλῳ τοῦ ἀγάλματος αὐτοῦ ἀφίδρυσις ἔχει μὲν ἐν

The image of him which is set up at Delos holds in its right hand a bow and

τῇ δεξιᾷ τόξον, ἐν δὲ τῇ ἀρισ- τερᾷ Χάριτας, τῶν τῆς μου- σικῆς ὀργάνων ἑκάστην τι ἔχουσαν· ἡ μὲν γὰρ λύραν κρατεῖ, ἡ δὲ αὐλούς, ἡ δὲ ἐν μέσῳ προκειμένην ἔχει τῷ στόματι σύριγγα.

in its left the Graces, each of whom has a musical instrument : one holds the lyre, another the flutes, while she that is in the midst presses a pipe to her lips.

This statue of the Delian Apollo is represented on several coins of Athens, *Num. Comm. CC.* xi–xiv.

Athenagoras mentions an Artemis (apparently also at Delos) by the same artists. Their date may be fixed by that of their pupil Kallon (v. infr. No. 52), and the style of the Apollo at about 540 B.C.

6. KLEARCHOS.

21. Paus. iii. 17. 6 τῆς Χαλκιοίκου δὲ ἐν δεξιᾷ Διὸς ἄγαλμα Ὑπάτου πεποί- ηται, παλαιότατον πάντων ὁ- πόσα ἐστὶ χαλκοῦ· δι' ὅλου γὰρ οὐκ ἔστιν εἰργασμένον, ἐληλαμένου δὲ ἰδίᾳ τῶν μερῶν καθ' αὑτὸ ἑκάστου συνήρμοσταί τε πρὸς ἄλληλα, καὶ ἧλοι συνέχουσιν αὐτὰ μὴ διαλυθῆναι. Κλέαρχον δὲ ἄνδρα Ῥηγῖνον τὸ ἄγαλμα ποιῆσαι λέγουσιν, ὃν Διποίνου καὶ Σκύλλιδος, οἱ δὲ αὑτοῦ Δαιδά- λου φασὶν εἶναι μαθητήν.

On the right hand of the goddess of the Brasen House there is an image of Zeus the Highest, the oldest of all works in bronze ; for it is not wrought all of one piece, but each part is separately beaten out, and all are held together by rivets that they may not fall asunder. They say that the image was made by Klearchos of Rhegion, who (according to some) was a pupil of Dipoinos and Skyllis, but according to others of Daidalos himself.

The technique here described was known as 'σφυρήλατον.' The best-known example was the golden colossus of Zeus, dedicated by

Periander at Olympia. A divergent tradition as to Klearchos is preserved by Paus. vi. 4, 4, who states that Klearchos was the pupil of Eucheir, and Eucheir of Syadras and Chartas, the Spartans. He also states that Klearchos was the master of Pythagoras of Rhegion (Part II. § 2. 1), which would fix his date approximately at 520 B.C.

With the Daidalidai we may class the two artists whose names follow.

7. SMILIS.

22. Paus. vii. 4. 4 τὸ δ' ἱερὸν τὸ ἐν Σάμῳ τῆς "Ηρας . . . ἐν τοῖς μάλιστα ἀρχαῖον οὐχ ἥκιστα ἄν τις καὶ ἐπὶ τῷ ἀγάλματι τεκμαίροιτο· ἔστι γὰρ δὴ ἀνδρὸς ἔργον Αἰγινη- τοῦ, Σμίλιδος τοῦ Εὐκλείδου. οὗτος ὁ Σμίλις ἐστιν ἡλικίαν κατὰ Δαίδαλον, δόξης δὲ οὐκ ἐς τὸ ἴσον ἀφίκετο.

The temple of Hera at Samos may be reasonably thought one of the oldest in existence, notably because of the statue; for it is the work of an Aeginetan, Smilis the son of Eukleides. This Smilis was a contemporary of Daidalos, but never attained the same height of fame.

The statue is represented on coins of Samos (Gardner, *Samos and Samian Coins*, Pl. v, 1–9); it was richly draped, and held fillets in each hand. Smilis was perhaps a Samian by birth, as is indicated by the statement of Pliny, *N. H.* xxxvi. 90, that the 'labyrinth of Lemnos,' i. e. the Heraion of Samos, was the work of 'Smilis et Rhoecus et Theodorus indigenae' (v. infr. No. 32 note).

23. Paus. v. 17. 1 (τῆς "Ηρας δὲ ἐν τῷ ναῷ) καθη- μένας ἐπὶ θρόνων "Ωρας ἐποίη- σεν ὁ Σμίλις.

(In the temple of Hera) are the Seasons seated on thrones, the work of Smilis.

At Olympia, v. supr. No. 18.

8. CHEIRISOPHOS.

24. Paus. viii. 53. 7 (At Tegea) Ἀπόλλωνος ναὸς καὶ ἄγαλμα ἐπίχρυσον· Χειρίσοφος δὲ ἐποίησε, Κρὴς μὲν γένος, ἡλικίαν δὲ αὐτοῦ καὶ τὸν διδάξαντα οὐκ ἴσμεν. ἡ δὲ δίαιτα ἡ ἐν Κνωσῷ Δαιδάλῳ παρὰ Μίνῳ συμβᾶσα ἐπὶ μακρότερον δόξαν τοῖς Κρησὶ καὶ ἐπὶ ξοάνων ποιήσει παρεσκεύασε. παρὰ δὲ τῷ Ἀπόλλωνι ὁ Χειρίσοφος ἔστηκε λίθου πεποιημένος.

(At Tegea) there is a temple of Apollo and a gilded image, made by Cheirisophos, a Cretan by birth, whose date and teacher I do not know. But the residence of Daidalos at the court of Minos made the Cretans long famous for the making of wooden images. Beside the Apollo stands a portrait of Cheirisophos in marble.

§ 2. THE SCULPTORS OF CHIOS.

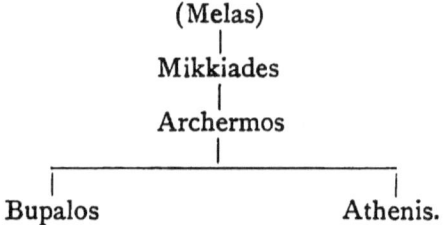

25. Plin. N. H. xxxvi. 11 Cum hi essent, iam fuerat in Chio insula Melas sculptor, dein filius eius Micciades, ac deinde nepos Archermus, cuius filii Bupalus et Athenis uel clarissimi in ea scientia fuere

Before their time the sculptor Melas had already lived on the island of Chios, and after him his son Mikkiades and his grandson Archermos, whose sons Bupalos and Athenis were the most famous masters

Hipponactis poetae aetate, quem certum est LX. Olympiade fuisse. Quodsi quis horum familiam ad proauom usque retro agat, inueniat artis eius originem cum Olympiadum initio coepisse. 12. Hipponacti notabilis foeditas uoltus erat, quam ob rem imaginem eius lasciuia iocorum hi proposuere ridentium circulis, quod Hipponax indignatus destrinxit amaritudinem carminum in tantum, ut credatur aliquîs ad laqueum eos compulisse. Quod falsum est. Complura enim in finitimis insulis simulacra postea fecere, sicut in Delo, quibus subiecerunt carmen, non uitibus tantum censeri Chion, sed et operibus Archermi filiorum. 13. Ostendunt et Lasii Dianam manibus eorum factam ; in ipsa Chio narrata est operis eorum Dianae facies in sublimi posita, cuius uoltum intrantes tristem, exeuntes hilarem putant. Romae signa eorum sunt in Palatina aede Apollinis in fas-

of their craft in the time of the poet Hipponax, who is known to have lived in the 60th Olympiad (540 B.C.). If their line is traced back to the great-grandfather, it will be found that the art took its rise at the beginning of the Olympiads. Hipponax was remarkable for the ugliness of his face, for which reason they exposed his portrait in wanton mockery to jesting crowds, until Hipponax in indignation turned the weapons of his bitterest satire against them with such effect that—as some believe—he drove them to hang themselves. This is not the case : for they afterwards made many statues in the neighbouring islands, as for example in Delos, where their work bore a metrical inscription, stating that Chios was famed not only for its vines but also for the works of the sons of Archermos. The people of Lasos display an Artemis fashioned by their hands ;

C

tigio et omnibus fere quae fecit diuos Augustus. Patris quoque eorum et Deli fuere opera et in Lesbo insula.

and it is stated that in Chios itself there is a figure of Artemis, made by them and set on a high pedestal, whose expression seems gloomy as one enters her shrine, and cheerful as one departs. At Rome their statues stand on the gable of the temple of Apollo on the Palatine, and on almost all the temples built by Augustus the Divine. Their father's works, too, were to be seen both in Delos and on the island of Lesbos.

hi] Dipoinos and Skyllis. The words follow No. 11.

Melas] In all probability the local hero of Chios, son of Oinopion. The confusion may have arisen from the misunderstanding of a phrase in a metrical inscription, *perhaps* of ' Μέλανος πατρώϊον ἄστυ' in the inscription quoted below (No. 26 note).

Olympiadum initio] Pliny erroneously reckons 60 years (a full life) to a generation.

Lasii] A variant is 'Iasii.' Iasos is in Caria, Lasos in Crete.

in fastigio] Either (1) 'on the gable.' The figures would then be ἀκρωτήρια such as those from the temple of Aegina, *F. W.* 84, 85. Or (2) 'in the pediment.' Petersen conjectures that a fragmentary kneeling Amazon from the Villa Ludovisi (*Röm. Mitth.* iv. 86 f.) formed part of the group.

26. Schol. Ar. Av. 573
νεωτερικὸν τὸ τὴν Νίκην καὶ τὸν Ἔρωτα ἐπτερῶσθαι· Ἀρχερμον γάρ φασι τὸν Βουπάλου

The representation of Victory and Love with wings is of recent origin : for according to some it

καὶ Ἀθήνιδος πατέρα, οἱ δὲ
Ἀγλαοφῶντα τὸν Θάσιον ζώ-
γραφον, πτηνὴν ἐργάσασθαι
τὴν Νίκην.

was Archermos, the father
of Bupalos and Athenis,
according to others, Aglao-
phon the Thasian painter,
who represented Victory
winged.

It is natural to combine with this notice the so-called 'Nike of
Delos,' now in the Central Museum at Athens (Brunn-Bruckmann,
36). The plinth, which *almost* certainly belongs to it, bears an
inscription variously restored (Löwy 1). Lolling's restoration
reads :—

Μικκιά[δης τόδ' ἄγαλ]μα καλόν [μ' ἀνέθηκε καὶ υἱός]
Ἄ]ρχερμος (σ)ο[φ]ίησιν Ἐκηβόλ[ῳ ἐκτελέσαντες]
Οἱ Χῖοι Μέ[λ]α[ν]ος πατρώϊον ἄσ[τυ νέμοντες].

But Mr. Ernest Gardner (*Class. Rev.* 1893, p. 140) has shown
cause for regarding the readings [ἄγαλ]μα in l. 1 and Μέλανος l. 3
(for which he reads μεγάλως) as impossible. An inscription from
the Akropolis (Δελτ. Ἀρχ. 1889, p. 119) reads Ἄρχερμος ἐποίησεν ὁ
Χῖος | Ἰφιδίκη μ' ἀνέθηκεν Ἀθηναίᾳ πολιούχῳ. Both inscriptions date
from the second half of the sixth century B.C.

Ἀρχερμον] A certain correction for Ἀρχεννον MSS.
φασι] For the omission of οἱ μέν cf. No. 21 ad fin.
Ἀγλαοφῶντα] The father of Polygnotos. See Brunn, *K. G.* II². 10.

27. Paus. iv. 30. 6 Βού-
παλος δέ, ναούς τε οἰκοδομή-
σασθαι καὶ ζῷα ἀνὴρ ἀγαθὸς
πλάσαι, Σμυρναίοις ἄγαλμα
ἐργαζόμενος Τύχης πρῶτος
ἐποίησεν ὧν ἡμεῖς ἴσμεν πόλον
τε ἔχουσαν ἐπὶ τῇ κεφαλῇ καὶ
τῇ ἑτέρᾳ χειρὶ τὸ καλούμενον
Ἀμαλθείας κέρας ὑπὸ Ἑλ-
λήνων.

Bupalos, a celebrated
temple-architect and sculptor, in making a statue of
Fortune for the people of
Smyrna, was the first, so
far as I know, to represent
her with a circular crown
on her head and that which
the Greeks call 'Amalthea's
horn' in one hand.

ζῷα . . . πλάσαι] Of sculpture generally, as ζῷα γράφειν, later
ζωγραφεῖν, of painting. ζῷα = 'figures' in art generally, so of
a statue in No. 35, where see note.

C 2

28. Paus. ix. 35. 6 ὅστις δὲ ἦν ἀνθρώπων ὁ γυμνὰς πρῶτος Χάριτας ἤτοι πλάσας ἢ γραφῇ μιμησάμενος, οὐχ οἷόν τε ἐγένετο πυθέσθαι με· ἐπεὶ τά γε ἀρχαιότερα ἐχούσας ἐσθῆτα οἵ τε πλάσται καὶ κατὰ ταὐτὰ ἐποίουν οἱ ζώγραφοι· καὶ Σμυρναίοις . . . . ἐν τῷ ἱερῷ τῶν Νεμέσεων ὑπὲρ τῶν ἀγαλμάτων χρυσοῦ Χάριτες ἀνάκεινται, τέχνη Βουπάλου . . . Περγαμηνοῖς δὲ ὡσαύτως ἐν τῷ Ἀττάλου θαλάμῳ, Βουπάλου καὶ αὗται.

I could not discover who was the first man to represent the Graces nude, either in sculpture or in painting. For in old times both sculptors and painters represented them draped. And at Smyrna in the temple of the Nemeseis there stand dedicated golden Graces above the images, the work of Bupalos. There are also statues of the Graces by Bupalos in the chamber of Attalos at Pergamon.

A base with the fragmentary inscription . . . [εἰργ]άσ(σ)ατο Χίος found at Pergamon (Fränkel, *Die Inschriften von Pergamon*, No. 46) may have belonged to the latter group.

§ 3. EARLY WORK IN METAL.

1. GLAUKOS OF CHIOS.

29. Hdt. i. 25 ἀνέθηκε δὲ (ὁ Ἀλυάττης) ἐς Δελφοὺς κρητῆρά τε ἀργύρεον μέγαν καὶ ὑποκρητηρίδιον σιδήρεον κολλητόν, θέης ἄξιον διὰ πάντων τῶν ἐν Δελφοῖσι ἀναθημάτων,

(Alyattes) dedicated at Delphi a large silver bowl and a stand of soldered iron, one of the most remarkable offerings to be seen at Delphi, the work of Glaukos

Γλαύκου τοῦ Χίου ποίημα, ὃς
μοῦνος δὴ πάντων ἀνθρώπων
σιδήρου κόλλησιν ἐξεῦρε.

of Chios, who was the sole
inventor of the soldering of
iron.

Alyattes reigned 617–560 B.C. The date given by the chrono-
logers for Glaukos (Ol. 22 = 672 B.C.) is consequently too high.

30. Paus. x. 16. 1 τῶν δὲ
ἀναθημάτωι, ἃ οἱ βασιλεῖς
ἀπέστειλαν οἱ Λυδῶν, οὐδὲν ἔτι
ἦν αὐτῶν εἰ μὴ σιδηροῦν μόνον
τὸ ὑπόθημα τοῦ ᾿Αλυάττου
κρατῆρος. τοῦτο Γλαύκου μέν
ἐστιν ἔργον τοῦ Χίου, σιδήρου κόλλησιν ἀνδρὸς εὑρόντος·
ἔλασμα δὲ ἕκαστον τοῦ ὑποθήματος ἐλάσματι ἄλλῳ προσ-
εχὲς οὐ περόναις ἐστὶν ἢ
κέντροις, μόνη δὲ ἡ κόλλα
συνέχει τε καί ἐστιν αὕτη τῷ
σιδήρῳ δεσμός· σχῆμα δὲ τοῦ
ὑποθήματος κατὰ πύργον μάλιστα ἐς μύουρον ἀνιόντα ἀπὸ
εὐρυτέρου τοῦ κάτω· ἑκάστη δὲ
πλευρὰ τοῦ ὑποθήματος οὐ διὰ
πάσης πέφρακται, ἀλλά εἰσιν
αἱ πλάγιαι τοῦ σιδήρου ζῶναι
ὥσπερ ἐν κλίμακι οἱ ἀνα-
βασμοί· τὰ δὲ ἐλάσματα τοῦ
σιδήρου τὰ ὀρθὰ ἀνέστραπται
κατὰ τὰ ἄκρα ἐς τὸ ἐκτός· καὶ
ἕδρα τοῦτο ἦν τῷ κρατῆρι.

Of the offerings sent by
the kings of Lydia none
remained but the iron
stand of the bowl of
Alyattes. This is the work
of Glaukos of Chios, the
inventor of the soldering of
iron; and each plate of the
stand is joined to the next,
not with pins or rivets, but
with solder alone, which
holds them together and
acts as a binding material
to the iron: and the form
of the stand is like that of
a tower in the shape of
a truncated cone resting on
the broader base: the sides
of the stand are not entirely
closed, but there are cross-
bars of iron like the rungs
of a ladder, while the upright plates are bent out-
wards at the top, and thus
form a support, on which
the bowl rests.

31. Ath. v. 210 C Γλαύκου .. τοῦ Χίου τὸ ἐν Δελφοῖς
ὑπόστημα .. ὡς ἀληθῶς θέας
ἄξιον διὰ τὰ ἐν αὐτῷ ἐντετο-
ρευμένα ζῳδάρια καὶ ἄλλα
τινὰ ζωΰφια καὶ φυτάρια, ἐπιτί-
θεσθαι ἐπ' αὐτῷ δυνάμενα καὶ
κρατῆρας καὶ ἄλλα σκεύη.

The stand of Glaukos of
Chios at Delphi is really
remarkable, by reason of
the small figures carved
upon it as well as other
animal and vegetable forms,
while bowls and other
vessels can be placed on it.

Instances of similar forms are found in early pottery and bronze ;
cp. the representation on a Phoenician silver bowl (*M. d. I.* ix. 31. 1).
The decoration (friezes of animals, plant-forms, &c.) is in the style
of Phoenician metal-work and Corinthian vases (cp. Brunn,
Griechische Kunstgeschichte, I. chap. 3).

2. THE SCULPTORS OF SAMOS.

(RHOIKOS, THEODOROS, TELEKLES.)

32. Paus. viii. 14. 8
διέχεαν δὲ χαλκὸν πρῶτοι καὶ
ἀγάλματα ἐχωνεύσαντο 'Ροῖ-
κός τε Φιλέου καὶ Θεόδωρος
Τηλεκλέους Σάμιοι.

The first to cast statues
in molten bronze were the
Samians Rhoikos, the son
of Phileas, and Theodoros,
the son of Telekles.

Rhoikos and Theodoros were architects as well as sculptors.
Hdt. iii. 60 states that Rhoikos built the Heraion at Samos, while
Plin. *N. H.* xxxvi. 90 attributes what is probably the same building
under the name of the 'labyrinth of Lemnos' to Rhoikos, Theodoros, and Smilis. Theodoros made a silver bowl for Croesus
(conquered 546 B.C.), and the famous ring of Polykrates (died
circ. 520 B.C.) ; and this date accords with an inscription found on
the Akropolis of Athens ('Εφ. 'Αρχ. 1886, Pl. vi. 5, *Coll.* I, Fig. 72),
which reads Θεό[δωρ]ος ἄγ[αλμα ἐποίησεν] in Ionic characters.

33. Paus. x. 38. 6 Θεοδώρου μὲν δὴ οὐδὲν ἔτι οἶδα
ἐξευρὼν ὅσα γε χαλκοῦ
πεποιημένα· ἐν δὲ 'Αρτέμιδος

I can find no trace of
any work by Theodoros, at
least in bronze ; but in
the temple of Artemis at

τῆς Ἐφεσίας πρὸς τὸ οἴκημα
ἐρχομένῳ τὸ ἔχον τὰς γραφὰς
λίθου θριγκός ἐστιν ὑπὲρ τοῦ
βωμοῦ τῆς Πρωτοθρονίας
καλουμένης Ἀρτέμιδος· ἀγάλματα δὲ ἄλλα τε ἐπὶ τοῦ θριγ-
κοῦ καὶ γυναικὸς εἰκὼν πρὸς
τῷ πέρατι ἔστηκε, τέχνη τοῦ
Ῥοίκου, Νύκτα δὲ οἱ Ἐφέσιοι
καλοῦσι.

Ephesos, at the approach
to the chamber containing
the paintings, there is a
marble cornice above the altar of Artemis Protothronia,
as she is called, and among
other statues on the cornice
there is a figure of a woman,
standing close to the end,
which the Ephesians call
Night. This is the work of
Rhoikos.

34. Plin. *N. H.* xxxiv.
83 Theodorus, qui labyrin-
thum fecit, Sami ipse se
ex aere fudit, praeter similitudinis mirabilem famam
magna subtilitate celebra-
tus ; dextra limam tenet,
laeua tribus digitis quad-
rigulam tenuit translatam
Praeneste, tantae paucitatis
ut miraculo fictam eam
currumque et aurigam in-
tegeret alis simul facta
musca.

Theodoros, the builder
of the labyrinth, cast his
own portrait in bronze at
Samos. This is famous, not
only because of the marvellous likeness, but also because of the minuteness of
the work ; in the right hand
is a file, while the left held
in three fingers a tiny four-
horse chariot, now removed
to Praeneste, so minute and
marvellously wrought that
a fly, made with it, covered
team, car, and driver with
its wings.

The rationalistic explanation of this story is that the statue held
the symbols of Theodoros' cunning as goldsmith and gem-engraver
—the latter being a scarab engraved with the design of a chariot.
As, however, a precisely similar object is attributed to one Myr-
mekides, an artist of unknown date, whose skill in minute

workmanship was proverbial (cp. vii. 85 Myrmecides . . . inclaruit quadriga . . . quam musca integeret alis. xxxvi. 43 M. cuius quadrigam cum agitatore operuit alis musca), and (doubtfully) to Pheidias himself by Julian, *Epist.* 8, p. 377 A, the story is in all probability entirely apocryphal.

miraculo fictam] Sillig's correction of 'miraculo pictam' of the best MS. The rest have 'totam.' For 'miraculo' cp. ix. 93 reliquiae . . . miraculo pependere pondo DCC.

35. Diod. i. 98 Τηλεκλέα καὶ Θεόδωρον τοὺς Ῥοίκου μὲν υἱούς, κατασκευάσαντας δὲ τοῖς Σαμίοις τὸ τοῦ Ἀπόλλωνος τοῦ Πυθίου ξόανον. τοῦ γὰρ ἀγάλματος ἐν Σάμῳ μὲν ὑπὸ Τηλεκλέους ἱστορεῖται τὸ ἥμισυ δημιουργηθῆναι, κατὰ δὲ τὴν Ἔφεσον ὑπὸ τοῦ ἀδελφοῦ Θεοδώρου τὸ ἕτερον μέρος συντελεσθῆναι, συντεθέντα δὲ πρὸς ἄλληλα τὰ μέρη συμφωνεῖν οὕτως ὥστε δοκεῖν ὑφ' ἑνὸς τὸ πᾶν σῶμα κατεσκευάσθαι. τοῦτο δὲ τὸ γένος τῆς ἐργασίας παρὰ μὲν τοῖς Ἕλλησι μηδαμῶς ἐπιτηδεύεσθαι, παρὰ δὲ τοῖς Αἰγυπτίοις μάλιστα συντελεῖσθαι . . . τὸ δὲ ἐν τῇ Σάμῳ ξόανον συμφώνως τῇ τῶν Αἰγυπτίων φιλοτεχνίᾳ κατὰ τὴν κορυφὴν διχοτομούμενον διορίζειν τοῦ ζῴου τὸ μέσον μέχρι τῶν αἰδοίων, ἰσάζον ὁμοίως ἑαυτῷ πάντοθεν. εἶναι δ' αὐτὸ λέγουσι

Telekles and Theodoros the sons of Rhoikos, who made the statue of the Pythian Apollo for the Samians. The story runs that one half of the image was made at Samos by Telekles, while the other half was fashioned at Ephesos by his brother Theodoros, and that when the parts were joined together they fitted so exactly that the whole figure appeared to be the work of one artist. This method of working was never practised by the Greeks, but was in common use among the Egyptians. And the statue at Samos, being made in accordance with the Egyptian system, is bisected by a line which runs from the crown of the head through the centre of the figure to

κατὰ τὸ πλεῖστον παρεμφερὲς τοῖς Αἰγυπτίοις, ὡς ἂν τὰς μὲν χεῖρας ἔχον παρατεταμένας, τὰ δὲ σκέλη διαβεβηκότα.

the groin, and divides it into precisely equal and similar halves. They say that it resembled Egyptian works as closely as possible, with its arms hanging by its sides and its legs parted.

ξόανον] The word is used not in the restricted sense of a *wooden* image found in Pausanias, but with the general meaning 'statue.' Cp. No. 112.

ζῷον] Like ζῴδιον, a 'figure,' here 'statue.' Thus the figures in the frieze of the Erechtheum are called ζῷα *CIA*. I. 322, ζῴδια *CIA*. I. 324C.

3. GITIADAS OF SPARTA.

36. Paus. iii. 17. 2 ἐνταῦθα ᾿Αθηνᾶς ἱερὸν πεποίηται, Πολιούχου καλουμένης καὶ Χαλκιοίκου τῆς αὐτῆς . . . Λακεδαιμόνιοι . . . τόν τε ναὸν ὁμοίως καὶ τὸ ἄγαλμα ἐποιήσαντο ᾿Αθηνᾶς χαλκοῦν· Γιτιάδας δὲ εἰργάσατο ἀνὴρ ἐπιχώριος . . . ἐπείργασται δὲ τῷ χαλκῷ πολλὰ μὲν τῶν ἄθλων ῾Ηρακλέους, πολλὰ δὲ καὶ ὧν ἐθελοντὴς κατώρθωσε, Τυνδάρεω τε τῶν παίδων ἄλλα τε καὶ ἡ τῶν Λευκίππου θυγατέρων ἁρπαγή· καὶ ῞Ηφαιστος τὴν μητέρα ἐστὶν ἀπολύων τῶν δεσμῶν . . . Περσεῖ δ' ἐς Λιβύην καὶ ἐπὶ Μέδουσαν ὡρμημένῳ διδοῦσαι

Here there is a temple of Athena, who is called Wardress of the city and also Goddess of the Brasen House. The Spartans caused both the temple and the image of Athena to be made of bronze. The work was done by Gitiadas, a native of Sparta. On the bronze there are wrought in relief many of the labours of Herakles, and of the exploits which he performed of his free will, and the deeds of the sons of Tyndareos, amongst others the rape of the daughters of Leukippos:

νύμφαι δῶρά εἰσι κυνῆν καὶ
τὰ ὑποδήματα, ὑφ᾽ ὧν οἰσθή-
σεσθαι διὰ τοῦ ἀέρος ἔμελλεν.
ἐπείργασται δὲ καὶ τὰ ἐς τὴν
'Αθηνᾶς γένεσιν, καὶ 'Αμφι-
τρίτη καὶ Ποσειδῶν, ἃ δὴ
μέγιστα καὶ μάλιστα ἦν ἐμοὶ
δοκεῖν θέας ἄξια.

and there is Hephaistos releasing his mother from her bonds. Perseus is bound for Libya to fight with Medusa, and the Nymphs are giving him gifts—a helmet, and the sandals which were to bear him through the air. The story of the birth of Athena is also represented, and Amphitrite and Poseidon. These are the most prominent, and, to my thinking, the most remarkable of the reliefs.

ἐνταῦθα] On the Akropolis of Sparta. The statue is represented on coins of Sparta and Melos (*Num. Comm. N.* xiii–xv). The body is in the form of a column divided into horizontal bands. It is uncertain whether the reliefs decorated these bands—representing woven patterns—or the walls of the temple.

Ἥφαιστος] Hera hurled Hephaistos down from heaven, and in revenge he presented her with a chair from which she could not rise. Dionysos made him drunk, and brought him back to heaven to release her.

37. Paus. iii. 18. 7 τὰ δὲ
ἐν 'Αμύκλαις θέας ἄξια, . . .
τρίποδες χαλκοῖ . . . ὑπὸ μὲν
δὴ τῷ πρώτῳ τρίποδι 'Αφροδίτης ἄγαλμα ἔστηκεν, Ἄρτεμις
δὲ ὑπὸ τῷ δευτέρῳ· Γιτιάδα
καὶ αὐτοὶ τέχνη καὶ τὰ
ἐπειργασμένα.

Among the notable sights of Amyklai are certain bronze tripods. The first tripod is supported by an image of Aphrodite, the second by one of Artemis. Both the tripods and the sculptures which adorn them are the work of Gitiadas.

Paus. mentions a story that these tripods were dedicated from the spoil taken in the first Messenian war (in the eighth or seventh century B.C.), but this is clearly impossible. There was a third tripod, the work of Kallon of Aegina (v. infr. No. 53) ; but we cannot be certain that it was dedicated at the same time.

4. BATHYKLES OF MAGNESIA.

38. Paus. iii. 18. 9
Βαθυκλέους δὲ Μάγνητος ὃς τὸν θρόνον ἐποίησε τοῦ Ἀμυκλαίου, ἀναθήματα ἐπεξειργασμένα τῷ θρόνῳ Χάριτες καὶ ἄγαλμα δὲ Λευκοφρύνης ἐστὶν Ἀρτέμιδος.

By the hand of Bathykles the Magnesian, who made the throne of Apollo at Amyklae, are certain votive offerings made after the completion of the throne — Graces and an image of Artemis Leukophryne.

The throne is described at length by Pausanias in the following sections (see the reconstruction by Furtw., *Meisterwerke*, p. 706). Bathykles was employed to utilize the present of gold sent by Croesus to Sparta in the decoration of the temple of Apollo at Amyklai.

Λευκοφρύνης] Artemis Leukophryne (or Leukophryene) had a famous temple at Magnesia on the Maeander, the home of Bathykles (Dittenberger, *Syll.* 171, 84, Tac. *Ann.* iii. 62).

§ 4. THE EARLIEST PORTRAITS OF ATHLETES.

39. Plin. *N. H.* xxxiv. 16
Effigies hominum non solebant exprimi nisi aliqua illustri causa perpetuitatem merentium, primo sacrorum

It was not the custom to represent the features of individuals unless they had earned immortality . by some special distinction.

certaminum uictoria maxu-
meque Olympiae, ubi om-
nium qui uicissent statuas
dicari mos erat, eorum uero
qui ter ibi superauissent ex
membris ipsorum simili-
tudine expressa, quas ico-
nicas uocant.

The first of such was a
victory in the sacred games,
and especially at Olympia,
where it was the custom to
dedicate statues of all victors, while in the case of
those thrice victorious the
actual features were por-
trayed. Such statues are
called 'iconic.'

40. Paus. vi. 18. 7 πρῶται
δὲ ἀθλητῶν ἀνετέθησαν ἐς
'Ολυμπίαν εἰκόνες Πραξιδά-
μαντός τε Αἰγινητοῦ νικήσαντος
πυγμῇ τὴν ἐνάτην 'Ολυμπιάδα
ἐπὶ ταῖς πεντήκοντα, καὶ
'Οπουντίου 'Ρηξιβίου παγκρα-
τιαστὰς καταγωνισαμένου, μιᾷ
πρὸς ταῖς ἑξήκοντα 'Ολυμπιάδι.
αὗται κεῖνται μὲν αἱ εἰκόνες οὐ
πρόσω τῆς Οἰνομάου κίονος,
ξύλου δέ εἰσιν εἰργασμέναι,
'Ρηξιβίου μὲν συκῆς, ἡ δὲ τοῦ
Αἰγινητοῦ κυπαρίσσου, καὶ
ἧσσον τῆς ἑτέρας πεπονηκυῖά
ἐστιν.

The first portraits of
athletes dedicated at Olympia were those of Praxida-
mas of Aegina, victorious
in boxing in the 59th
Olympiad (544 B.C.) and
Rhexibios of Opus, victo-
rious in the pankration in
the 61st Olympiad (536 B.C.).
These figures stand not far
from the pillar of Oinomaos,
and are made of wood. The
portrait of Rhexibios is of
fig-wood, while that of the
Aeginetan is of cypress,
and has suffered less than
the other.

τῆς Οἰνομάου κίονος] A wooden column at Olympia, carefully
preserved as a relic of the palace of Oinomaos (Paus. v. 20. 6).

41. Paus. viii. 40. 1
Φιγαλεῦσι δὲ ἀνδριάς ἐστιν ἐπὶ
τῆς ἀγορᾶς 'Αρραχίωνος τοῦ

In the market-place at
Phigaleia stands a portrait
of Arrhachion, the pankra-

παγκρατιαστοῦ, τά τε ἄλλα tiast, which is archaic in
ἀρχαῖος καὶ οὐχ ἥκιστα ἐπὶ style, and especially in
τῷ σχήματι· οὐ διεστᾶσι μὲν attitude. The feet are not
πολὺ οἱ πόδες, καθεῖνται δὲ far apart, and the hands
παρὰ πλευρᾷ αἱ χεῖρες ἄχρι hang down by the sides as
τῶν γλουτῶν· πεποίηται μὲν far as the buttocks. The
δὴ ἡ εἰκὼν λίθου, λέγουσι δὲ portrait is made of marble,
καὶ ἐπίγραμμα ἐπ' αὐτῇ γρα- and it is alleged that there
φῆναι· καὶ τοῦτο μὲν ἠφάνισται was an inscription painted
ὑπὸ τοῦ χρόνου. τῷ δὲ Ἀρραχί- upon it ; but this has dis-
ωνι ἐγένοντο Ὀλυμπικαὶ νῖκαι appeared through lapse of
δύο μὲν Ὀλυμπιάσι ταῖς πρὸ time. Arrhachion gained
τῆς τετάρτης καὶ πεντηκοστῆς. two Olympic victories in
the Olympiads which pre-
ceded the 54th (564 B.C.).

Paus. (vi. 15. 8) also mentions a portrait of the Spartan Eutelidas,
victorious as a boy in wrestling and the five contests in the 38th
Olympiad (628 B.C.). But the date rests on his own inference, and
is inconsistent with the statement of No. 40. The statue was, however, archaic, and the inscription no longer legible.

PART II

ARCHAIC AND TRANSITIONAL SCULPTURE

Nos. 42-95.

§ I. THE ARCHAIC SCHOOLS.

1. ARGOS.

(a) AGELADAS.

Date.—Determined by (1) his statues of Olympic victors—
Anochos 520, Kleosthenes 516, Timasitheos executed in 507
(Hdt. v. 72); (2) the inscription of his son (or slave) Argeiadas on
the base of a chariot-group dedicated at Olympia by Praxiteles,
Συρακύσιος . . . καὶ Καμαριναῖος (Löwy 30). Kamarina was destroyed
and its inhabitants removed to Syracuse in 484 B.C. Pliny states
that he was the teacher of Myron and Polykleitos, but this is improbable in the first case, and impossible in the second. The statement
that he was the teacher of Pheidias (No. 43) has no early authority.

42. Paus. iv. 33. 2. (At Ithome.) τὸ δὲ ἄγαλμα τοῦ Διὸς Ἀγελάδα μέν ἐστιν ἔργον, ἐποιήθη δὲ ἐξ ἀρχῆς τοῖς οἰκήσασιν ἐν Ναυπάκτῳ Μεσσηνίων.

(At Ithome.) The image of Zeus is the work of Ageladas, and was origin-ally made for the Mes-senians who settled at Nau-paktos.

The Messenians were probably transferred to Naupaktos about
46⅓ (whether we read τετάρτῳ ἔτει in Thuc. i. 103. 1 or adopt the
earlier date (46⅘) for the revolt of the Helots, as is done by Wilamowitz, *Aristoteles und Athen*, ii. 295), so that we must not take
the words of Pausanias as a note of chronology. The statue is
represented on the coins of Messene, *Num. Comm. PP.* iv, v.

43. Schol. Ar. Ran. 504 ἡ Μελίτη δῆμος τῆς Ἀττικῆς . . . ἔστι δὲ καὶ ἐκεῖ Ἡρα-

Melite is a deme of Attica, where there is a celebrated temple of Hera-

D

κλέους ἐπιφανέστατον ἱερὸν Ἀλεξικάκου· τὸ δὲ τοῦ Ἡρακλέους ἄγαλμα ἔργον Ἀγελάδου τοῦ Ἀργείου τοῦ διδασκάλου Φειδίου. ἡ δὲ ἵδρυσις ἐγένετο κατὰ τὸν μέγαν λοιμόν.

kles, the Averter of Ill. The image of Herakles is the work of Ageladas of Argos, the teacher of Pheidias, and it was set up at the time of the great plague.

The Scholiast refers to the plague of 4²⁹⁄₂₈, but this would give far too late a date. A plague about 500 B.C. is attested by the epitaph λοι]μῷ θανούσης εἰμὶ [σῆ]μα Μυρ(ρ)ίνης (*CIA*. i. 475).

44. Anth. Plan. iv. 220.
Ἀντιπάτρου Σιδωνίου.
Τρίζυγες αἱ Μοῦσαι τᾷδ' ἔσταμεν· ἁ μία λωτούς,
ἁ δὲ φέρει παλάμαις βάρβιτον, ἁ δὲ χέλυν.
ἁ μὲν Ἀριστοκλῆος ἔχει χέλυν,
ἁ δ' Ἀγελάδα
βάρβιτον, ἁ Καναχᾶ δ'
ὑμνοπόλους δόνακας.

ANTIPATER OF SIDON.
Here stand we Muses three; one bears in her hand the flutes, one the barbitos, one the lyre. The Muse of Aristokles holds the lyre, that of Ageladas the barbitos, that of Kanachos the reeds that make music.

On Kanachos and Aristokles of Sicyon v. infr. Nos. 49 ff. The χέλυς may be illustrated by the 'School' vase of Duris (*M. d. I.* ix. 54); the βάρβιτος by Benndorf, *Griech. und sicil.Vasenbilder*, xli. 2.

45. Paus. x. 10. 6 Ταραντίνων δὲ οἱ ἵπποι οἱ χαλκοῖ καὶ αἰχμάλωτοι γυναῖκες ἀπὸ Μεσσαπίων εἰσίν, ὁμόρων τῇ Ταραντίνων βαρβάρων, Ἀγελάδα δὲ ἔργα τοῦ Ἀργείου.

The bronze horses of the Tarentines and the captive women are offerings from the spoils of the Messapians, who are barbarous neighbours of Tarentum; they are the work of Ageladas of Argos.

At Delphi.

46. Paus. vi. 10. 6 ἐπὶ δὲ τῷ Παντάρκει Κλεοσθένους ἐστὶν ἅρμα ἀνδρὸς Ἐπιδαμνίου. τοῦτο ἔργον . . . ἐστὶν Ἀγελάδα . . . ἐνίκα μὲν δὴ τὴν ἕκτην Ὀλυμπιάδα καὶ ἑξηκοστὴν ὁ Κλεοσθένης, ἀνέθηκε δὲ ὁμοῦ τοῖς ἵπποις αὐτοῦ τε εἰκόνα καὶ τὸν ἡνίοχον. ἐπιγέγραπται δὲ καὶ τῶν ἵππων τὰ ὀνόματα, Φοῖνιξ καὶ Κόραξ, ἑκατέρωθεν δὲ οἱ παρὰ τὸ ζυγόν, κατὰ μὲν τὰ δεξιὰ Κνακίας, ἐν δὲ τῇ ἀριστέρᾳ Σάμος· καὶ ἐλεγεῖον τόδ᾽ ἐστὶν ἐπὶ τῷ ἅρματι

Κλεοσθένης μ᾽ ἀνέθηκεν ὁ Πόν-
τιος ἐξ Ἐπιδάμνου
νικήσας ἵπποις καλὸν ἀγῶνα
Διός.

Next to Pantarkes is the chariot of Kleosthenes the Epidamnian. This is the work of Ageladas. Kleosthenes was victorious in the 66th Olympiad (516 B.C.), and dedicated portraits of himself and his charioteer along with his team. The names of the horses also are inscribed, Phoinix and Korax, and the trace-horses on either side, Knakias on the right and Samos on the left. And on the chariot is the following couplet :—

Kleosthenes of Pontos from Epidamnos dedicated me, when his team won the victory in the noble games of Zeus.

Other works :—
ZEUS as a child and HERAKLES as a beardless youth, in bronze, at Aigion (Paus. vii. 24. 4).
Athlete-statues at Olympia :—
Anochos of Tarentum, victorious in the foot-race, Ol. 65 (520 B.C.) (Paus. vi. 14. 11).
Timasitheos of Delphi, twice victorious in the pankration, executed at Athens in 507 B.C. for participation in the treason of Isagoras (Paus. vi. 8. 6).

(b) Glaukos and Dionysios (Simon).

Date.—See notes on Nos. 47, 48.

47. Paus. v. 26. 2 τὰ δὲ ἀναθήματα Μικύθου πολλά τε ἀριθμὸν καὶ οὐκ ἐφεξῆς ὄντα εὕρισκον, ἀλλὰ Ἰφίτου. μὲν ... ἔχεται τοσάδε ἀναθήματα τῶν Μικύθου, Ἀμφιτρίτη τε καὶ Ποσειδῶν καὶ Ἑστία, Γλαῦκος δὲ ὁ ποιήσας ἐστιν Ἀργεῖος. παρὰ δὲ τοῦ ναοῦ τοῦ μεγάλου τὴν ἐν ἀριστερᾷ πλευρὰν ἀνέθηκεν ἄλλα, Κόρην τὴν Δήμητρος καὶ Ἀφροδίτην Γανυμήδην τε καὶ Ἄρτεμιν, ποιητῶν δὲ Ὅμηρον καὶ Ἡσίοδον, καὶ θεοὺς αὖθις Ἀσκληπιὸν καὶ Ὑγίειαν. 3. Ἀγών τε ἐν τοῖς ἀναθήμασίν ἐστι τοῖς Μικύθου φέρων ἁλτῆρας ... παρὰ δὲ τοῦ Ἀγῶνος τὴν εἰκόνα Διόνυσος καὶ ὁ Θρᾷξ ἐστὶν Ὀρφεὺς καὶ ἄγαλμα Διός ... ταῦτα ἔργα ἐστὶν Ἀργείου Διονυσίου, τεθῆναι δὲ ὑπὸ τοῦ Μικύθου καὶ ἄλλα ὁμοῦ τούτοις λέγουσι, Νέρωνα δὲ ἀφελέσθαι φασὶ καὶ ταῦτα. τοῖς δὲ ἐργασαμένοις αὐτά, γένος οὖσιν Ἀργείοις, Διονυσίῳ τε καὶ Γλαύκῳ, διδάσκαλόν σφισιν οὐδένα ἐπιλέγουσιν· ἡλι-

The offerings of Mikythos I discovered to be many in number and separated from each other. Close to the statue of Iphitos stand the following offerings of Mikythos—Amphitrite, Poseidon, and Hestia. They are the work of Glaukos of Argos. On the left-hand side of the great temple he dedicated another group of figures— Kore the daughter of Demeter and Aphrodite and Ganymede and Artemis, the poets Homer and Hesiod, and again the gods Asklepios and Hygieia. Among the offerings of Mikythos is a figure of Agon bearing leaping-weights. And beside this figure are Dionysos and Orpheus the Thracian and an image of Zeus. These are the work of Dionysios of Argos. It is said that other statues were dedicated by Mikythos at the same time, but that they (like others) were

κίαν δὲ αὐτῶν ὁ τὰ ἔργα ἐς Ὀλυμπίαν ἀναθεὶς ἐπιδείκνυσιν ὁ Μίκυθος.

carried away by Nero. Nothing is recorded as to the teacher of the artists Dionysios and Glaukos, who were Argives by birth; but their date is shown by the fact that Mikythos dedicated their works at Olympia.

Mikythos reigned at Rhegion as guardian of the sons of Anaxilas 478–467 B.C., and then retired to Tegea. Fragments of the inscription have been found (Löwy 31) ; it appears that the statues were erected about 460 B. C.

Ἀγών] A personification of ' Contest.'

ἀλτῆρας] The leaping-weights used by the Greeks resembled dumb-bells. They are frequently represented on vases, e. g. Gerhard, A. V. 260.

ἄγαλμα Διός Beardless (Paus. v. 24. 6).

48. Paus. v. 27. 1 ἐν δὲ αὐτοῖς καὶ τὰ ἀνατεθέντα ἐστὶν ὑπὸ τοῦ Φόρμιδος, ὃς ἐκ Μαινάλου διαβὰς ἐς Σικελίαν παρὰ Γέλωνα τὸν Δεινομένους, καὶ ἐκείνῳ τε αὐτῷ καὶ Ἱέρωνι ὕστερον ἀδελφῷ τοῦ Γέλωνος ἐς τὰς στρατείας ἀποδεικνύμενος λαμπρὰ ἔργα, ἐς τοσοῦτο προῆλθεν εὐδαιμονίας, ὡς ἀναθεῖναι μὲν ταῦτα ἐς Ὀλυμπίαν, ἀναθεῖναι δὲ καὶ Ἀπόλλωνι ἄλλα ἐς Δελφούς. 2. τὰ δὲ ἐς Ὀλυμπίαν δύο τέ εἰσιν ἵπποι καὶ ἡνίοχοι δύο, ἑκατέρῳ τῶν ἵππων παρεστὼς ἀνὴρ

Among them are the offerings dedicated by Phormis, who crossed over from Mainalos to Sicily and joined Gelon the son of Deinomenes, in whose service and afterwards in that of his brother Gelon he performed remarkable exploits in war and raised his fortunes to such a height that he was enabled to dedicate these offerings at Olympia, and others to Apollo at Delphi. His offerings at Olympia consist

ἡνίοχος. ὁ μὲν δὴ πρότερος τῶν ἵππων καὶ ὁ ἀνὴρ Διονυσίου τοῦ Ἀργείου, τὰ δεύτερα δὲ ἔργα ἐστὶν Αἰγινητοῦ Σίμωνος. τῷ προτέρῳ δὲ τῶν ἵππων ἐπίγραμμα ἔπεστιν ἐπὶ τῇ πλευρᾷ, τὰ πρῶτα οὐ σὺν μέτρῳ· λέγει γὰρ δὴ οὕτω

Φόρμις ἀνέθηκε
Ἀρκὰς Μαινάλιος, νῦν δὲ
Συρακόσιος.

in two horses and two charioteers, one of whom stands beside each horse. The first of the two horses with its groom is the work of Dionysios of Argos, while the second pair are by Simon of Aegina. The first of the two horses has an inscription on its side, of which the former part is unmetrical, running as follows :—

Phormis dedicated me, once an Arkadian of Mainalos, but now a Syracusan.

Gelon reigned 485–476 B. C., Hieron 476–467 B. C.

2. SIKYON.

KANACHOS.

Date.—He is coupled with Ageladas in No. 44, and with Kallon of Aegina by Paus. vii. 18. 10; cp. Cicero's criticism, quoted Introd. § 3. The temple of Apollo at Branchidai (v. No. 49) was destroyed by Darius in 493 B. C. (Hdt. vi. 19). His brother Aristokles (Paus. vi. 9. 1) was the founder of a school which Paus. traces to the seventh generation.

49. Plin. N. H. xxxiv. 75 Canachus (fecit) Apollinem nudum qui Philesius cognominatur in Didymaeo Aeginetica aeris temperatura, ceruomque una ita uestigiis suspendit ut linum

Kanachos made a nude Apollo, which bears the name of Philesios and stands in the Didymaion, in bronze of Aeginetan composition, and with it a stag, supported on its

subter pedes trahatur, alterno morsu calce digitisque retinentibus solum, ita uertebrato dente utrisque in partibus ut a repulsu per uices resiliat. Idem et κελητίζοντας pueros.

feet in such a way that a string can be passed beneath them, while heel and toe alternately retain their grip. The teeth of the mechanism are jointed in such a manner that each recoils in turn when driven home. He also made statues of boys riding on racehorses.

The statue is represented on coins of Miletos (Overbeck, *Kunstmyth.*, Apollon, Münztafel i. 22 ff.) holding stag in r., bow in l., and there is a small copy (without the bow) in the Brit. Mus· Bronze Room.

suspendit] Used in the less common sense 'supported from below,' not 'dependent from above.' Cp. xxxiii. 69 tellus ligneis columnis suspenditur (in mines).

solum] sōlum 'only' and sŏlum 'the surface of the hand' (lit. ground), are both possible.

repulsu] For this use cp. xi. 164 (of a snake) dentium repulsu uirus fundit in morsus (quoted by Petersen, *A. Z.* 1880, p. 23). The principle of the mechanism described seems to be that 'heel and toe' were provided with 'teeth' which fitted a semicircular groove in the hollow of the hand. Thus, while the foot could not be dislodged, 'heel' and 'toe' could be *alternately* set free, and the string passed from end to end. The temple of Apollo Philesios was at Branchidai, near Miletos. The statue was removed by Darius (not Xerxes, as stated by Paus. viii. 46. 3, cp. Hdt. vi. 19), but restored by Seleukos Nikator (312–281 B.C.).

50. Paus. ix. 10. 2 (At Thebes) ἔστι δὲ λόφος ἐν δεξιᾷ τῶν πυλῶν ἱερὸς Ἀπόλλωνος· καλεῖται δὲ ὅ τε λόφος καὶ ὁ θεὸς Ἰσμήνιος, παραρρε-

(At Thebes) there is a hill on the right of the gate, sacred to Apollo: both the hill and the god are called Ismenian, because the river

ὄντος τοῦ ποταμοῦ ταύτῃ τοῦ Ἰσμήνου . . . τὸ δὲ ἄγαλμα μεγέθει τε ἴσον τῷ ἐν Βραγχίδαις ἐστὶ καὶ τὸ εἶδος οὐδὲν διαφόρως ἔχον· ὅστις δὲ τῶν ἀγαλμάτων τούτων τὸ ἕτερον εἶδε καὶ τὸν εἰργασμένον ἐπύθετο, οὐ μεγάλη οἱ σοφία καὶ τὸ ἕτερον θεασαμένῳ Κανάχου ποίημα ὃν ἐπίστασθαι. διαφέρουσι δὲ τοσόνδε· ὁ μὲν γὰρ ἐν Βραγχίδαις χαλκοῦ, ὁ δὲ Ἰσμήνιός ἐστι κέδρου.

Ismenos passes by it. The image is equal in size to that at Branchidai and exactly similar in appearance; and whoever has seen one of the images and learnt the artist's name needs no great skill to discern that the other is the work of Kanachos, when he sees it; there is this difference, that the statue at Branchidai is of bronze, while the Ismenian Apollo is of cedarwood.

51. Paus. ii. 10. 4 (At Sikyon) ἄλλος ἐστὶν Ἀφροδίτης ἱερός . . . 5. τὸ μὲν δὴ ἄγαλμα καθήμενον Κάναχος Σικυώνιος ἐποίησεν· . . . πεποίηται δὲ ἐκ χρυσοῦ καὶ ἐλέφαντος, φέρουσα ἐπὶ τῇ κεφαλῇ πόλον, τῶν χειρῶν δὲ ἔχει τῇ μὲν μήκωνα, τῇ δὲ ἑτέρᾳ μῆλον.

(At Sikyon) there is another shrine of Aphrodite. . . . The seated image was made by Kanachos of Sikyon. It is wrought of gold and ivory, and wears a circular crown on its head, while it holds in the one hand a poppy and in the other an apple.

For the MUSES of Kanachos and Aristokles, v. No. 44.

3. AEGINA.

(a) KALLON.

Date.—An inscription found on the Akropolis of Athens (Löwy 27) reads Κάλων ἐποίησε Αἰ[γινήτης], and may be assigned to the opening years of the fifth century B.C. He is coupled with Kanachos by Paus. vii. 18. 10 and with Hegesias by Quintilian (v. Introd. § 3).

52. Paus. ii. 32. 5 (At Troizen) ἐν δὲ τῇ ἀκροπόλει τῆς Σθενιάδος καλουμένης ναός ἐστιν ᾿Αθηνᾶς. αὐτὸ δὲ εἰργάσατο τῆς θεοῦ τὸ ξόανον Κάλλων Αἰγινήτης. μαθήτης δὲ ὁ Κάλλων ἦν Τεκταίου καὶ ᾿Αγγελιῶνος.

(At Troizen) on the Akropolis is a temple of Athena, called Sthenias. The wooden image of the goddess was made by Kallon of Aegina, who was a pupil of Tektaios and Angelion.

V. supr. No. 19.

53. Paus. iii. 18. 7 ἐν ᾿Αμύκλαις . . . τρίποδες χαλκοῖ . . . ὁ τρίτος δέ ἐστιν Αἰγινήτου Κάλλωνος· ὑπὸ τούτῳ δὲ ἄγαλμα Κόρης τῆς Δήμητρος ἕστηκεν.

At Amyklai are tripods of bronze; the third is by Kallon of Aegina, and beneath it stands an image of Kore the daughter of Demeter.

The others were by Gitiadas, v. supr. No. 37 note.

(b) Onatas.

Date.—(1) An inscription found on the Akropolis of Athens (*CIA*. iv. 2. 373, 399 ; cp. *Jahrb*. 1888, p. 271) reads ᾿Ονάτας ἐποίησεν, and is earlier than the Persian destruction in 480 B.C. (2) The base of No. 59 lies partly under the foundations of the temple of Zeus at Olympia, begun circ. 460 B.C. (3) No. 58 was dedicated after the death of Hieron in 467 B.C. (4) O. is coupled with Hegias and Ageladas by Paus., and dated in the generation succeeding the Persian wars (Nos. 54, 58).

54. Paus. viii. 42. 1 τὸ δὲ ἕτερον τῶν ὀρῶν, τὸ ᾿Ελάϊον, ἀπωτέρω μὲν Φιγαλίας ὅσον τε σταδίοις τριάκοντά ἐστι, Δήμητρος δὲ ἄντρον αὐτόθι ἱερὸν

The other mountain, Elaïon by name, is about thirty stades further removed from Phigalia, and there is a cave there sacred to

ἐπίκλησιν Μελαίνης . . . 3.
. . πεποιῆσθαι δὲ οὕτω σφίσι
τὸ ἄγαλμα. 4. καθέζεσθαι μὲν
ἐπὶ πέτρᾳ, γυναικὶ δὲ ἐοικέναι
τἆλλα πλὴν κεφαλήν· κεφα-
λὴν δὲ καὶ κόμην εἶχεν ἵππου,
καὶ δρακόντων τε καὶ ἄλλων
θηρίων εἰκόνες προσεπεφύκε-
σαν τῇ κεφαλῇ· χιτῶνα δὲ
ἐνεδέδυτο καὶ ἐς ἄκρους τοὺς
πόδας· δελφὶς δὲ ἐπὶ τῆς
χειρὸς ἦν αὐτῇ, περιστερὰ δὲ
ἡ ὄρνις ἐπὶ τῇ ἑτέρᾳ . . .
Μέλαιναν δὲ ἐπονομάσαι φασὶν αὐτήν, ὅτι καὶ ἡ θεὸς μέλαιναν τὴν ἐσθῆτα εἶχε.

Demeter, who is called 'the Black.' They describe the original image as follows. The goddess was seated on a rock, and was in form like a woman except for her head : she had the head and mane of a horse, and forms of serpents and other creatures sprang from her head ; she was dressed in a tunic which reached to her feet ; in one hand was a dolphin, while the bird in the other was a dove. They say that she got the name 'Black' because the goddess herself wore black raiment.

The statue was destroyed by fire, and the worship neglected by the Phigaleans, who were visited with famine, and commanded by the Pythian Apollo to renew the cult. Paus. continues :—

'Ονάταν τὸν Μίκωνος Αἰ-
γινήτην πείθουσιν ἐφ' ὅσῳ δὴ
μισθῷ ποιῆσαί σφισιν ἄγαλμα
Δήμητρος . . . τότε δὴ ὁ ἀνὴρ
οὗτος ἀνευρὼν γραφὴν ἢ μί-
μημα τοῦ ἀρχαίου ξοάνου, τὰ
πλείω δέ, ὡς λέγεται, καὶ κατὰ
ὀνειράτων ὄψιν, ἐποίησε χαλκοῦν Φιγαλεῦσιν ἄγαλμα, γενεᾷ
μάλιστα ὕστερον τῆς ἐπὶ τὴν

They persuaded Onatas, the son of Mikon of Aegina, to make them an image of Demeter for a certain sum of money. Then this man discovered a painting or copy of the old wooden image, and partly with the aid of this, but chiefly, as the story goes, by visions

Ἑλλάδα ἐπιστρατείας τοῦ Μήδου.

revealed to him, made a bronze image for the Phigaleans, about a generation later than the Persian invasion of Greece.

Brunn thinks that the visions were designed to cover an adaptation of the statue to more advanced artistic canons.
The cult of the Black Demeter was a relic of primitive horse-worship, v. *J. H. S.* xiv. pp. 138 ff. (Cook). The statue was destroyed by the falling in of part of the cave's roof before Pausanias' time.

55. Paus. viii. 42. 7 τοῦ δὲ Ὀνάτα τούτου Περγαμηνοῖς ἐστὶν Ἀπόλλων χαλκοῦς, θαῦμα ἐν τοῖς μάλιστα μεγέθους τε ἕνεκα καὶ ἐπὶ τῇ τέχνῃ.

The Pergamenes possess a bronze Apollo by this Onatas, which is very remarkable both for its size and its artistic excellence.

This work may be referred to in an Epigram of Antipater (*Anth. Pal.* ix. 238), who addresses it as 'βούπαις'='hulking lad.' A base from Pergamon (Fränkel, *Inschriften von Pergamon*, 48) appears to have belonged to this statue, which was no doubt acquired by Attalos I, who bought Aegina in 210 B.C. for thirty tal. (Polyb. xxii. 18). The inscription may be restored ['Ονάτας] Σμίκωνος Αἰγινήτης [ἐποίησεν]. (Σμίκων is a bye-form of Μίκων, cp. σμικρός, μικρός.)

56. Paus. v. 27. 8 ὁ δὲ Ἑρμῆς ὁ τὸν κριὸν φέρων ὑπὸ τῇ μασχάλῃ καὶ ἐπικείμενος τῇ κεφαλῇ κυνῆν, καὶ χιτῶνά τε καὶ χλαμύδα ἐνδεδυκώς . . . ὑπό . . . Ἀρκάδων ἐκ Φενεοῦ δέδοται τῷ θεῷ. Ὀνάταν δὲ τὸν Αἰγινήτην, σὺν δὲ αὐτῷ Καλλιτέλην ἐργάσασθαι λέγει

The Hermes, who carries the ram under his arm, and has a leathern cap on his head, and wears a tunic and cloak, was given to the god by the Arcadians of Pheneos. The inscription states that Onatas of Aegina made it, assisted by Kalliteles. I

τὸ ἐπίγραμμα. δοκεῖν δέ μοι
τοῦ 'Ονάτα μαθητὴς ἢ παῖς ὁ
Καλλιτέλης ἦν.

suppose that Kalliteles was
a pupil or son of Onatas.

At Olympia.

57. Paus. v. 25. 12 Θάσιοι
δέ . . . ἀνέθεσαν Ἡρακλέα
ἐς 'Ολυμπίαν, τὸ βάθρον
χαλκοῦν ὁμοίως τῷ ἀγάλματι.
μέγεθος μὲν δὴ τοῦ ἀγάλματός
εἰσι πήχεις δέκα, ῥόπαλον δὲ
ἐν τῇ δεξιᾷ, τῇ δὲ ἀριστερᾷ
χειρὶ ἔχει τόξον . . . 13. τῷ
δὲ ἀναθήματι ἔπεστιν ἐλε-
γεῖον
    υἱὸς μέν γε Μίκωνος 'Ονάτας
        ἐξετέλεσσεν
    αὐτὸς ἐν Αἰγίνῃ δώματα
        ναιετάων.
τὸν δὲ 'Ονάταν τοῦτον ὅμως,
καὶ τέχνης ἐς τὰ ἀγάλματα
ὄντα Αἰγιναίας, οὐδενὸς ὕστερον θήσομεν τῶν ἀπὸ Δαιδάλου τε καὶ ἐργαστηρίου τοῦ
'Αττικοῦ.

The Thasians dedicated
at Olympia a statue of
Herakles: both the figure
and the base were of
bronze. The statue is ten
cubits in height, and holds
a club in its right hand and
a bow in its left. On the
offering is inscribed the following couplet:—

Onatas, son of Mikon,
fashioned me, himself a
dweller in Aegina.

This Onatas, though the
style of his sculpture is
that of Aegina, I should
place second to none of
Daidalos' successors and
the Attic school.

The distinction between the Aeginetan and Attic schools is presupposed by several passages of Pausanias, collected by Overbeck,
Schriftquellen, pp. 81 f. Klein thinks that οἱ ἀπὸ Δαιδάλου are
a third school, that of Argos and Sikyon; the words τε καί, however, are clearly not disjunctive, but serve to identify the descendants of Daidalos with the ἐργαστήριον 'Αττικόν.

58. Paus. viii. 42. 8
'Ιέρωνος δὲ ἀποθανόντος πρό-

Hieron died before dedi-
cating the offerings, which

τερον πρὶν ἢ τῷ 'Ολυμπίῳ Διΐ
ἀναθεῖναι τὰ ἀναθήματα ἃ
εὔξατο ἐπὶ τῶν ἵππων ταῖς
νίκαις, οὕτω Δεινομένης ὁ
'Ιέρωνος ἀπέδωκεν ὑπὲρ τοῦ
πατρός· 'Ονάτα καὶ ταῦτα
ποιήματα. καὶ ἐπιγράμματα
ἐν 'Ολυμπίᾳ, τὸ μὲν ὑπὲρ τοῦ
ἀναθήματός ἐστιν αὐτῶν

σόν ποτε νικήσας, Ζεῦ 'Ολύμ-
πιε, σεμνὸν ἀγῶνα
τεθρίππῳ μὲν ἅπαξ μουνοκέ-
λητι δὲ δίς,
δῶρ' 'Ιέρων τάδε σοι ἐχαρίσ-
σατο· παῖς δ' ἀνέθηκε
Δεινομένης πατρὸς μνῆμα
Συρακοσίου.

τὸ δὲ ἕτερον λέγει τῶν ἐπι-
γραμμάτων

υἱὸς μέν γε Μίκωνος 'Ονάτας
ἐξετέλεσσεν
νάσῳ ἐν Αἰγίνῃ δώματα
ναιετάων.

ἡ δὲ ἡλικία τοῦ 'Ονάτα κατὰ
τὸν 'Αθηναῖον 'Ηγίαν καὶ
'Αγελάδαν ἂν συμβαίνοι τὸν
'Αργεῖον.

he vowed to Olympian Zeus in return for the victories of his horses, and Deinomenes his son fulfilled his father's vow : these offerings are also works of Onatas. At Olympia there are two inscriptions, one above the offering, running as follows :—

Hieron, erstwhile victorious at thy solemn games, Olympian Zeus, once with the chariot, twice with the single horse, bestowed these gifts on thee, and Deinomenes his son set them up to be a memorial of his father, the Syracusan.

And the other reads thus :—

Onatas, son of Mikon, fashioned me, having his dwelling in the island of Aegina.

It would follow that Onatas was contemporary with Hegias of Athens and Ageladas of Argos.

Hieron died 467 B.C. He was victorious with the single horse, Ol. 73 and 77 (488 and 472 B.C.), with the chariot, Ol. 78 = 468 B.C. The chariot only was by Onatas, the other figures by Kalamis (v. No. 85).

59. Paus. v. 25. 8 ἔστι δὲ καὶ ἀναθήματα ἐν κοινῷ τοῦ Ἀχαιῶν ἔθνους, ὅσοι προκαλεσαμένου τοῦ Ἕκτορος ἐς μονομαχίαν ἄνδρα Ἕλληνα τὸν κλῆρον ἐπὶ τῷ ἀγῶνι ὑπέμειναν. οὗτοι μὲν δὴ ἑστήκασι τοῦ ναοῦ τοῦ μεγάλου πλησίον, δόρασι καὶ ἀσπίσιν ὡπλισμένοι· ἀπαντικρὺ δὲ ἐπὶ ἑτέρου βάθρου πεποίηται Νέστωρ τὸν ἑκάστου κλῆρον ἐσβεβληκὼς ἐς τὴν κυνῆν. τῶν δὲ ἐπὶ τῷ Ἕκτορι κληρουμένων ἀριθμὸν ὄντων ὀκτώ, τὸν γὰρ ἔνατον αὐτῶν, τὴν τοῦ Ὀδυσσέως εἰκόνα, Νέρωνα κομίσαι λέγουσιν ἐς Ῥώμην, 9. τῶν δὲ ὀκτὼ τούτων ἐπὶ μόνῳ τῷ Ἀγαμέμνονι τὸ ὄνομά ἐστι γεγραμμένον. γέγραπται δὲ καὶ τοῦτο ἐπὶ τὰ λαιὰ ἐκ δεξιῶν. ὅτου δὲ ὁ ἀλεκτρύων ἐστὶν ἐπίθημα τῇ ἀσπίδι, Ἰδομενεύς ἐστιν ὁ ἀπόγονος Μίνω· τῷ δὲ Ἰδομενεῖ γένος ἀπὸ τοῦ Ἡλίου τοῦ πατρὸς Πασιφάης· Ἡλίου δὲ ἱερόν φασιν εἶναι τὸν ὄρνιθα καὶ ἀγγέλλειν ἀνιέναι μέλλοντος τοῦ ἡλίου. 10. γέγραπται δὲ καὶ ἐπίγραμμα ἐπὶ τῷ βάθρῳ τῷ Διὶ τἀχαιοὶ τἀγάλματα ταῦτ' ἀνέθηκαν

There are also offerings dedicated in common by the whole Achaean race: they represent the warriors who accepted Hector's challenge to meet a Greek in single combat and faced the drawing of lots. They stand near the great temple, armed with spear and shield: and opposite them on another base is set Nestor, who has cast each man's lot into the helmet. Those for whom lots are being drawn are eight in number, for the ninth, viz. Odysseus, is said to have been removed by Nero to Rome. Of these eight, Agamemnon's name only is inscribed: and that is written from right to left. The warrior, who bears a cock as the device on his shield, is Idomeneus, the descendant of Minos. Idomeneus traced his descent to Helios, the father of Pasiphae: and the bird is said to be sacred to Helios, and to give warning when the sun is about

ἔγγονοι ἀντιθέου Τανταλίδα
Πέλοπος.
τοῦτο μὲν δὴ ἐνταῦθά ἐστι γεγραμμένον, ὁ δὲ ἀγαλματοποιὸς
ὅστις ἦν, ἐπὶ τοῦ 'Ιδομενέως
γέγραπται τῇ ἀσπίδι
πολλὰ μὲν ἄλλα σοφοῦ ποιή-
μ̣ατα καὶ τόδ' 'Ονάτα
ἔργον, ὃν Αἰγίνῃ γείνατο
παῖδα Μίκων.

to rise. There is an in-
scription, too, on the base
which runs as follows :—

To Zeus the Achaeans
dedicated these statues,
descendants of Pelops the
godlike, son of Tantalos.

Such is the inscription
on the base, and the artist's
name may be read on the
shield of Idomeneus :—

Many are the works of
Onatas, the cunning crafts-
man, whom Mikon begat
in Aegina, and this is
among them.

At Olympia. Fragments of the bases have been found, v. *A. Z.*
1879, p. 44. The nine heroes stood on a semicircular base,
Nestor on a round one.

60. Paus. x. 13. 10 Ταραν-
τῖνοι δὲ καὶ ἄλλην δεκάτην
ἐς Δελφοὺς ἀπὸ βαρβάρων
Πευκετίων ἀπέστειλαν· τέχνη
μὲν τὰ ἀναθήματα 'Ονάτα τοῦ
Αἰγινητοῦ, καὶ *Καλλιτέλους
τοῦ συνεργοῦ*· εἰκόνες δὲ
καὶ πεζῶν καὶ ἱππέων, βασι-
λεὺς 'Ιαπύγων'Ωπις ἥκων τοῖς
Πευκετίοις σύμμαχος, οὗτος
μὲν δὴ εἴκασται τεθνεῶτι ἐν
τῇ μάχῃ, οἱ δὲ αὐτῷ κειμένῳ
ἐφεστηκότες ὁ ἥρως Τάρας

The Tarentines also de-
dicated at Delphi a tithe of
the spoil taken from the
barbarous Peuketians : the
offerings are the work of
Onatas of Aegina and his
assistant Kalliteles. There
are figures of horsemen and
footmen, and of Opis, king
of the Iapygians, who came
to the aid of the Peuke-
tians. He is represented
as having been killed in

ἐστὶ καὶ Φάλανθος ὁ ἐκ Λακεδαίμονος, καὶ οὐ πόρρω τοῦ
Φαλάνθου δελφίς.

the fight, and over his dead body stand the hero Taras and Phalanthos of Lakedaimon, and not far from Phalanthos is a dolphin.

*Κ. τοῦ συνεργοῦ *] MSS. Καλύνθου τε ἐστικωσι ἔργου. The text is suggested by No. 56. Phalanthos, the founder of Tarentum, was shipwrecked and carried ashore by a dolphin, which he rides on the coins of Tarentum.

(c) GLAUKIAS.

Date.—See notes on his works, all of which were at Olympia. The alphabet of the Theagenes inscription would date it circ. 450 B.C.

61. Paus. vi. 9. 4 τὸ ἅρμα τοῦ Γέλωνος . . ἐπίγραμμα μὲν δή ἐστιν αὐτῷ Γέλωνα Δεινομένους ἀναθεῖναι Γελῷον· καὶ ὁ χρόνος τούτῳ τῷ Γέλωνί ἐστι τῆς νίκης τρίτη πρὸς τὰς ἑβδομήκοντα Ὀλυμπιάδας. 5. . . Γλαυκίας δὲ Αἰγινήτης τό τε ἅρμα καὶ αὐτῷ τῷ Γέλωνι ἐποίησε τὴν εἰκόνα.

The chariot of Gelon bears an inscription, stating that Gelon, the son of Deinomenes, of Gela, dedicated it: and the date of this Gelon's victory is the 73rd Olympiad (488 B.C.). Glaukias of Aegina made both the chariot and the portrait of Gelon himself.

Gelon became tyrant of Syracuse and ceased to be Γελῷος in 485 B.C. Paus., believing that this took place in 491 B.C., argues that this must be a private person.

The inscription, found at Olympia, reads Γέλων Δεινομένεος Γέλω|νος ἀνέθηκεν | Γλαυκίας Αἰγινάτας ἐ|ποίησε. (Löwy 28 gives the second line only.) Paus. therefore misread the third word. The tyrant's chariot was victorious, Ol. 73=488 B.C.

62. Paus. vi. 10. 1 ἐπὶ δὲ τοῖς κατειλεγμένοις ἔστηκεν

Next to those above-mentioned stands Glaukos

ὁ Καρύστιος Γλαῦκος . . 3. .
τοῦ Γλαύκου δὲ τὴν εἰκόνα
ἀνέθηκε μὲν ὁ παῖς αὐτοῦ,
Γλαυκίας δὲ Αἰγινήτης ἐποί-
ησε· σκιαμαχοῦντος δὲ ὁ ἀνδριὰς παρέχεται σχῆμα, ὅτι
ὁ Γλαῦκος ἦν ἐπιτηδειότατος
τῶν κατ' αὐτὸν χειρονομῆσαι
πεφυκώς.

of Karystos. His portrait was dedicated by his son and made by Glaukias of Aegina; the figure presents the appearance of a man boxing for practice, since Glaukos was the most consummate boxer of his time in the art of using his arms.

Other athlete-statues by Glaukias were those of
THEAGENES of Thasos, victorious in the pankration, Ol. 75 and 76 (480 and 476 B.C.) (Paus. v. 11. 2). A fragment of the base was found at Olympia (Löwy 29).
PHILON of Korkyra, victorious in boxing twice (epitaph by Simonides, who died 467 B.C.) (Paus. vi. 9. 9).

(d) ANAXAGORAS.

63. Paus. v. 23. 1 (At Olympia) παρεξιόντι δὲ παρὰ τὴν ἐς τὸ βουλευτήριον ἔσοδον, Ζεύς τε ἕστηκεν ἐπίγραμμα ἔχων οὐδέν, καὶ αὖθις ὡς πρὸς ἄρκτον ἐπιστρέψαντι ἄγαλμά ἐστι Διός. τοῦτο τέτραπται μὲν πρὸς ἀνίσχοντα ἥλιον, ἀνέθεσαν δὲ Ἑλλήνων ὅσοι Πλαταιᾶσιν ἐμαχέσαντο ἐναν-τία Μαρδονίου τε καὶ Μήδων. εἰσὶ δὲ καὶ ἐγγεγραμμέναι κατὰ τοῦ βάθρου τὰ δεξιὰ αἱ μετασχοῦσαι πόλεις τοῦ ἔργου . . . 3. . . τὸ δὲ ἄγαλμα ἐν

(At Olympia) Passing by the entrance to the council-chamber, one may see a statue of Zeus, bearing no inscription, and turning to the north, another statue of Zeus, which faces the east, and was dedicated by the Greeks who fought at Plataea against Mardonios and the Persians. On the right hand of the base are inscribed the names of the cities which took part in the battle. The image

E

Ὀλυμπίᾳ τὸ ἀνατεθὲν ὑπὸ τῶν
Ἑλλήνων ἐποίησεν Ἀναξαγό-
ρας Αἰγινήτης.

dedicated by the Greeks
at Olympia was made by
Anaxagoras of Aegina.

After 479 B. C.

4. ATHENS.

(a) ANTENOR.

Date.—(1) An inscription from the Akropolis of Athens (Ἐφ. Ἀρχ. 1886, Pl. vi. 4, cp. *Jahrb.* 1887, p. 146) reads Νέαρχος ἀν[έθηκεν ὁ κεραμε]|ὺς? ἔργων ἀπαρχήν.|Ἀντήνωρ ἐπ[οίησεν] | ὁ Εὐμάρους τὸ [ἄγαλμα], and probably dates from the close of the sixth century. On Eumares the painter, see *O. S.* 377. It cannot be proved that the statue published with this base in *Antike Denkmäler*, i. 53, was originally connected with it. (2) No. 64 must have been erected after 510 B. C.

64. Paus. i. 8. 5 οὐ πόρρω δὲ ἑστᾶσιν Ἁρμόδιος καὶ Ἀριστογείτων οἱ κτείναντες Ἵππαρχον ... τῶν δὲ ἀνδριάντων οἱ μὲν εἰσὶ Κριτίου τέχνη, τοὺς δὲ ἀρχαίους ἐποίησεν Ἀντήνωρ. Ξέρξου δέ, ὡς εἷλεν Ἀθήνας ἐκλιπόντων τὸ ἄστυ Ἀθηναίων, ἐπαγαγομένα καὶ τούτους ἅτε λάφυρα, κατέπεμψεν ὕστερον Ἀθηναίοις Ἀντίοχος.

Not far off are the statues of Harmodios and Aristogeiton, who slew Hipparchos. The one pair are the work of Kritios, while the older ones were made by Antenor. When Xerxes captured Athens after the Athenians had deserted the city, he carried them away as spoils, and Antiochos afterwards restored them to the Athenians.

Antiochos Soter, 281–261 B. C. According to others Seleukos (Val. Max.) or Alexander himself (Pliny, Arrian) restored the statues, which stood in the upper part of the Kerameikos on the ascent to the Akropolis.

(b) Kritios and Nesiotes.

Date.—Three inscriptions have been found on the Akropolis (Löwy 38-40), of which the first is from the base of No. 66. From these we recover the true form of the name Kritios (Kritias in the MSS. of Plin., Paus., and Lucian). Their date is 460 B.C. or earlier. No. 65 is dated 477 B.C. by the Parian marble.

65. Lucian, Philops. 18
ἀλλὰ τοὺς μὲν ἐπὶ τὰ δεξιὰ
εἰσιόντων ἄφες, ἐν οἷς καὶ τὰ
Κριτίου καὶ Νησιώτου πλάσ-
ματα ἔστηκεν, οἱ τυραννο-
κτόνοι.

Pass by the statues on the right as you enter, amongst which stand the slayers of the tyrant, the handiwork of Kritios and Nesiotes.

Paus. mentions Kritios only in No. 64. On the date v. supr. They replaced the portraits removed by Xerxes. Restored copies exist at Naples and elsewhere, and the group is depicted on Athenian coins and on Panathenaic amphora. See *Ov.* I⁴, Figs. 26–28.

66. Paus. i. 23. 9 ἀνδριάντων δὲ ὅσοι μετὰ τὸν ἵππον
ἑστήκασιν Ἐπιχαρίνου μὲν
ὁπλιτοδρομεῖν ἀσκήσαντος τὴν
εἰκόνα ἐποίησε Κρίτιος.

Among the portrait-statues which stand next to the horse is that of Epicharinos, who practised the race in armour, by Kritios.

The inscription (v. supr.) gives both names. The nature of the contest must have been inferred from the attitude and costume of the figure, since the inscription does not read (as was formerly supposed) Ἐπιχαρῖνος ὁπλιτοδρόμος. The second word gave the father's name.

67. Lucian, Rhet. Prae-
cept. 9 εἶτά σε κελεύσει
ζηλοῦν ἐκείνους τοὺς ἀρχαίους
ἄνδρας, ἕωλα παραδείγματα
παρατιθεὶς τῶν λόγων οὐ ῥᾴδια

Then he will bid you imitate those ancient ora-tors, setting before you stale models of speeches hard to imitate, like the

E 2

μιμεῖσθαι, οἷα τὰ τῆς παλαιᾶς ἐργασίας ἐστίν, Ἡγησίου καὶ τῶν ἀμφὶ Κρίτιον καὶ Νησιώτην, ἀπεσφιγμένα καὶ νευρώδη καὶ σκληρὰ καὶ ἀκριβῶς ἀποτεταμένα ταῖς γραμμαῖς.

works of archaic art, by Hegesias and the school of Kritios and Nesiotes, closely knit and sinewy and stiff, and severe in outline.

On Hegesias, v. infr.

ἀκρ. ἀποτ. ταῖς γραμμαῖς] refers to the prominent use of *straight* lines and surfaces, imparting severity of outline to the figure. Cf. Lucian, *Zeuxis* 5 τὸ ἀποτεῖναι τὰς γραμμὰς ἐς τὸ εὐθύτατον (in painting).

(c) HEGIAS (HEGESIAS).

Date.—An inscription from the Acropolis (Δελτ. ᾿Αρχ. 1889, p. 37 f.) reads ῾Ηγίας ἐποίησεν, and appears to be of the same period as Löwy 38 (Kritios and Nesiotes). The stone was damaged by fire, probably in the Persian destruction (480 B. C.). The artist is coupled with Kritios and Nesiotes by Lucian in No. 67, and with Kallon by Quintilian, and was the teacher of Pheidias according to a certain emendation by Otfried Müller of the text of Dion Chrys. 55, p. 169, 4 Dind. (ΗΓΙΟΥ for ΗΠΟΥ). The form Hegesias is found in Lucian, Quintilian, and Pliny.

68. Plin. *N. H.* xxxiv. 78
Hegiae Minerua Pyrrhusque rex laudatur, et κελητίζοντες pueri, et Castor et Pollux ante aedem Jouis Tonantis; Hegesiae in Pario colonia Hercules.

The Athena and King Pyrrhos of Hegias are noted works, also his boys riding race-horses, and his Kastor and Polydeukes, which stand before the temple of Jupiter the Thunderer; by Hegesias is a Herakles in the colony of Parium.

Hegesiae] Hagesiae MSS. Pliny has derived notes from different sources referring to the artist under two names. ' Pyrrhus *rex'* must be a mistake of Pliny, and refers to Neoptolemos, the son of Achilles, by his second name.

κελητίζοντες **pueri**] Overbeck suggests a comparison with funeral monuments, such as the 'rider of Vari' (*Ath. Mitth.* 1879, Pl. iii), but Olympic victors are equally probable. Cp. Nos. 85, 239.

in Pario colonia] Augustus founded a military colony at Parium on the Propontis.

5. ELIS.

KALLON.

Date.—The inscription of No. 70 from Olympia (Löwy 33) is posterior to 496 B.C., showing the influence of the Samian immigrants at Rhegion in its Ionic dialect.

69. Paus. v. 25. 4 οἱ Μεσσήνιοι . . . εἰκόνας ἐς Ὀλυμπίαν ἀνέθεσαν χαλκᾶς, σὺν δὲ αὐτοῖς τὸν διδάσκαλον τοῦ χοροῦ καὶ τὸν αὐλητήν. τὸ μὲν δὴ ἐπίγραμμα ἐδήλου τὸ ἀρχαῖον ἀναθήματα εἶναι τῶν ἐν πορθμῷ Μεσσηνίων· χρόνῳ δὲ ὕστερον Ἱππίας ὁ λεγόμενος ὑπὸ Ἑλλήνων γενέσθαι σοφὸς τὰ ἐλεγεῖα ἐπ' αὐτοῖς ἐποίησεν. ἔργα δέ εἰσιν Ἠλείου Κάλλωνος αἱ εἰκόνες.

The Messenians dedicated statues of bronze at Olympia, representing the chorus, the trainer and the flute-player. The original inscription indicated that they were offerings of the Messenians dwelling on the strait : afterwards Hippias, called by the Greeks the Wise, composed the elegiac lines inscribed on the monument. The statues are the work of Kallon of Elis.

The chorus was lost by the foundering of the ship which carried it across the straits of Rhegion. Zankle became Messene in 494 B.C.

70. Paus. v. 27. 8 (At Olympia) οὐ πόρρω δὲ τοῦ

Not far from the offering of the people of Pheneos is

Φενεατῶν ἀναθήματος ἄλλο ἐστὶν ἄγαλμα, κηρύκειον Ἑρμῆς ἔχων. ἐπίγραμμα δὲ ἐπ' αὐτῷ Γλαυκίαν ἀναθεῖναι γένος Ῥηγῖνον, ποιῆσαι δὲ Κάλλωνα Ἠλεῖον.

another statue representing Hermes holding the herald's wand. The inscription upon it states that Glaukias of Rhegion dedicated it, and Kallon of Elis made it.

The inscription reads [Γλαυκί]αι με Κάλων γενε[ᾶ Ϝ]αλεῖ[ο]ς ἐποίει | [Γλ]αυκίης ὁ Λυκκίδεω | [τῶ]ι Ἑρμῇ Ῥ[η]γῖνος.

6. NAUPAKTOS.

MENAICHMOS AND SOIDAS.

71. Paus. vii. 18. 9 Πατρεῦσι δὲ ὁ Αὔγουστος ἄλλα τε τῶν ἐκ Καλυδῶνος λαφύρων καὶ δὴ καὶ τῆς Λαφρίας ἔδωκε τὸ ἄγαλμα, ὃ δὴ καὶ ἐς ἐμὲ ἔτι ἐν τῇ ἀκροπόλει τῇ Πατρέων εἶχε τιμάς. . . 10. τὸ μὲν σχῆμα τοῦ ἀγάλματος θηρεύουσά ἐστιν, ἐλέφαντος δὲ καὶ χρυσοῦ πεποίηται, Ναυπάκτιοι δὲ Μέναιχμος καὶ Σοίδας εἰργάσαντο· τεκμαίρονται δὲ σφᾶς Κανάχου τοῦ Σικυωνίου καὶ τοῦ Αἰγινήτου Κάλλωνος οὐ πολλῷ γενέσθαι τινὶ ἡλικίαν ὑστέρους.

Augustus bestowed on the people of Patrai, amongst other treasures from the spoil of Kalydon, the image of Artemis Laphria, which was held in honour on the Akropolis of Patrai down to my own time. The goddess is represented as a huntress, and the statue was made in gold and ivory by Menaichmos and Soidas of Naupaktos: it is inferred that they were slightly later in time than Kanachos of Sikyon and Kallon of Aegina.

Studniczka (*Röm. Mitth.* 1886, p. 277 ff.) maintains that the Artemis of Naples (*F. W.* 442) is a copy of this work, and that it is represented on coins of Augustus (*loc. cit.* Pl. x. infr.). But there seems no doubt that the true type is given by the coins of Patrai (*Num. Comm. Q.* vi-x). For Artemis· represented as an Amazon at this early period, cp. the relief from Asopos, *A. Z.* 1882, Pl. vi.

§ 2. THE SCULPTORS OF THE TRANSITIONAL PERIOD.

1. PYTHAGORAS.

Date.—(1) The inscription on the base of the portrait of Euthymos (v. infr.) (Löwy 23) reads Πυθαγόρας Σάμιος. This shows that Pliny and Diogenes Laertius are wrong in distinguishing two sculptors of the name, one from Rhegion and the other from Samos. Pythagoras was doubtless one of the Samians who emigrated to Zankle on the fall of Samos in 496 B.C., and became subject to Anaxilas of Rhegion. (2) Astylos (v. infr.) was victorious Ol. 73-75 (488-480 B.C.); as he described himself as a Syracusan in Ol. 74-75, and Paus. says that the statue was of Astylos Κροτωνιάτης, it must have commemorated the first victory. (3) Euthymos (v. infr.) was victorious Ol. 74, 76, 77 (484, 476, 472 B.C.). On his supposed teacher Klearchos, v. supr. No. 21 note.

72. Plin. *N. H.* xxxiv. 59 Uicit eum (Myronem) Pythagoras Rheginus ex Italia pancratiaste Delphis posito, eodem uicit et Leontiscum; fecit et σταδιόδρομον Astylon, qui Olympiae ostenditur, et Libyn ⟨et⟩ puerum tenentem flagellum eodem loco, et mala ferentem

Pythagoras of Rhegion surpassed him (Myron) with his pankratiast dedicated at Delphi, with which he outdid Leontiskos also; he also represented the runner Astylos, a work which is shown at Olympia, also a Libyan and a boy holding a whip, likewise at Olympia,

nudum, Syracusis autem claudicantem, cuius ulceris dolorem sentire etiam spectantes uidentur, item Apollinem serpentemque eius sagittis configi, citharoedum qui Δίκαιος appellatus est, quod, cum Thebae ab Alexandro caperentur, aurum a fugiente conditum sinu eius celatum esset. Hic primus neruos et uenas expressit capillumque diligentius. 60. Fuit et alius Pythagoras, Samius, initio pictor, cuius signa ad aedem Fortunae huiusce diei septem nuda et senis unum laudata sunt; hic supra dicto facie quoque indiscreta similis fuisse traditur.

and a nude figure bearing apples, a lame man at Syracuse, the pain of whose wound seems to be felt by the spectator, also an Apollo transfixing the serpent with his arrows, and a musician with his lyre, which was called 'the Just,' because, when Thebes was taken by Alexander, a fugitive hid his gold in its bosom, where it remained concealed. He was the first to represent sinews and veins, and to bestow attention on the treatment of hair. There was another Pythagoras, a Samian, who began life as a painter. His works, seven nude figures and one old man, stand by the temple of Fortune to this day and are famous; the story runs that his countenance too precisely resembled that of the other Pythagoras.

Leontiscum] Pliny seems to regard Leontiskos as an artist. He was really. a native of Messina, victorious in wrestling at Olympia, whose portrait was made by Pythagoras (Paus. vi. 4. 3).

Astylon] A Krotoniate runner, thrice victorious in the single and double course. On the two latter occasions he proclaimed himself a Syracusan as a compliment to Hieron (Paus. vi. 13. 1).

Libyn ... flagellum] Two alterations are here made in the text—*et* inserted, and *flagellum* for MSS. *tabellam*. Furtwängler suggested similar but somewhat more violent changes. 'Libys' must be Mnaseas 'the Libyan' of Kyrene, a victor in the race in armour, whose portrait by Pythagoras stood at Olympia (Paus. vi. 13. 7); 'puer tenens flagellum,' his son Kratisthenes, on whom v. infr. No. 73. Pliny translated παῖδα in his Greek authority by 'puerum,' instead of 'filium.'

claudicantem] Generally supposed (after Lessing, *Laokoon* c. 2) to mean Philoktetes. The participle in Pliny's use often covers a proper name, and probably points to a Greek source. Cf. catagusa (=κατάγουσα) in No. 189, which may mean Hekate.

citharoedum] The κιθαρῳδός both played and sang to the lyre. This was a portrait of one Kleon of Thebes (Ath. i. 19 B).

hic primus] v. Introduction, § 2.

alius] Probably identical with the first. See the explanation given above.

---

73. Paus. vi. 18. 1 ἔστι δὲ καὶ τοῦ Κυρηναίου Κρατισθέ-νους χαλκοῦν ἅρμα, καὶ Νίκη τε ἐπιβέβηκε τοῦ ἅρματος καὶ αὐτὸς ὁ Κρατισθένης. δῆλα μὲν δὴ ὅτι ἵππων γέγονεν αὐτῷ νίκη· λέγεται δὲ καὶ ὡς Μνα-σέου τοῦ δρομέως, ἐπικλη-θέντος δὲ ὑπὸ Ἑλλήνων Λίβυος, εἴη παῖς ὁ Κρατισθένης. τὰ δὲ ἀναθήματα αὐτῷ τὰ ἐς Ὀλυμ-πίαν ἐστὶ τοῦ Ῥηγίνου Πυθα-γόρου τέχνη.

There is also the bronze chariot of Kratisthenes the Kyrenian; both Victory and Kratisthenes himself are mounted on the car. It is plain that his team has won a victory; and it is said that Kratisthenes was the son of the runner Mnaseas, to whom the Greeks gave the surname of 'the Libyan.' His offerings at Olympia are the work of Pythagoras of Rhegion.

V. supra note on No. 72, Libyn ... flagellum.

---

74. Dion Chrys. 37. 10 μένουσι μέντοι οὗτοι πάντες

But these all remain in their position and place,

κατὰ σχῆμα καὶ κατὰ χώραν
. . . τό γε ἐπ' αὐτοῖς εἶναι
χαλκὸς ἄδραστος, ἂν καὶ πτερὰ
ἔχῃ, ὥσπερ ὁ τοῦ Πυθαγόρου
Περσεύς.

being for their own part of
bronze immoveable, even
though they have wings,
like the Perseus of Pythagoras.

οὗτοι] = statues (οἱ ἀνδριάντες).
Πυθαγόρου] It is possible that the name is merely a slip, and that
Dion was really thinking of the Perseus of Myron (No. 88, note).

75. Tatian, c. Graec. 54
πῶς γὰρ οὐ χαλεπὸν ἀδελφο-
κτονίαν παρ' ὑμῖν τετιμῆσθαι,
οἱ Πολυνείκους καὶ 'Ετεο-
κλέους ὁρῶντες τὰ σχήματα
[καὶ] μὴ σὺν τῷ ποιήσαντι
Πυθαγόρᾳ καταβοθρώσαντες
συναπόλλυτε τῆς κακίας τὰ
ὑπομνήματα;

Is it not shameful that
ye honour among yourselves
the shedding of brothers'
blood, when ye look upon
the figures of Eteokles and
Polyneikes, and do not
bury them and Pythagoras
who made them and destroy
therewith the memorial of
their crime?

76. Varro, L. L. v. 31
Europa . . . quam ex
Phoenice Mallius scribit
taurum exportasse, quorum
egregiam imaginem ex aere
Pythagoras Tarenti fecit.

Europa, who, as Mallius
says, was carried away from
Phoenicia by a bull; both
were represented by Pythagoras in a magnificent
bronze group at Tarentum.

77. Diog. Laert. viii. 46
οἱ δὲ καὶ ἄλλον ἀνδριαντοποιὸν
'Ρηγῖνον γεγονέναι φασὶ Πυθαγόραν, πρῶτον δοκοῦντα ῥυθμοῦ καὶ συμμετρίας ἐστοχάσθαι, καὶ ἄλλον, ἀνδριαντοποιὸν
Σάμιον.

Some say that there
was another Pythagoras, a
sculptor, of Rhegion, who
is thought to have been the
first to aim at rhythm and
proportion, and yet another,
a sculptor of Samos.

ῥυθμοῦ καὶ συμμετρίας] The latter is the system of proportions observable in the human frame at rest, the former the system of changes producing a constant harmony of the parts of the body when in motion. The knowledge of the one is the static, of the other the dynamic, of sculpture. See Introduction, § 2.

Other portraits of Olympic victors by Pythagoras :—

EUTHYMOS of Lokroi Epizephyroi, victorious in boxing, Ol. 74, 76, 77 (484, 476, 472 B.C.) (Paus. vi. 6. 4). The inscription (Löwy 23) reads :—

> Εὔθυμος Λοκρὸς 'Αστυκλέος τρὶς 'Ολύμπι' ἐνίκων,
> εἰκόνα δ' ἔστησεν τήνδε βροτοῖς ἐσορᾶν.
> Εὔθυμος Λοκρὸς ἀπὸ Ζεφυρίου ἀνέθηκε.
> Πυθαγόρας Σάμιος ἐποίησεν.

DROMEUS of Stymphalos in Arkadia, victorious in the long foot-race (Paus. vi. 7. 10).

PROTOLAOS of Mantineia, victorious in the boys' boxing match (Paus. vi. 6. 1).

2. KALAMIS.

Date.—(1) He was employed with Onatas on the offerings of Hieron dedicated by Deinomenes after 467 B.C. (2) He was employed by Pindar, who died at a great age in 441 B.C. (3) His place is next to Kanachos and Kallon in the Canon of Sculptors (v. Introd. § 3). See notes on Nos. 78 and 83.

78. Paus. i. 3. 4 πρὸ δὲ τοῦ νεὼ ὃν . . . καλοῦσιν 'Αλεξίκακον, Κάλαμις ἐποίησε. τὸ δὲ ὄνομα τῷ θεῷ γενέσθαι λέγουσιν, ὅτι τὴν λοιμώδη σφίσι νόσον ὁμοῦ τῷ Πελοποννησίων πολέμῳ πιεζουσαν κατὰ μάντευμα ἔπαυσεν ἐκ Δελφῶν.

Before the temple is an image of Apollo who is called the Averter of Ill, made by Kalamis. They say that this name was given to the god because he put an end to the plague which afflicted them at the time of the Peloponnesian war by means of an oracle from Delphi.

τοῦ νεώ] The temple of Apollo Patroos in the Kerameikos at

Athens. Paus. reproduces a common error founded on the vivid impression left by the great plague of 4$\frac{30}{29}$, which effaced all others from the popular memory. V. note on No. 43.

79. Strab. vii. 319 Ἀπολλωνία . . . ἔχουσα ἐν νησίῳ τινὶ ἱερὸν τοῦ Ἀπόλλωνος, ἐξ οὗ Μάρκος Λεύκολλος τὸν κολοσσὸν ἦρε καὶ ἀνέθηκεν ἐν τῷ Καπετωλίῳ τὸν τοῦ Ἀπόλλωνος, Καλάμιδος ἔργον.

Apollonia possessed a shrine of Apollo on a small island from which M. Lucullus carried away the colossal statue of Apollo, the work of Kalamis, and dedicated it on the Capitol.

Apollonia] On the Black Sea, a colony of Miletos.
τὸν κολοσσόν] According to Pliny, *N. H.* xxxiv. 39, it was 30 cubits in height, and cost 500 talents (£125,000).

80. Paus. ix. 22. 1 ἐς δὲ τοῦ Ἑρμοῦ . . . τοῦ Κριοφόρου τὴν ἐπίκλησιν λέγουσιν, ὡς ὁ Ἑρμῆς σφίσιν ἀποτρέψαι νόσον λοιμώδη περὶ τὸ τεῖχος κριὸν περιενεγκών, καὶ ἐπὶ τούτῳ Κάλαμις ἐποίησεν ἄγαλμα Ἑρμοῦ φέροντα κριὸν ἐπὶ τῶν ὤμων.

As to the surname of Hermes 'the Bearer of the Ram' their story is that Hermes averted a plague from them by carrying a ram round the city wall: to commemorate this, Kalamis made an image of Hermes carrying a ram on his shoulders.

At Tanagra, where the ceremony was repeated yearly by a youth re resenting Hermes.
On monuments supposed to represent this statue, v. *F. W.* 418, 419, and *Ov.* I⁴. 280 (figs. 75, 76).

81. Paus. ii. 10. 3 ἐσελθοῦσι δὲ ὁ θεός ἐστιν οὐκ ἔχων πω γένεια, χρυσοῦ καὶ ἐλέφαντος, Καλάμιδος δὲ ἔργον·

At the entrance is a statue of the god, beardless, in gold and ivory, by Kalamis: he holds a sceptre

ἔχει δὲ καὶ σκῆπτρον, καὶ ἐπὶ τῆς ἑτέρας χειρὸς πίτυος καρπὸν τῆς ἡμέρου.

in one hand, and in the other a cone of the cultivated pine.

In the temple of Asklepios at Sikyon.

82. Paus. v. 26. 6 παρὰ δὲ τὴν ᾿Αθηνᾶν πεποίηται Νίκη· ταύτην Μαντινεῖς ἀνέθεσαν ... Κάλαμις δὲ οὐκ ἔχουσαν πτερὰ ποιῆσαι λέγεται ἀπομιμούμενος τὸ ᾿Αθήνησι τῆς ᾿Απτέρου καλουμένης ξόανον.

Beside the Athena stands a statue of Victory, dedicated by the Mantineans. It is said that Kalamis represented her without wings in imitation of the old image of the so-called 'Wingless Victory' at Athens.

At Olympia.

τῆς ᾿Απτέρου] Really Athena Nike, popularly called 'Νίκη ῎Απτερος.' Her temple stands on the south-west bastion of the Akropolis.

83. Lucian, Εἰκόνες 6 ἡ Σώσανδρα δὲ καὶ Κάλαμις αἰδοῖ κοσμήσουσιν αὐτήν, καὶ τὸ μειδίαμα σεμνὸν καὶ λεληθὸς ὥσπερ τὸ ἐκείνης ἔσται, καὶ τὸ εὐσταλὲς δὲ καὶ κόσμιον τῆς ἀναβολῆς παρὰ τῆς Σωσάνδρας πλὴν ὅτι ἀκατακάλυπτος αὕτη ἔσται τὴν κεφαλήν.

Kalamis and the Saviour of Men shall adorn her with shamefacedness, and she shall have the noble, unconscious smile of the goddess, and shall borrow the trim and modest folds of her garment from the Saviour of Men ; only she shall not, like her, have her head covered.

From Lucian's picture of an ideal beauty, 'Panthea.' This so-called 'Sosandra' is generally identified with a statue of Aphrodite, which, according to Paus. i. 23. 2, was dedicated by Kallias

(possibly the wealthy Athenian of that name known as ὁ λακκό-
πλουτος, who flourished circ. 480 B.C.) at the entrance to the
Akropolis; since Lucian speaks of the 'Sosandra' as seen by all
who ascended the Akropolis. In *Dial. Meretr.* iii. 2 he speaks of
a dancer, praised for the beauty of her ankles and her rhythmical
motions, as though she were the Sosandra of Kalamis.

84. Paus. v. 25. 5 τοῖς
ἐν Μοτύῃ βαρβάροις 'Ακρα-
γαντῖνοι καταστάντες ἐς πόλεμον καὶ λείαν τε καὶ λάφυρα
ἀπ' αὐτῶν λαβόντες ἀνέθεσαν
τοὺς παῖδας ἐς 'Ολυμπίαν τοὺς
χαλκοῦς, προτείνοντάς τε τὰς
δεξιὰς καὶ εἰκασμένους εὐχο-
μένοις τῷ θεῷ .... Καλά-
μιδος δὲ εἶναι σφᾶς ἔργα ἐγώ τε
εἴκαζον, καὶ ἐς αὐτοὺς κατὰ τὰ
αὐτὰ εἶχεν ὁ λόγος.

The Agrigentines having
gone to war with the bar-
barians of Motya, and taken
much booty and spoil from
them, dedicated at Olympia
the bronze boys, who are
extending their right hands,
and seem to be addressing
prayer to the god. I con-
jectured them to be the
work of Kalamis, and such
was the tradition concern-
ing them.

In a previous section (§ 2) Paus. ascribes to Motya (the later
Lilybaeum) the geographical situation of Motyca (the modern
Modica, in the S.E. corner of Sicily); but the first named must
be the town here referred to. It is, however, suggested that Motya
was misread by Paus. for Motyon, a fort in Agrigentine territory
recaptured from Duketios in 451 B.C. (Diod. xi. 92).

85. Paus. vi. 12. 1 πλησίον
δὲ ἅρμα ἐστὶ χαλκοῦν, καὶ
ἀνὴρ ἀναβεβηκὼς ἐπ' αὐτό,
κέλητες δὲ ἵπποι παρὰ τὸ ἅρμα
εἷς ἑκατέρωθεν ἔστηκε, καὶ
ἐπὶ τῶν ἵππων καθέζονται
παῖδες. ὑπομνήματα δὲ ἐπὶ
νίκαις 'Ολυμπιακαῖς ἐστιν
'Ιέρωνος τοῦ Δεινομένους

Hard by is a chariot of
bronze, and a man mounted
upon it, and beside the
chariot stand race-horses on
either hand, and boys are
seated upon the horses.
These commemorate the
Olympic victories of Hieron,
the son of Deinomenes,

τυραννήσαντος Συρακουσίων
. . τὰ δὲ ἀναθήματα οὐχ Ἱέρων
ἀπέστειλεν, ἀλλ' ὁ μὲν ἀποδοὺς
τῷ θεῷ Δεινομένης ἐστὶν ὁ
Ἱέρωνος· ἔργα δέ, τὸ μὲν
Ὀνάτα τοῦ Αἰγινήτου τὸ ἅρμα,
Καλάμιδος δὲ οἱ ἵπποι τε οἱ
ἑκατέρωθεν καὶ ἐπ' αὐτῶν εἰσὶν
οἱ παῖδες.

tyrant of Syracuse. The offerings were not sent by Hieron himself, but the debt was paid to the god by Deinomenes, the son of Hieron. The chariot is the work of Onatas of Aegina, while the horses on either side and the boys seated on them are by Kalamis.

Cp. No. 58 note.

86. Plin. *N. H.* xxxiv. 71 Habet simulacrum et benignitas eius. Calamidis enim quadrigae aurigam suum imposuit, ne melior in equorum effigie defecisse in homine crederetur.

There is also a statue which bears witness to his kindness. For he placed a charioteer of his own on a four-horse chariot of Kalamis, lest the artist who excelled in representing horses should be thought to have failed in his treatment of the human figure.

Praxiteles (perhaps the elder of that name, v. infr. No. 189 note) is referred to. Kalamis was specially renowned for his horses, Plin. *N. H.* xxxiv. 71 Equis semper sine aemulo expressis, Prop. iii. 9. 10 Exactis Calamis se mihi iactat equis.

87. Dion. Hal. de Isocr. p. 522 R. δοκεῖ δέ μοι μὴ ἀπὸ σκοποῦ τις ἂν εἰκάσαι τὴν μὲν Ἰσοκράτους ῥητορικὴν τῇ Πολυκλείτου τε καὶ Φειδίου

I think that it would not be wide of the mark to compare the oratory of Isokrates to the art of Polykleitos and Pheidias,

τέχνη, κατὰ τὸ σεμνὸν καὶ μεγαλότεχνον καὶ ἀξιωματικόν· τὴν δὲ Λυσίου τῇ Καλάμιδος καὶ Καλλιμάχου τῆς λεπτότητος ἕνεκα καὶ τῆς χάριτος.

with its grandeur and breadth of style and sublimity, and that of Lysias to the art of Kalamis and Kallimachos, with its delicacy and grace.

On Kallimachos, v. No. 153.

Other works by Kalamis :—
ZEUS AMMON at Thebes, executed for Pindar (Paus. ix. 16. 1).
DIONYSOS at Tanagra, of Parian marble (Paus. ix. 20. 4).
An ERINNYS at Athens, v. infr. No. 208.
ALKMENE (Plin. *N. H.* xxxiv. 71).
HERMIONE, dedicated by the Spartans at Delphi (Paus. x. 16. 4).

3. MYRON.

Date.—According to Pliny he was the pupil of Ageladas and rival of Pythagoras, on whom v. supra. His son Lykios seems to have been employed on work of importance in 446 B.C. (infr. No. 147).

88. Plin. *N. H.* xxxiv. 57
Myronem Eleutheris natum, Ageladae et ipsum discipulum, bucula maxime nobilitauit celebratis uersibus laudata (quando alieno plerique ingenio magis quam suo commendantur). Fecit et canem et discobolum et Perseum et pristas et satyrum admirantem tibias et Mineruam, Delphicos pentathlos, pancratiastas, Herculem qui est

Myron, born at Eleutherai, also a pupil of Ageladas, was made famous chiefly by his cow, whose praises are sung in wellknown lines—for there are many whose fame rests not on their own genius, but on that of others. He also made a dog and a quoit-thrower, and Perseus and sawyers, and a satyr gazing in wonderment at the flutes and Athena,

apud Circum maximum in aede Pompei Magni. Fecisse et cicadae monumentum ac lucustae carminibus suis Erinna significat. 58. fecit et Apollinem quem ab triumuiro Antonio sublatum restituit Ephesiis diuos Augustus admonitus in quiete. Primus hic multiplicasse ueritatem uidetur, numerosior in arte quam Polyclitus et in symmetria diligentior, et ipse tamen corporum tenus curiosus animi sensus non expressisse, capillum quoque et pubem non emendatius fecisse quam rudis antiquitas instituisset.

winners in the five contests at Delphi, pankratiasts, a Herakles which stands by the great Circus in the temple of Pompey the Great. Erinna too mentions in her poems that he made the gravestone of a cicada and a locust. He also made an Apollo, which was carried away by Antony the triumvir and restored to the Ephesians by Augustus, after a warning conveyed in a dream. He is thought to have been the first to extend the province of lifelike representation in art; his art was more rhythmical than that of Polykleitos, and his proportions more carefully studied, yet he too expended his care on the bodily frame, and did not represent the emotions of the mind. His treatment too of the hair of the head and body showed no advance on the rude attempts of early art.

Ageladae . . . discipulum] Possible, but not very probable, since the similar statement in regard to Polykleitos (No. 160) cannot be true.

bucula] The cow stood on the Akropolis of Athens, but was afterwards removed to the Forum Pacis at Rome. Thirty-six epigrams upon it are preserved in the *Anthology*, but they give no information of any value.

canem] Benndorf corrects this to 'Ladam,' thinking the mention of an important work called for in this place. V. infr. No. 92.

discobolum] V. infr. No. 93.

Perseum] Paus. i. 23. 7 mentions Μύρωνος Περσέα τὸ ἐς Μέδουσαν ἔργον εἰργασμένον in describing the Akropolis of Athens. From the use of the perfect participle ('P. *after* his exploit') we learn that this was a single figure. For another explanation v. the following note.

pristas] Some editors translate 'sea-monsters,' which would be 'pristes.' If the reading is right we may (1) connect the word with 'Perseum,' the carpenters forming part of a group representing the enclosure of Danae and Perseus in the chest (Mayer, *Ath. Mitth.* 1891, p. 246), or (2) interpret with reference to the game of see-saw (Murray, *Class. Rev.* 1887, p. 3). Löschcke corrects 'pyctas,' 'boxers.'

satyrum ... Mineruam] The words of Pliny leave it an open question whether 'Mineruam' is governed by 'admirantem' or by 'fecit.' In the latter case it is still possible to combine both figures in a group. Paus. i. 24. 1 describes a group on the Akropolis of Athens as follows :—

ἐνταῦθα . . . 'Αθηνᾶ πεποίηται τὸν Σιληνὸν Μαρσύαν παίουσα, ὅτι δὴ τοὺς αὐλοὺς ἀνέλοιτο, ἐρρῖφθαι σφᾶς τῆς θεοῦ βουλομένης.	Here Athena is represented in the act of striking the Satyr Marsyas, because he took up the flutes when the goddess wished them to be thrown aside.

Brunn would read ἐπιοῦσα 'advancing upon' for παίουσα, which might however have an inceptive sense (='on the point of striking'). A group of monuments figured in *Ov.* I⁴, Fig. 73 (p. 269) seems to represent the group alluded to by Pausanias and Pliny.

cicadae monumentum] An epigram in *Anth. Pal.* vii. 190 by Anyte mentions a tomb erected to a locust and cicada by a girl named Myro, whom Pliny has confused with the sculptor.

multiplicasse ueritatem] This seems to mean that M. increased the number of situations in which the human figure could be represented with truth to nature beyond those current in his time. And this interpretation is certainly borne out by what we know of his works. It is also held to mean that he, as it were, 'raised nature to a higher power'—i. e. seized the moments when nature displays an abnormal activity. This might pass as a fair criticism of his works, but is hardly contained in the words of Pliny.

numerosior in arte] Probably to be explained with Overbeck as a translation of εὐρυθμώτερος τὴν τέχνην. On the sense of ῥυθμός in sculpture, see No. 77 note. It could also mean (1) that there was more *variety* in his subjects than in those of P. (cp. Quint. v. 10. 10 numerosum opus), though this seems to be already implied in the previous words, or (2) that he was more *prolific* (cp. Plin. *N. H.* xxxv. 130 (Antidotus) diligentior quam numerosior).

et ... diligentior] These words have created much difficulty since the 'canon' of Polykleitos was renowned as a model of proportions. Several alterations of the text have been proposed, of which the simplest is the omission of 'et'; the words will then mean 'his mastery of rhythm was greater than Polykleitos' accuracy in proportion'; but it seems doubtful whether this expression is good Latin; it would be improved by the further omission of 'Polykleitos.' (Substitute 'his' for 'Polykleitos' in the translation given above.) But the true solution of the difficulty seems to be that the series of criticisms which Pliny borrows (v. Introduction, § 2), proceeds from a pupil or admirer of Lysippos, and places Myron higher than Polykleitos, whose proportions are disapproved (v. infr. No. 241).

---

89. Paus. ii. 30. 2 θεῶν δὲ Αἰγινῆται τιμῶσιν Ἑκάτην μάλιστα . . . ξόανον δὲ ἔργον Μύρωνος, ὁμοίως ἐν πρόσωπόν τε καὶ τὸ λοιπὸν σῶμα.

The Aeginetans honour Hekate above all deities. Their image is the work of Myron; it has but one face, and the rest of the body is likewise one.

Alkamenes (v. infr. No. 129) was said to be the first to represent Hekate in threefold form.

---

90. Strab. xiv. 637 τρία Μύρωνος ἔργα κολοσσικὰ ἱδρυμένα ἐπὶ μιᾶς βάσεως, ἃ ἦρε μὲν Ἀντώνιος, ἀνέθηκε δὲ πάλιν ὁ Σεβαστὸς Καῖσαρ εἰς

There were three colossal statues by Myron, standing on one base, which Antony removed. Augustus, however, restored two

τὴν αὐτὴν βάσιν τὰ δύο, τὴν
'Αθηνᾶν καὶ τὸν 'Ηρακλέα· τὸν
δὲ Δία εἰς τὸ Καπετώλιον
μετήνεγκε κατασκευάσας αὐτῷ
ναΐσκον.

of them, the Athena and the Herakles, and set them up on the same base, but removed the Zeus to the Capitol, where he had built a shrine for it.

Originally at Samos.

91. Paus. ix. 30. 1 τὸ
δὲ ἄγαλμα ἀνέθηκε Σύλλας
τοῦ Διονύσου τὸ ὀρθόν, ἔργων
τῶν Μύρωνος θέας μάλιστα
ἄξιον μετά γε τὸν 'Αθήνησιν
'Ερεχθέα· ἀνέθηκε δὲ οὐκ οἴκο-
θεν, 'Ορχομενίους δὲ ἀφελό-
μενος τοὺς Μινύας.

The standing image of Dionysos, which is the most remarkable of the works of Myron after the Erechtheus at Athens, was dedicated by Sulla. It was not his own property, but was taken by him from the Minyai of Orchomenos.

On Mount Helikon. The Erechtheus here referred to is supposed to have formed part of a group on the Akropolis described by Paus. i. 27. 4 as 'ἀγάλματα μέγαλα χαλκᾶ, διεστῶτες ἄνδρες εἰς μάχην— large statues of bronze, representing men facing each other in single combat.' The combatants were Erechtheus and Eumolpos.

92. Anth. Plan. iv. 54.
(a) οἷος ἔης φεύγων τὸν ὑπή-
νεμον, ἔμπνοε Λάδα,
Θυμόν, ἐπ' ἀκροτάτῳ
νευρὰ ταθεὶς ὄνυχι,
τοῖον ἐχάλκευσέν σε
Μύρων, ἐπὶ παντὶ
χαράξας
σώματι Πισαίου προσ-
δοκίην στεφάνου.
(b) πλήρης ἐλπίδος ἐστίν,

As once thou wast, O Ladas, instinct with life, when thou didst fly from Thymos swift as the wind, on tiptoe, with every muscle at full strain—even so did Myron fashion thee in bronze, and stamp on thy whole frame eager yearning for the crown that Pisa gives.

ἄκροις δ' ἐπὶ χείλε-
σιν ἆσθμα
ἐμφαίνει κοίλων ἔνδο-
θεν ἐκ λαγόνων.
πηδήσει τάχα χαλκὸς
ἐπὶ στέφος, οὐδὲ
καθέξει
ἁ βάσις· ὢ τέχνη πνεύ-
ματος ὠκυτέρα.

He is full of hope, and
on his lips is seen the
breath that comes from
the hollow flanks ; anon the
bronze will leap to seize
the crown, and the base
will hold it no longer ; see
how art is swifter than the
wind !

Ladas was probably an Argive (since Paus. saw his statue in the
temple of Apollo Lykios at Argos), and was victorious in the long
foot-race at Olympia.

93. Lucian, Philops. 18
μῶν τὸν δισκεύοντα, ἦν δ' ἐγώ,
φὴς τὸν ἐπικεκυφότα κατὰ τὸ
σχῆμα τῆς ἀφέσεως, ἀπεστραμ-
μένον εἰς τὴν δισκοφόρου,
ἠρέμα ὀκλάζοντα τῷ ἑτέρῳ,
ἐοικότα ξυναναστησομένῳ μετὰ τῆς βολῆς ; οὐκ ἐκεῖνον,
ἦ δ' ὅς, ἐπεὶ τῶν Μύρωνος
ἔργων ἓν καὶ τοῦτό ἐστιν ὁ
δισκοβόλος ὃν σὺ λέγεις.

Surely, said I, you do
not speak of the quoit-
thrower who stoops in the
attitude of one who is making his cast, turning round
toward the hand that holds
the quoit, and bending the
other knee gently beneath
him, like one who will rise
erect as he hurls the quoit?
No, said he, for that quoit-
thrower of whom you speak
is one of the works of
Myron.

Reproduced in many copies, of which the best is in the Palazzo
Lancelotti, Rome (*Coll.* I, Pl. xi).

Quintilian (ii. 13. 8) says of it, 'Quid tam distortum et elabora-
tum, quam est ille discobolus Myronis'—'What can be more
strained and artificial in its attitude than the famous quoit-thrower
of Myron?'

94. Prop. ii. 31. 7
Atque aram circum stete-
rant armenta Myronis
Quattuor artifices, uiuida
signa, boues.

And about the altar
stood Myron's herd, four
kine from the master's
hand, statues full of life.

aram] In the colonnade of the temple of Apollo on the Palatine.

95. Petron. 88 Myron,
qui paene hominum ani-
mas ferarumque aere com-
prehenderat, non inuenit
heredem.

Myron, who could almost
catch the souls of men and
beasts and enchain them in
bronze, found no heir.

animas] The principle of *animal* life, not the mind ; hence there
is no contradiction with Pliny's 'animi sensus non expressisse.' Cp.
the epithets 'ἔμπνοε,' No. 92, 'uiuida,' No. 94.

Other works by Myron :—
APOLLO at Agrigentum, carried away by Verres (Cic. *Verr*. iv.
43. 93).
HERAKLES, taken from Heius the Mamertine by Verres (Cic.
Verr. iv. 3. 5).
Olympic victors :—
LYKINOS of Sparta, victorious in the chariot-race.
TIMANTHES of Kleonai, victorious in the pankration.
PHILIPPOS of Pellana in Arkadia, victorious in the boys' boxing-
match.
CHIONIS of Sparta, victorious in the foot-race, Ol. 29–31 (664–
656).
[The 'drunken old woman' attributed to Myron by Plin. *N. H.*
xxxvi. 32 belongs to a later artist of the same name ; see Weiss-
häupl, 'Εφ. 'Αρχ. 1891, p. 143.]

PART III

THE AGE OF PHEIDIAS
AND POLYKLEITOS

Nos. 96–181.

§ 1. THE ATTIC SCHOOL.

1. PHEIDIAS.

(a) LIFE.

The statements that he was the pupil of Hegias (Part I. § 1.4 (c)) and Ageladas (No. 43) rest on the authority of Dion Chrysostom (as emended) and the Scholia on Aristophanes respectively. Pliny's 'floruit' (Ol. 83=448 B.C.) may be based (1) on that of Perikles, (2) on the completion of the Olympian Zeus.

96. Plin. *N. H.* xxxv. 54 Cum et Phidiam ipsum initio pictorem fuisse tradatur clipeumque Athenis ab eo pictum.

For tradition tells that Pheidias himself began life as a painter, and that there is a shield at Athens painted by him.

clipeum] It is suggested by Urlichs that this refers to the inner surface of the shield of Parthenos. This is, however, in contradiction to the words of Pliny in No. 106. Panainos, the brother of Pheidias, painted the inner surface of the shield carried by the Athena of Kolotes at Elis.

97. Plut. Perikl. 13 ᾿Αναβαινόντων δὲ τῶν ἔργων, ὑπερηφάνων μὲν μεγέθει, μορφῇ δ᾿ ἀμιμήτων καὶ χάριτι, τῶν δημιουργῶν ἁμιλλωμένων ὑπερβάλλεσθαι τὴν δημιουργίαν τῇ καλλιτεχνίᾳ, μάλιστα θαυμάσιον ἦν τὸ τάχος . . .

As the buildings rose, stately in size and unsurpassed in form and grace, the workmen vied with each other that the quality of their work might be enhanced by its artistic beauty. Most wonderful of all was

πάντα δὲ διεῖπε καὶ πάντων ἐπίσκοπος ἦν αὐτῷ (Περικλεῖ) Φειδίας.

the rapidity of construction. Pheidias managed everything, and was his (Perikles') overseer in all the work.

Plut. refers to the architectural and artistic works carried out under Perikles.

98. Plut. Perikl. 31

Φειδίας ὁ πλάστης ἐργολάβος μὲν ἦν τοῦ ἀγάλματος ... φίλος δὲ τῷ Περικλεῖ γενόμενος καὶ μέγιστον παρ' αὐτῷ δυνηθεὶς τοὺς μὲν δι' αὐτὸν ἔσχεν ἐχθροὺς φθονούμενος, οἱ δὲ τοῦ δήμου ποιούμενοι πεῖραν ἐν ἐκείνῳ ποῖός τις ἔσοιτο Περικλεῖ κριτής, Μένωνά τινα τῶν Φειδίου συνεργῶν πείσαντες, ἱκέτην ἐν ἀγορᾷ καθίζουσιν, αἰτούμενον ἄδειαν ἐπὶ μηνύσει καὶ κατηγορίᾳ τοῦ Φειδίου. προσδεξαμένου δὲ τοῦ δήμου τὸν ἄνθρωπον καὶ γενομένης ἐν ἐκκλησίᾳ διώξεως κλοπαὶ μὲν οὐκ ἠλέγχοντο· τὸ γὰρ χρυσίον οὕτως εὐθὺς ἐξ ἀρχῆς τῷ ἀγάλματι προσειργάσατο καὶ περιέθηκεν ὁ Φειδίας, γνώμῃ τοῦ Περικλέους, ὥστε πάνυ δυνατὸν εἶναι περιελοῦσιν ἀποδεῖξαι τὸν σταθμόν· ὃ καὶ τότε τοὺς κατηγόρους ἐκέλευσε ποιεῖν ὁ Περικλῆς. ἡ δὲ δόξα τῶν

Pheidias the sculptor accepted the contract for the statue ; and being a friend of Perikles, with considerable influence over him, he became an object of jealousy and acquired many enemies, while the democratic party made his case a test of the probable disposition of the jurors towards Perikles. They suborned one Menon, an assistant of Pheidias, and caused him to sit as a suppliant in the market-place and demand assurance of pardon, in order that he might accuse Pheidias or give evidence against him. The people listened to the man's charges, and there was a trial in the assembly ; but the charge of theft was not proved ; for Pheidias had by Perikles' advice originally fitted the gold

ἔργων ἐπίεζε φθόνῳ τὸν
Φειδίαν καὶ μάλισθ' ὅτι τὴν
πρὸς 'Αμάζονας μάχην ἐν τῇ
ἀσπίδι ποιῶν αὐτοῦ τινὰ
μορφὴν ἐνετύπωσε, πρεσβυτοῦ
φαλακροῦ, πέτρον ἐπηρμένου
δι' ἀμφοτέρων τῶν χειρῶν,
καὶ τοῦ Περικλέους εἰκόνα
παγκάλην ἐνέθηκε μαχομένου
πρὸς 'Αμαζόνα. τὸ δὲ σχῆμα
τῆς χειρός, ἀνατεινούσης δόρυ
πρὸ τῆς ὄψεως τοῦ Περι-
κλέους, πεποιημένον εὐμηχά-
νως, οἷον ἐπικρύπτειν βούλεται
τὴν ὁμοιότητα παραφαινομέ-
νην ἑκατέρωθεν. ὁ μὲν οὖν
Φειδίας εἰς τὸ δεσμωτήριον
ἀπαχθεὶς ἐτελεύτησε νοσήσας,
ὡς δέ φασιν ἔνιοι, φαρμάκοις,
ἐπὶ διαβολῇ τοῦ Περικλέους
τῶν ἐχθρῶν παρασκευασάντων.

to the statue, and fastened
it upon it in such a manner
that it was quite possible
to take it off and deter-
mine its weight, which
Perikles ordered the ac-
cusers to do. But the
fame of his works caused
Pheidias to be the victim
of jealousy, notably be-
cause, in representing the
battle of the Amazons on
the shield, he had intro-
duced a figure of himself
as a bald old man lifting
up a stone in both hands,
and a very fine portrait of
Perikles fighting with an
Amazon. The attitude of
the arm, however, which is
levelling a spear across the
face of Perikles, is in-
geniously contrived with
the intention, as it were, of
concealing the likeness of
which a glimpse is shown
on either side. Pheidias
then was cast into prison,
where he fell sick and died
—or, as some say, was
poisoned by his enemies,
in order to bring discredit
upon Perikles.

τοῦ ἀγάλματος] The Parthenos.

αὐτοῦ τινὰ μορφήν] Clearly seen on the so-called 'Strangford shield' in the British Museum (*Brit. Mus. Catalogue of Greek Sculpture*, p. 99), where, however, the figure holds an axe. Aristotle, περὶ οὐρανοῦ 399ᵇ, tells a story to the effect that the shield contained a hidden mechanism by which, if the head were removed, the whole statue would fall to pieces.

99. Schol. Ar. Pax 605

Φιλόχορος ἐπὶ Θεοδώρου ἄρχοντος ταῦτά φησι· καὶ τὸ ἄγαλμα τὸ χρυσοῦν τῆς Ἀθηνᾶς ἐστάθη εἰς τὸν νεὼν τὸν μέγαν ... καὶ Φειδίας ὁ ποιήσας, δόξας παραλογίζεσθαι τὸν ἐλέφαντα τὸν εἰς τὰς φολίδας ἐκρίθη. καὶ φυγὼν ἐς Ἦλιν ἐργολαβῆσαι τὸ ἄγαλμα τοῦ Διὸς τοῦ ἐν Ὀλυμπίᾳ λέγεται, τοῦτο δὲ ἐξεργασάμενος ἀποθανεῖν ὑπὸ Ἠλείων ἐπὶ Πυθοδώρου.

Philochoros, writing of the archonship of Theodoros, says :—' The golden image of Athena was placed in the great temple. The artist, Pheidias, was thought to have been guilty of peculation in respect of the ivory used for the serpent's scales, and was put on his trial. He fled to Elis, where he is said to have accepted the contract for the image of Zeus at Olympia, and, after completing it, to have been put to death by the Eleans in the archonship of Pythodoros.'

Theodoros was archon 438 B.C., Pythodoros 432 B.C. Both names are corrupt in the text. It is impossible to reconcile this story with that given by Plutarch. From the words of Ar. *Pax* 605 πρῶτα μὲν γὰρ ἦρξεν ἄτης Φειδίας πράξας κακῶς, which relate to the outbreak of the Peloponnesian war, we may infer that the later date (432 B.C.) for the trial of Pheidias is the correct one. The question, however, still remains whether the Olympian Zeus is earlier (456–448 B.C.) or later (438–432 B.C.) than the Parthenos. On the one hand, (1) it seems improbable that the temple at Olympia, completed in 456 B.C., should have remained for eighteen years without a statue; (2) Pliny dates Panainos, the brother of

Pheidias, Ol. 83=448 B.C., possibly by the completion of the statue, in the construction of which he took part; on the other, (1) Dörpfeld (*Olympia*, Textband ii. pp. 16, 20) considers that some architectural peculiarities of the base are *imitated* from that of the Parthenos; (2) Pliny may simply date Panainos by his brother.

(b) WORKS.

I. IN ATHENS.

100. Paus. i. 28. 2 χωρὶς δὲ ἢ ὅσα κατέλεξα, δύο μὲν Ἀθηναίοις εἰσὶ δεκάται πολεμήσασιν, ἄγαλμα Ἀθηνᾶς χαλκοῦν ἀπὸ Μήδων τῶν ἐς Μαραθῶνα ἀποβάντων, τέχνη Φειδίου· καί οἱ τὴν ἐπὶ τῆς ἀσπίδος Λαπιθῶν πρὸς Κενταύρους μάχην καὶ ὅσα ἄλλα ἐστὶν ἐπειργασμένα λέγουσι τορεῦσαι Μῦν· τῷ δὲ Μυὶ ταῦτά τε καὶ τὰ λοιπὰ τῶν ἔργων Παρράσιον καταγράψαι τὸν Εὐήνορος. ταύτης τῆς Ἀθηνᾶς ἡ τοῦ δόρατος αἰχμὴ καὶ ὁ λόφος τοῦ κράνους ἀπὸ Σουνίου προσπλέουσίν ἐστιν ἤδη σύνοπτα.

Beside those which I have enumerated, the Athenians have two offerings from the tithes of spoil taken in war; one is a bronze image of Athena from the spoils of the Persians who landed at Marathon, the work of Pheidias; the battle of the Lapithai and Centaurs on the shield, and the other reliefs are said to be the work of the engraver Mys; and both these and his other works are said to have been designed for him by Parrhasios, the son of Evenor. The point of the spear and crest of the helmet of this Athena are visible even to mariners, as they approach from the side of Sunion.

This statue is usually called the Athena Promachos, a name directly applied to it only by the Scholiast on Dem. *Androt.* 597 R, and in *CIA.* iii. 1. 638 (circ. 410 A.D.). The epithet is inappropriate to the pose of the statue, which is represented on coins of Athens (*Num. Comm. Z.* iii–vii) standing between the Propylaia and Erechtheion.

λέγουσι τορεῦσαι Μῦν] Mys and Parrhasios both belonged to the generation following Pheidias, and contemporary with the Peloponnesian war. The designs on the shield were therefore a later addition. The Scholiast on Aristid. *Panath.* p. 320. attributes it to Praxiteles, which Furtwängler accepts as the true tradition, referring to the elder Praxiteles.

ἀπὸ Σουνίου . . . σύνοπτα] The Akropolis being invisible from Sunium, we must not connect ἤδη with the words ἀπὸ Σουνίου, which give the *direction* of approach only, but take it closely with προσπλέουσιν. It merely emphasises the idea that the statue could be seen before landing.

101. Niket. Chon. Isaac. Ang. et Alex. F. p. 738 B ἀλλὰ καὶ τῶν ἀγοραίων οἱ φιλοινότεροι τὸ ἑστὸς ἐπὶ στήλης ἐν τῷ Κωνσταντινείῳ φόρῳ τῆς ᾿Αθηνᾶς ἄγαλμα εἰς πλεῖστα διεῖλον τμήματα . . . ἀνέβαινε μὲν τὴν ἡλικίαν ὄρθιον ὡς ἐς τριακάδα ποδῶν, ἠμφίεστο δὲ στολὴν ἐξ ὁποίας ὕλης ὅλον τὸ ἰνδαλλόμενον κεχαλκούργητο. ποδήρης δ᾿ ἦν ἡ στολὴ καὶ συμπτυσσομένη πολλαχῇ τῶν μερῶν. . . . μίτρα δ᾿ ῎Αρεως τὴν ἰξὺν διειληφυῖα ἱκανῶς αὐτὴν περιέσφιγγεν. εἶχε δὲ κἀπὶ τοῖς στέρνοις ὀρθότιτθον ὂν ποικίλον αἰγιδῶδες ἐπένδυμα, τῶν ὤμων διεξικνούμενον, τὴν τῆς Γοργόνης τυποῦν κεφαλήν. ὁ δέ γε αὐχὴν

But the more drunken among the crowd also dashed in pieces the image of Athena, which stood on a column in the forum of Constantine. In stature it rose to the height of about 30 feet, and was clothed in garments of the same material as the whole statue, namely, of bronze. The robe reached to the feet, and was gathered up in several places. A warrior's baldric passed round her waist and clasped it tightly. Over her prominent breasts she wore a cunningly-wrought garment, like an aegis, suspended from her shoulders,

ἀχίτων ὢν καὶ πρὸς τὸ δολι-
χόδειρον ἀνατεινόμενος ἄμα-
χον εἰς ἡδονὴν θέαμα ἦν. . . .
καὶ φλεβῶν δὲ διεκτάσεις ὑπε-
κρίνοντο, καὶ ὡς ὑγρὸν ὅλον
τὸ σῶμα ἐν οἷς ἔδει περιεκλᾶτο.
. . . ἵππουρις δ' ἐπικειμένη τῇ
κεφαλῇ δεινὸν καθύπερθεν
ἔνευεν. ἡ δὲ κόμη εἰς πλέγμα
διεστραμμένη καὶ δεσμουμένη
ὄπισθεν, ὅση κέχυτο ἐκ μετώ-
πων, τροφή τις ἦν ὀφθαλμῶν,
μὴ ἐπίπαν τῷ κράνει συνε-
χομένη, ἀλλὰ καί τι παρεμ-
φαίνουσα τοῦ πλοχμοῦ. τῶν
δὲ χειρῶν ἡ μὲν λαιὰ τὰ συν-
επτυγμένα τῆς ἐσθῆτος ἀν-
έστελλε, ἀτέρα δ' ἐκτεινομένη
πρὸς κλίμα τὸ νότιον εἶχε τὴν
κεφαλὴν ἠρέμα πως ἐγκλινο-
μένην ἐκεῖ καὶ τὰς τῶν ὀφθαλμῶν ἐπ' ἴσης τεινομένας βολάς.

and representing the Gor-
gon's head. Her neck,
which was undraped and
of great length, was a sight
to cause unrestrained de-
light. Her veins stood out
prominently, and her whole
frame was supple and, where
need was, well - jointed.
Upon her head a crest of
horse-hair 'nodded fear-
fully from above.' Her
hair was twisted in a plait
and fastened at the back,
while that which streamed
from her forehead was a
feast for the eyes : for it
was not altogether con-
cealed by the helmet,
which allowed a glimpse of
her tresses to be seen. Her
left hand held up the folds
of her dress, while the right
was extended towards the
south and supported her
head, slightly inclined in
the same direction, with
the gaze of both eyes fixed
on that quarter.

Gurlitt (*Analecta Graeciensia*, Graz, 1893, p. 99 ff.) has shown
that a note by Arethas (archbishop of Caesarea 907 A.D.) on Aristid.
Or. 50, p. 408, 15 J (quoted by Overbeck, *Schriftquellen* 690, cp.
640) refers to the 'bronze Athena' of Pheidias, then in the Forum of

Constantine. Niketas describes the destruction of the same statue by rioters in 1203 A. D. The description seems to be accurate, with the exception of the closing words; the right hand originally held a lance.

102. Paus. i. 28. 2 τῶν ἔρ-γων τῶν Φειδίου θέας μάλιστα ἄξιον, 'Αθηνᾶς ἄγαλμα, ἀπὸ τῶν ἀναθέντων καλουμένης Λημνίας.

The most remarkable of the works of Pheidias, an image of Athena, called the Lemnian, after the dedicators.

On the Akropolis. The dedicators were no doubt the Athenian colonists sent to Lemnos between 451 and 448 B. C. A statue at Dresden, combined with a head at Bologna, seems to represent the type (Furtwängler, *Meisterwerke*, Pl. I, II. pp. 4–36).

103. Lucian, Εἰκόνες 4 ΛΥΚ. τῶν δὲ Φειδίου ἔργων τί μάλιστα ἐπῄνεσας; ΠΟΛ. τί δ' ἄλλο ἢ τὴν Λημνίαν, ᾗ καὶ ἐπιγράψαι τοὔνομα Φειδίας ἠξίωσε; ... 6. τὴν δὲ τοῦ παντὸς προσώπου περιγραφὴν καὶ παρειῶν τὸ ἀπαλὸν καὶ ῥῖνα σύμμετρον ἡ Λημνία παρέ-ξει καὶ Φειδίας.

Lyk. Which of the works of Pheidias do you praise most highly? *Pol.* Which but the goddess of Lemnos, whereon Pheidias deigned to inscribe his name? ... Pheidias and the Lemnian goddess shall bestow on her the outline of her countenance, her delicate cheeks and finely proportioned nose.

References to this statue have been found in the words of Pliny (v. infr., No. 119) as to an Athena called 'the Beautiful,' and in a passage of Himerios to the effect that Pheidias did not always represent Athena armed, but also without a helmet.

104. Plin. *N. H.* xxxiv. 54 Phidias praeter Iouem Olympium quem nemo

Pheidias, beside the unrivalled Zeus of Olympia, made also of ivory the

aemulatur fecit ex ebore aeque Mineruam Athenis quae est in Parthenone stans.

Athena which is at Athens, and stands erect in the Parthenon.

On the Athena Parthenos (the name is applied by Paus. v. 11. 10), see *Ov.* I⁴. 350 ff., *Coll.* I. 538 ff., where references are given to the earlier literature of the subject.

105. Paus. i. 24. 5 αὐτὸ δὲ ἔκ τε ἐλέφαντος τὸ ἄγαλμα καὶ χρυσοῦ πεποίηται. μέσῳ μὲν οὖν ἐπίκειταί οἱ τῷ κράνει Σφιγγὸς εἰκών· . . καθ᾽ ἑκάτερον δὲ τοῦ κράνους γρῦπές εἰσιν ἐπειργασμένοι . . 7. τὸ δὲ ἄγαλμα τῆς Ἀθηνᾶς ὀρθόν ἐστιν ἐν χιτῶνι ποδήρει, καί οἱ κατὰ τὸ στέρνον ἡ κεφαλὴ Μεδούσης ἐλέφαντός ἐστιν ἐμπεποιημένη καὶ Νίκη ὅσον τε τεσσάρων πηχῶν ⟨ἐπὶ τῆς χειρός ἐστιν αὐτῇ,⟩ ἐν δὲ τῇ ⟨ἑτέρᾳ⟩ χειρὶ δόρυ ἔχει, καὶ οἱ πρὸς τοῖς ποσὶν ἀσπίς τε κεῖται, καὶ πλησίον τοῦ δόρατος δράκων ἐστίν· εἴη δ᾽ ἂν Ἐριχθόνιος οὗτος ὁ δράκων· ἔστι δὲ τῷ βάθρῳ τοῦ ἀγάλματος ἐπειργασμένα Πανδώρας γένεσις.

The statue itself is made of gold and ivory. On the middle of the helmet rests the figure of a Sphinx; and on either side of the helmet griffins are represented. The image of Athena stands erect, and wears a tunic reaching to the feet. On its breast is represented in ivory the head of Medusa, and a Victory about 4 cubits in height stands on one of its hands, while in the other it holds a spear: at its feet rests a shield, and close to the shield is a serpent, which no doubt represents Erichthonios; on the base of the statue the birth of Pandora is wrought in relief.

106. Plin. *N. H.* xxxvi. 18 Phidiam clarissimum esse per omnis gentes, quae

No one doubts that Pheidias' renown extends through all lands where

Iouis Olympii famam in-
tellegunt, nemo dubitat,
sed ut laudari merito sciant
etiam qui opera, eius non
uidere proferemus argu-
menta parua et ingeni
tantum. Neque ad hoc
Iouis Olympii pulchritu-
dine utemur, non Miner-
uae Athenis factae ampli-
tudine, cum sit ea cubi-
torum uiginti sex,—ebore
haec et auro constat,—sed
in scuto eius Amazonum
proelium caelauit intumescente ambitu parmae, eiusdem concaua parte deorum
et Gigantum dimicationes,
in soleis uero Lapitharum
et Centaurorum, adeo mo-
menta omnia capacia artis
illi fuere. In basi autem
quod caelatum est Πανδώ-
ρας γένεσιν appellant ; di
sunt nasce⟨nti adsta⟩ntes
xx numero. Uictoria prae-
cipue mirabili, periti mi-
rantur et serpentem sub
ipsa cuspide aureum ac
sphingem.

the fame of his Olympian
Zeus is heard ; but in order
that those too who have
not seen his works may
know that his praises are
merited, I will bring forward some minor proofs
which establish only the
fertility of his invention.
And to this end I shall em-
ploy, not the beauty of the
Olympian Zeus, nor the
grandeur of the Athena
which he made at Athens,
though she is 26 cubits in
height, all of ivory and
gold—but the fact that on
her shield he wrought in
relief the battle of the
Amazons on the convex
surface, and the combats of
gods and giants on the
concave side, while on her
sandals he represented
those of the Lapithai and
Centaurs ; so true was it
that every spot furnished
a field for his art to fill.
The subject of the reliefs
on the base they call ' Pandora's birth' ; Gods, twenty
in number, are present at
the scene. The Victory is

specially marvellous, but
connoisseurs admire also
the golden serpent at the
foot of the spear, and the
sphinx.

intumescente ambitu parmae] If the sense of 'ambitus'=
'circumference' be pressed, this will mean that a band of relief
ran round the edge of the shield; but Pliny may have strained
language in order to obtain an antithesis to 'concava parte' in
different words, and used 'ambitus' like the Greek ἀψίς, possibly
even as a translation of that word, which is used both of the tyre of
a wheel and of a closed circle like the sun's orb. The Strangford
shield represents the whole surface as covered with reliefs. See
A. H. Smith, *Brit. Mus. Catalogue of Greek Sculpture*, p. 99.

dimicationes] The plural seems to point to single duel-scenes,
and it is *a priori* probable that only the inner edge was decorated.
The same will apply to the groups of Lapithai and Centaurs.

momenta] Lit. a particle sufficient to turn the scale, and so
a mathematical particle or point; cp. xviii. 333 sol cotidie ex
alio caeli momento oritur. Then, in the language of literary criticism, a division of a subject. Quint. v. 10. 71 ordo rerum tribus
momentis consertus est. Hence its use in art-criticism, as here.

nasce⟨nti adsta⟩ntes] MSS. nascentes. Al. corr. ⟨ad⟩sunt
nascenti.

sub ipsa ... sphingem] MSS. ac sub ipsa cuspide aeream
sphingem.

107. Plut. Perikl. 13 ὁ δὲ   Pheidias made the golden
Φειδίας εἰργάζετο μὲν τῆς θεοῦ   image of the goddess, and
τὸ χρυσοῦν ἕδος, καὶ τούτου   his name is inscribed as the
δημιουργὸς ἐν τῇ στήλῃ γέ-   artist's on the slab.
γραπται.

ἐν τῇ στήλῃ] The words have been supposed to show that the
column which supports the right hand of the 'Varvakeion' statuette
(*Ov.* I⁴, Fig. 94), and appears on other monuments (*op. cit.* p. 352),
represents an original support. But this would be expressed by
κίων, not στήλη.

108. Thuc. ii. 13 ἀπέφαινε δ' ἔχον τὸ ἄγαλμα τεσσαρά-κοντα τάλαντα σταθμὸν χρυσοῦ ἀπέφθου καὶ περιαιρετὸν εἶναι ἅπαν.

He (Pericles) pointed out that the image bore 40 talents' weight of refined gold, which was all removeable.

Thucydides, as a contemporary authority, is no doubt right as to the weight (later authorities give 44–50 tal.).

ἀπέφθου] Lit. 'boiled down.'

109. Paus. i. 14. 7 πλησίον δὲ ἱερόν ἐστιν 'Αφροδίτης Οὐρανίας ... τὸ δὲ ἐφ' ἡμῶν ἔτι ἄγαλμα λίθου Παρίου καὶ ἔργον Φειδίου.

Hard by is a temple of Aphrodite Urania. Even in my time it contained an image of Parian marble, the work of Pheidias.

In the deme of Melite. The temple was built by Perikles (Curtius, *Stadtgeschichte von Athen*, p. 177).

110. Paus. i. 24. 8 τοῦ ναοῦ ἐστὶ πέραν 'Απόλλων χαλκοῦς, καὶ τὸ ἄγαλμα λέγουσι Φειδίαν ποιῆσαι· Παρνόπιον δὲ καλοῦσιν, ὅτι σφίσι παρνόπων βλαπτόντων τὴν γῆν ἀποτρέψειν ὁ θεὸς εἶπεν ἐκ τῆς χώρας.

Beyond the temple is an Apollo of bronze: the statue is said to be the work of Pheidias; it is called the Apollo of the Locusts, because, when the land of Attica was ravaged by locusts, the god promised to drive them away.

II. IN ELIS.

111. Paus. v. 10. 2 ἐποιήθη δὲ ὁ ναὸς καὶ τὸ ἄγαλμα τῷ Διὶ ἀπὸ λαφύρων, ἡνίκα Πίσαν οἱ 'Ηλεῖοι καὶ ὅσον τῶν περι-

The temple and image of Zeus were erected from the spoil taken by the Eleans, when they reduced Pisa and

οἴκων ἄλλο συναπέστη Ἠλείοις πολέμῳ καθεῖλον. Φειδίαν δὲ τὸν ἐργασάμενον τὸ ἄγαλμα εἶναι καὶ ἐπίγραμμά ἐστιν ἐς μαρτυρίαν ὑπὸ τοῦ Διὸς γεγραμμένον τοῖς ποσί,
Φειδίας Χαρμίδου υἱὸς Ἀθηναῖός μ᾽ ἐποίησε.
... 11. 1 καθέζεται μὲν δὴ ὁ θεὸς ἐν θρόνῳ χρυσοῦ πεποιημένος καὶ ἐλέφαντος· στέφανος δὲ ἐπίκειταί οἱ τῇ κεφαλῇ μεμιμημένος ἐλαίας κλῶνας. ἐν μὲν δὴ τῇ δεξιᾷ φέρει Νίκην, ἐξ ἐλέφαντος καὶ ταύτην καὶ χρυσοῦ, ταινίαν τε ἔχουσαν καὶ ἐπὶ τῇ κεφαλῇ στέφανον· τῇ δὲ ἀριστερᾷ τοῦ θεοῦ χειρὶ ἔνεστι σκῆπτρον μετάλλοις τοῖς πᾶσι διηνθισμένον. ὁ δὲ ὄρνις ὁ ἐπὶ τῷ σκήπτρῳ καθήμενός ἐστιν ὁ ἀετός. χρυσοῦ δὲ καὶ τὰ ὑποδήματα τῷ θεῷ καὶ ἱμάτιον ὡσαύτως ἐστί. τῷ δὲ ἱματίῳ ζῴδιά τε καὶ τῶν ἀνθῶν τὰ κρίνα ἐστὶν ἐμπεποιημένα. 2. ὁ δὲ θρόνος ποικίλος μὲν χρυσῷ καὶ λίθοις, ποικίλος δὲ καὶ ἐβένῳ τε καὶ ἐλέφαντί ἐστι καὶ ζῷά τε ἐπ᾽ αὐτοῦ γραφῇ μεμιμημένα, καὶ ἀγάλματά ἐστιν εἰργασμένα. Νῖκαι μὲν δὴ τέσσαρες, χορευ-

the other dependent cities which joined in revolt against them. That Pheidias was the sculptor of the image is proved by the inscription graven beneath the feet of Zeus :
Pheidias, son of Charmides, the Athenian, made me.
Now the god is seated on his throne, and is made of gold and ivory : on his head rests a garland which imitates sprays of olive. In his right hand he bears a Victory, also of ivory and gold, which holds a fillet and has a garland on its head ; and in his left there is a sceptre inlaid with every kind of metal ; the bird which is perched on the sceptre is the eagle. The sandals of the god and likewise his robe are of gold. On the robe are wrought figures and flowers ; these latter are lilies. The throne is diversified with gold and precious stones and ebony and ivory ; and there are figures upon it, painted and sculptured.

ουσῶν παρεχόμεναι σχῆμα κατὰ ἕκαστον τοῦ θρόνου πόδα· δύο δὲ εἰσὶν ἄλλαι πρὸς ἑκάστου πέζῃ ποδός. τῶν ποδῶν δὲ ἑκατέρῳ τῶν ἔμπροσθεν παῖδές τε ἐπίκεινται Θηβαίων ὑπὸ Σφιγγῶν ἡρπασμένοι, καὶ ὑπὸ τὰς Σφίγγας Νιόβης τοὺς παῖδας Ἀπόλλων κατατοξεύουσι καὶ Ἄρτεμις. 3. τῶν δὲ τοῦ θρόνου μεταξὺ ποδῶν τέσσαρες κανόνες εἰσίν, ἐκ ποδὸς ἐς πόδα ἕτερον διήκων ἕκαστος. τῷ μὲν δὴ κατ' εὐθὺ τῆς ἐσόδου κανόνι, ἑπτά ἐστιν ἀγάλματα ἐπ' αὐτῷ. τὸ γὰρ ὄγδοον ἐξ αὐτῶν οὐκ ἴσασι τρόπον ὅντινα ἐγένετο ἀφανές. εἴη δ' ἂν ἀγωνισμάτων ἀρχαίων ταῦτα μιμήματα· οὐ γάρ πω τὰ ἐς τοὺς παῖδας ἐπὶ ἡλικίας ἤδη καθειστήκει τῆς Φειδίου. τὸν δὲ αὐτὸν ταινίᾳ τὴν κεφαλὴν ἀναδούμενον ἐοικέναι τὸ εἶδος Παντάρκει λέγουσιν, μειράκιον δὲ Ἠλεῖον τὸν Παντάρκην παιδικὰ εἶναι τοῦ Φειδίου. ἀνείλετο δὲ καὶ ἐν παισὶν ὁ Παντάρκης πάλης νίκην Ὀλυμπιάδι ἕκτῃ πρὸς ταῖς ὀγδοήκοντα. 4. ἐπὶ δὲ τῶν κανόνων τοῖς λοιποῖς ὁ λόχος ἐστὶν ὁ σὺν Ἡρακλεῖ μαχό-

There are four Victories in the attitudes of the dance on each leg of the throne; and two others at the foot of each leg. On each of the front legs rest Theban youths in the clutches of Sphinxes, and beneath the Sphinxes are the children of Niobe, whom Apollo and Artemis are shooting with arrows. Between the legs of the throne are four bars, each of which extends from one leg to the next. On the bar which faces the entry are wrought seven figures. For the eighth disappeared in some mysterious way. These must be representations of the old contests; for the contests for boys had not been instituted in Pheidias' time. They say that the boy who is binding his hair with a fillet is like Pantarkes in countenance, and that Pantarkes was a youth of Elis who was beloved by Pheidias. Pantarkes won the victory in the boys' wrestling-match

μενος πρὸς ᾿Αμαζόνας. ἀριθμὸς
μὲν δὴ συναμφοτέρων ἐς ἐννέα
ἐστὶ καὶ εἴκοσι· τέτακται δὲ
καὶ Θησεὺς ἐν τοῖς συμμάχοις
τῷ ῾Ηρακλεῖ. ἀνέχουσι δὲ οὐχ
οἱ πόδες μόνοι τὸν θρόνον,
ἀλλὰ καὶ κίονες ἴσοι τοῖς ποσὶ
μεταξὺ ἑστηκότες τῶν ποδῶν.
ὑπελθεῖν δὲ οὐχ οἷόν τέ ἐστι
ὑπὸ τὸν θρόνον, ὥσπερ γε καὶ
ἐν ᾿Αμύκλαις ἐς τὸ ἐντὸς τοῦ
θρόνου παρερχόμεθα· ἐν ᾿Ολυμ-
πίᾳ δὲ ἐρύματα τρόπον τοίχων
πεποιημένα τὰ ἀπείργοντά ἐστι.
5. τούτων τῶν ἐρυμάτων ὅσον
μὲν οὖν ἀπαντικρὺ τῶν θυρῶν
ἐστὶν ἀλήλιπται κυανῷ μόνον,
τὰ δὲ λοιπὰ αὐτῶν παρέχεται
Παναίνου γραφάς. . . . 7. ἐπὶ
δὲ τοῖς ἀνωτάτω τοῦ θρόνου
πεποίηκεν ὁ Φειδίας ὑπὲρ τὴν
κεφαλὴν τοῦ ἀγάλματος τοῦτο
μὲν Χάριτας τοῦτο δὲ ῞Ωρας,
τρεῖς ἑκατέρας. . . . τὸ ὑπόθημα δὲ τὸ ὑπὸ τοῦ Διὸς τοῖς
πόσιν, ὑπὸ τῶν ἐν τῇ ᾿Αττικῇ
καλούμενον θρανίον, λέοντάς
τε χρυσοῦς καὶ Θησέως ἐπειρ-
γασμένην ἔχει μάχην τὴν πρὸς
᾿Αμαζόνας, τὸ ᾿Αθηναίων πρῶτον ἀνδραγάθημα ἐς οὐχ ὁμο-
φύλους. 8. ἐπὶ δὲ τοῦ βάθρου
τοῦ τὸν θρόνον τε ἀνέχοντος

in the 86th Olympiad (436
B.C.) On the remaining bars
are represented Herakles
and his troop engaging the
Amazons in battle. The
number of both parties
amounts to twenty-nine;
and Theseus has a place
among the allies of Hera-
kles. The throne is sup-
ported not only by the legs,
but also by pillars standing
between the legs and equal
to them in number. It is
not possible to enter be-
neath the throne, as one
goes into the interior of the
throne at Amyklai; for at
Olympia there are screens
like walls which bar the
ingress. Of these screens
that which is opposite the
door is covered with plain
blue enamel; but the rest
of them are decorated with
paintings by Panainos. On
the uppermost part of the
throne Pheidias has represented above the head of
the image the Graces and
the Seasons each three in
number. The stool upon
which the feet of Zeus rest

καὶ ὅσος ἄλλος κόσμος περὶ τὸν Δία, ἐπὶ τούτου τοῦ βάθρου χρυσᾶ ποιήματα, ἀναβεβηκὼς ἐπὶ ἅρμα Ἥλιος, καὶ Ζεύς τέ ἐστι καὶ Ἥρα ⟨καὶ Ἥφαιστος⟩, παρὰ δὲ αὐτὸν Χάρις· ταύτης δὲ Ἑρμῆς ἔχεται, τοῦ Ἑρμοῦ δὲ Ἑστία· μετὰ δὲ τὴν Ἑστίαν Ἔρως ἐστὶν ἐκ θαλάσσης Ἀφροδίτην ἀνιοῦσαν ὑποδεχόμενος· τὴν δὲ Ἀφροδίτην στεφανοῖ Πειθώ. ἐπείργασται δὲ καὶ Ἀπόλλων σὺν Ἀρτέμιδι, Ἀθηνᾶ τε καὶ Ἡρακλῆς, καὶ ἤδη τοῦ βάθρου πρὸς τῷ πέρατι Ἀμφιτρίτη καὶ Ποσειδῶν, Σελήνη τε ἵππον ἐμοὶ δοκεῖν ἐλαύνουσα. τοῖς δέ ἐστιν εἰρημένον ἐφ᾽ ἡμιόνου τὴν θεὸν ὀχεῖσθαι καὶ οὐχ ἵππου, καὶ λόγον γέ τινα ἐπὶ τῷ ἡμιόνῳ λέγουσιν εὐήθη. 9. μέτρα δὲ τοῦ ἐν Ὀλυμπίᾳ Διὸς ἐς ὕψος τε καὶ εὖρος ἐπιστάμενος γεγραμμένα οὐκ ἐν ἐπαίνῳ θήσομαι τοὺς μετρήσαντας· ἐπεὶ καὶ τὰ εἰρημένα αὐτοῖς μέτρα πολύ τι ἀποδέοντά ἐστιν ἢ τοῖς ἰδοῦσι παρέστηκεν ἐς τὸ ἄγαλμα δόξα, ὅπου γε καὶ αὐτὸν τὸν θεὸν μάρτυρα ἐς τοῦ Φειδίου τὴν τέχνην γενέσθαι λέγουσιν. ὡς γὰρ δὴ ἐκ-

(which in the Attic dialect is called 'thranion') is decorated in relief with golden lions and the battle of Theseus and the Amazons, the first deed of valour performed by the Athenians against an alien race. On the base which supports the throne of Zeus and all its adornments, are figures of gold—Helios mounted on his chariot, Zeus, Hera, Hephaistos and beside him Charis : next to her is Hermes, and next to Hermes, Hestia ; after Hestia comes Eros, who is receiving Aphrodite as she rises from the sea ; and Persuasion is crowning her. Apollo, too, is represented on the base with Artemis, and Athena and Herakles, and at the end of the base are Amphitrite and Poseidon and Selene, riding on a horse, as I hold. Some, however, have said that the goddess is mounted on a mule, not a horse, and they tell a foolish tale about the mule. The measurements

τετελεσμένον ἤδη τὸ ἄγαλμα
ἦν, ηὔξατο ὁ Φειδίας ἐπιση-
μῆναι τὸν θεόν, εἰ τὸ ἔργον
ἐστὶν αὐτῷ κατὰ γνώμην· αὐ-
τίκα δ' ἐς τοῦτο τοῦ ἐδάφους
κατασκῆψαι κεραυνόν φασιν,
ἔνθα ὑδρία καὶ ἐς ἐμὲ ἐπίθημα
ἦν ἡ χαλκῆ. 10. ὅσον δὲ τοῦ
ἐδάφους ἐστὶν ἔμπροσθεν τοῦ
ἀγάλματος, τοῦτο οὐ λευκῷ,
μέλανι δὲ κατεσκεύασται τῷ
λίθῳ. περιθεῖ δὲ ἐν κύκλῳ τὸν
μέλανα λίθον Παρίου κρηπίς,
ἔρυμα εἶναι τῷ ἐλαίῳ τῷ
ἐκχεομένῳ. ἔλαιον γὰρ τῷ
ἀγάλματί ἐστιν ἐν 'Ολυμπίᾳ
σύμφερον, καὶ ἔλαιόν ἐστι τὸ
ἀπεῖργον μὴ γίνεσθαι τῷ ἐλέφαντι βλάβος διὰ τὸ ἑλῶδες
τῆς ῎Αλτεως. ἐν ἀκροπόλει δὲ
τῇ 'Αθηναίων τὴν καλουμένην
Παρθένον οὐκ ἔλαιον, ὕδωρ δὲ
τὸ ἐς τὸν ἐλέφαντα ὠφελοῦν
ἐστίν. ἅτε γὰρ αὐχμηρᾶς τῆς
ἀκροπόλεως οὔσης διὰ τὸ ἄγαν
ὑψηλόν, τὸ ἄγαλμα ἐλέφαντος
πεποιημένον ὕδωρ καὶ δρόσον
τὴν ἀπὸ τοῦ ὕδατος ποθεῖ. ἐν
'Επιδαύρῳ δὲ ἐρομένου μου
καθ' ἥντινα αἰτίαν οὔτε ὕδωρ
τῷ 'Ασκληπιῷ σφίσιν οὔτε
ἔλαιόν ἐστιν ἐγχεόμενον, ἐδί-
δασκόν με οἱ περὶ τὸ ἱερόν, ὡς

of the Olympian Zeus in height and breadth are, as I am aware, recorded, but I will not praise those who measured them; for the measurements which they give fall far short of the impression which the statue makes on a spectator. For they say that the god himself bore witness to the consummate art of Pheidias; when the statue was completed, Pheidias prayed the god to give a sign, if the work was well-pleasing to him; and immediately (they say) a thunderbolt fell on the very spot, on the floor, where the bronze urn stood in my own day. The whole of the floor in front of the image is paved not with white but with black marble. This black pavement is surrounded by a border of Parian marble, which keeps in the oil which streams from the statue. For it is oil which is best fitted to preserve the statue at Olympia, and protects the ivory against damage

καὶ τὸ ἄγαλμα τοῦ θεοῦ καὶ ὁ θρόνος ἐπὶ φρέατι εἴη πεποιημένα.

from the marshy atmosphere of the Altis. But in the case of the so-called Parthenos on the Akropolis of Athens it is not oil but water which keeps the ivory sound. For since the Akropolis is dry owing to its great height, the statue, being made of ivory, requires water and the moisture which water gives. At Epidauros, when I inquired as to the reason why they pour neither water nor oil into the Asklepios, the attendants of the temple told me that both the image of the god and his throne stood over a well.

On the Olympian Zeus and the monument representing it see *Ov.* I⁴. 356 ff., *Coll.* I. 528 ff. and references there given.

ἐποιήθη δὲ ὁ ναός] The victory over Pisa took place circ. 472 B. C., and the temple was completed in 456 B. C. (Purgold, *A. Z.* 1882, p. 184).

μετάλλοις τοῖς πᾶσι διηνθισμένον] Cp. No. 17 χρυσῷ διηνθισμένα of wood inlaid with gold. Others suggest decorative knobs.

Νῖκαι . . . καὶ Ἄρτεμις] The lower section of the leg was decorated with two Victories, probably back to back, above which were four others, no doubt in relief, with joined hands. The Sphinxes supported the side-rails and the Niobids decorated the side-surfaces of the seat.

ἀγωνισμάτων] Robert suggests ἀγωνιστῶν, since there were never eight 'ancient' contests.

οὐ γάρ πω . . . Φειδίου] The words are quite meaningless in the context, and the statement is entirely incorrect. Robert transfers the words to the end of the section and reads οὐκ ἄρα, regarding them as part of (Polemon's) argument *against* the identification of Pantarkes with the figure on the bar : ' P. was victorious *as a boy* in 436 B. C., he could not therefore have been a boy when Pheidias was at Olympia (sc. in 448 B. C.).' Late authorities repeat a story that Pheidias inscribed 'Παντάρκης κάλος' (after the fashion of the vase-painters and others) on the finger of Zeus.

ἐν 'Αμύκλαις] v. No. 38 note, and see Furtwängler's reconstruction, *Meisterwerke*, p. 706.

ἐρύματα] Murray, followed by the German excavators, interprets this of the barriers enclosing the section of the ' cella' in which the statue stood (see *Olympia*, Plates, I. xi, xii). It is supposed that the paintings were on the inner surfaces. But Mr. Ernest Gardner (*J. H. S.* xiv. 2) shows that the screens enclosed the space between the legs of the throne.

Ἔρως ἐστὶν . . . ὑποδεχόμενος] Possibly copied on the silver-gilt relief from Galaxidi, *Gaz. Arch.* 1879, Pl. xix.

τῷ 'Ασκληπιῷ] By Thrasymedes of Paros, v. No. 231.

112. Strab. viii. 353 μέγιστον δὲ τούτων ὑπῆρξε τὸ τοῦ Διὸς ξόανον ὃ ἐποίει Φειδίας Χαρμίδου 'Αθηναῖος ἐλεφάντινον, τηλικοῦτον τὸ μέγεθος, ὡς καίπερ μεγίστου ὄντος τοῦ νεὼ δοκεῖν ἀστοχῆσαι τῆς συμμετρίας τὸν τεχνίτην, καθήμενον ποιήσαντα, ἁπτόμενον δὲ σχεδόν τι τῇ κορυφῇ τῆς ὀροφῆς, ὥστ' ἔμφασιν ποιεῖν, ἐὰν ὀρθὸς γένηται, διαναστὰς ἀποστεγάσειν τὸν νεών. 354 ἀνέγραψαν δέ τινες τὰ μέτρα τοῦ ξοάνου καὶ Καλλίμαχος ἐν ἰάμβῳ τινὶ ἐξεῖπε. πολλὰ δὲ συνέπραξε τῷ Φειδίᾳ Πάναινος ὁ ζώγρα-

The greatest of these offerings was the statue of Zeus, made of ivory by Pheidias the son of Charmides the Athenian ; this is of such colossal size that, although the temple is a very large one, the artist seems to have failed to observe proportion, and has represented the god seated, but almost touching the roof with his head, thus creating the impression that should he rise and stand upright he would unroof the temple. Some writers have recorded the measure-

φος, ἀδελφιδοῦς ὢν αὐτοῦ καὶ
συνεργολάβος, πρὸς τὴν τοῦ
ξοάνου διὰ τῶν χρωμάτων
κόσμησιν καὶ μάλιστα τῆς
ἐσθῆτος. δείκνυνται δὲ καὶ
γραφαὶ πολλαί τε καὶ θαυμα-
σταὶ περὶ τὸ ἱερὸν ἐκείνου ἔργα.
ἀπομνημονεύουσι δὲ τοῦ Φειδίου, διότι πρὸς τὸν Πάναινον
εἶπε πυνθανόμενον, πρὸς τί
παράδειγμα μέλλοι ποιήσειν
τὴν εἰκόνα τοῦ Διός, ὅτι πρὸς
τὴν Ὁμήρου δι᾽ ἐπῶν ἐκτε-
θεῖσαν τούτων·

ἦ καὶ κυανέῃσιν ἐπ᾽ ὀφρύσι
    νεῦσε Κρονίων
ἀμβρόσιαι δ᾽ ἄρα χαῖται ἐπερ-
    ρώσαντο ἄνακτος
κρατὸς ἀπ᾽ ἀθανάτοιο, μέγαν
    δ᾽ ἐλέλιξεν Ὄλυμπον.

ments of the statue, and
Kallimachos mentioned
them in an iambic poem.
Pheidias received much
assistance from his nephew
and fellow contractor, the
painter Panainos, in the
decoration of the statue and
especially of the drapery in
colours. Several remark-
able paintings by him are
to be seen in the temple.
An anecdote is told of
Pheidias to the effect that
he replied to Panainos (who
inquired of him after what
pattern he intended to represent Zeus), 'by the
pattern exhibited by Homer
in the following lines :—

So spake the son of
Kronos and nodded his
dark brow, and the am-
brosial locks waved from
the king's undying head ;
and he made great Olympos
to quake.'

ξόανον] In the general sense 'statue,' not necessarily of wood.
Cp. No. 35.

μέτρα] Calculated by Adler (*Olympia*, Textband ii. p. 13, note 1)
at seven times life-size. The base measures 6·55 metres in breadth
and 9·93 metres in length.

Πάναινος] Paus. and Plin. agree that he was the brother of
Pheidias   See Brunn, *K. G.* II². 33.

113. Quint. x. 10. 9 Phidias tamen dis quam hominibus efficiendis melior artifex creditur, in ebore uero longe citra aemulum, uel si nihil nisi Mineruam Athenis aut Olympium in Elide Iouem fecisset, cuius pulchritudo adiecisse aliquid etiam receptae religioni uidetur; adeo maiestas operis deum aequauit.

Pheidias, however, is thought to have displayed higher art in his statues of gods than in those of mortals: in ivory indeed he would be without a rival, had he only made the Athena at Athens or the Olympian Zeus in Elis, whose beauty seems to have added somewhat to the received religion ; so adequate to the divine nature is the grandeur of his work.

114. Dion Chrys. xii. 14 ὁ δὲ ἡμέτερος (Ζεὺς) εἰρηνικὸς καὶ πανταχοῦ πρᾶος, οἷος ἀστασιάστου καὶ ὁμονοούσης τῆς Ἑλλάδος ἐπίσκοπος.

But our Zeus is peaceful and mild in every way, as it were the guardian of Hellas when she is of one mind and not distraught with faction.

115. Paus. vi. 4. 5 ὁ δὲ παῖς ὁ ἀναδούμενος ταινίᾳ τὴν κεφαλὴν ἐπεισήχθω μοι καὶ οὗτος ἐς τὸν λόγον Φειδίου τε ἕνεκα καὶ τῆς ἐς τὰ ἀγάλματα τοῦ Φειδίου σοφίας, ἐπεὶ ἄλλως γε οὐκ ἴσμεν ὅτου τὴν εἰκόνα ὁ Φειδίας ἐποίησε.

Let us also mention the youth binding his hair with a fillet for the sake of Pheidias and his skill in sculpture, since we have no means of knowing whose portrait it was that Pheidias here represented.

Identified by Löschcke and others with Pantarkes (v. No. 111).

116. Paus. vi. 25. 1 ἔστι δὲ
τῆς στοᾶς ὀπίσω τῆς ἀπὸ τῶν
λαφύρων τῶν ἐκ Κορκύρας
Ἀφροδίτης ναὸς ... καὶ τὴν
μὲν ἐν τῷ ναῷ καλοῦσιν Οὐ-
ρανίαν· ἐλέφαντος δέ ἐστι καὶ
χρυσοῦ, τέχνη Φειδίου, τῷ δὲ
ἑτέρῳ ποδὶ ἐπὶ χελώνης βέ-
βηκε.

At Elis.

Behind the colonnade
erected from the spoils of
Korkyra there is a temple of
Aphrodite; and the goddess
in the temple is called Urania and is made of ivory and
gold, the work of Pheidias.
With one foot she is tread-
ing on a tortoise.

Plut. *Coni. Praec.* 32 explains the tortoise as a symbol of silence
in the wife.

III. MISCELLANEOUS.

117. Plin. *N. H.* xxxiv.
53 Uenere autem in certa-
men laudatissimi quanquam
diuersis aetatibus geniti,
quoniam fecerant Ama-
zonas, quae cum in templo
Dianae Ephesiae dicarentur,
placuit eligi probatissimum
ipsorum artificum (qui
praesentes erant) iudicio,
cum apparuit, eam esse
quam omnes secundam a
sua quisque iudicassent;
haec est Polycliti, proxuma
ab ea Phidiae, tertia Cre-
silae, [quarta Cydonis],
quinta Phradmonis.

Sculptors of the highest
fame, though of different
ages, were brought into
rivalry, since all had made
statues of Amazons, which
were dedicated in the temple
of Artemis at Ephesus. It was
determined therefore that
the most highly approved
should be selected by the
decision of the artists themselves, who were present.
It then appeared that it
was the one which each
placed second to his own,
namely that of Polykleitos.
That of Pheidias came next,
that of Kresilas third, [that
of Kydon fourth], and that
of Phradmon fifth.

The anecdote is valueless; but statues of Amazons would be natural offerings to the temple which they were said to have founded, and Amazons by the artists named may well have stood there; possibly the four in question may have formed a single existing offering. On the types traceable to these statues see Michaelis, *Jahrb.* 1886, p. 14 ff., Pl. i–iv. and Furtwängler, *Meisterwerke*, p. 286 ff.

quarta Cydonis] Kresilas (No. 148) was a native of Kydonia in Crete, and hence might be called Κύδων. Pliny misinterpreted the term as the name of an artist.

Phradmonis] Dated Ol. 90=420 B.C. by Pliny. His other works were :—(1) Portrait of Amertas of Elis, victorious in the boys' wrestling-match at Olympia (Paus. vi. 8. 1) ; (2) a group of twelve kine, dedicated by the Thessalians to Athena Itonia from the spoils of the Illyrians, in bronze (*Anth. Pal.* ix. 743). He was a native of Argos.

118. Lucian, Εἰκόνες 4 τὴν Ἀμαζόνα τὴν ἐπερειδομένην τῷ δορατίῳ ... 6. ἔτι καὶ στόματος ἁρμογὴν ὁ αὐτὸς (Φειδίας) καὶ τὸν αὐχένα, παρὰ τῆς Ἀμαζόνος λαβών (παρέξει).

The Amazon who is leaning on her spear ... Pheidias too shall borrow from his Amazon the setting of her mouth and her neck and bestow them on her.

Cp. Nos. 83, 103, 127.

119. Plin. *N. H.* xxxiv. 54 Phidias . . . fecit . . . ex aere uero praeter Amazonem supra dictam Mineruam tam eximiae pulchritudinis ut formae cognomen acceperit ; fecit et cliduchum et aliam Mineruam quam Romae Paulus Aemilius ad aedem Fortunae huiusce diei dicauit, item duo signa quae Catulus in eadem aede

Beside the Amazon mentioned above, Pheidias made in bronze an Athena of such surpassing beauty that she received the surname of 'the Beautiful' ; he also made the Keeper of the Keys and another Athena which Aemilius Paulus dedicated at Rome close to the temple of Fortune, where it stands to this day,

palliataetalterumcolossicon nudum, primusque artem toreuticen aperuisse atque demonstrasse merito iudicatur.

two draped statues which Catulus dedicated in the same temple and a colossal nude figure. He is justly held to have been the first to reveal the art of sculpture and to point out the path to his successors.

This Athena is commonly identified with the Lemnia, No. 102.

formae] It is not necessary to emend 'formosae,' since 'cognomen formae,' 'the appellation of Beauty,' could mean 'the name Beautiful,' or 'forma' might mean 'Beauty itself'; cp. iracundiam, No. 223. Jahn suggests that Pliny is translating 'Μορφώ.'

cliduchum] κλειδοῦχον. Two interpretations are possible: (1) a priestess. The temple-key was the symbol of the priestess, and the adjective κλειδοῦχος is thus applied. Cp. No. 228, and for the use of the word in poetry Aesch. *Supp.* 291, Eur. *I. T.* 132. (2) The Athena Promachos. The work is mentioned in a list of Athena statues, and Ar. *Thesm.* 1140 speaks of Athena ἢ πόλιν ἡμετέραν ἔχει · · · κληδοῦχός τε καλεῖται. The name might be applied to the Promachos as 'keeper of the keys' of the Akropolis.

primusque . . . iudicatur] On the series of criticisms to which this belongs, v. Introduction, § 2.

toreuticen] τορευτικήν, sc. τέχνην. Pliny takes the word from Greek sources in which it has the general sense of sculpture, not the special sense of repoussé-work in metal. Thus in his list of authorities he mentions 'Antigonus qui de toreutice scripsit,' and cp. xxxv. 77 neque in hac (pictura) neque in toreutice ullius qui seruierit opera celebrantur.

120. Paus. x. 10. 1 τῷ βάθρῳ δὲ τῷ ὑπὸ τὸν ἵππον τὸν δούρειον ἐπίγραμμα μέν ἐστιν ἀπὸ δεκάτης τοῦ Μαραθωνίου ἔργου τεθῆναι τὰς εἰκόνας· εἰσὶ δὲ Ἀθηνᾶ τε καὶ Ἀπόλλων, καὶ ἀνὴρ τῶν στρα-

On the base of the wooden horse there is an inscription which states that the statues were set up from the tithe of the spoils of Marathon; they represent Athena and Apollo, and one human

τηγησάντων Μιλτιάδης· ἐκ δὲ τῶν ἡρώων καλουμένων Ἐρεχθεύς τε καὶ Κέκροψ καὶ Πανδίων καὶ Λεώς τε καὶ Ἀντίοχος ὁ ἐκ Μήδας Ἡρακλεῖ γενόμενος τῆς Φύλαντος, ἔτι δὲ Αἰγεύς τε καὶ παίδων τῶν Θησέως Ἀκάμας· οὗτοι μὲν καὶ φυλαῖς Ἀθήνησιν ὀνόματα κατὰ μάντευμα ἔδοσαν τὸ ἐκ Δελφῶν. ὁ δὲ Μελάνθου Κόδρος καὶ Θησεὺς καὶ Φιλέας, οὗτοι δὲ οὐκέτι τῶν ἐπωνύμων εἰσί. 2. τοὺς μὲν δὴ κατειλεγμένους Φειδίας ἐποίησε, καὶ ἀληθεῖ λόγῳ δεκάτη καὶ οὗτοι τῆς μάχης εἰσίν.

figure, .that of Miltiades the general, besides the so-called heroes Erechtheus, Kekrops, Pandion, Leos. Antiochos (the son of Herakles, by Meda the daughter of Phylas), also Aigeus and Akamas, one of the sons of Theseus ; these gave their names to the Attic tribes as the oracle of Delphi prescribed ; there are also Kodros the son of Melanthos and Theseus and Phileas, who are not among those by whose names the tribes were called. The above-mentioned were made by Pheidias, and are genuinely part of the offering from the spoils of Marathon.

At Delphi.

κατὰ μάντευμα] Kleisthenes submitted 100 names, from which the oracle selected ten (Aristotle, Ἀθ. Πολ. c. 21, 6).

Φιλέας] So Curtius for Φυλεύς of MSS.

ἀληθεῖ λόγῳ] Statues of the eponymi of the three new tribes Ἀντιγονίς, Δημητριάς, Πτολεμαΐς, were afterwards added. These were Antigonos I and his son Demetrios Poliorketes (added 307 B. C.) and Ptolemy Philadelphos (285-247 B. C.). (So Paus. ; Beloch believes that we should substitute the name of Ptolemy Euergetes (247-221 B. C.).

121. Paus. vii. 27. 2 κατὰ δὲ τὴν ὁδὸν ἐς αὐτὴν τὴν πόλιν ἐστὶν Ἀθηνᾶς λίθου μὲν ἐπι-

By the road to the town itself is a temple of Athena built of the local stone, and

H

χωρίου ναός, ἐλέφαντος δὲ τὸ
ἄγαλμα καὶ χρυσοῦ· Φειδίαν
δὲ εἶναι τὸν εἰργασμένον φασί,
πρότερον ἔτι ἢ ἐν τῇ ἀκροπόλει τε αὐτὸν τῇ Ἀθηναίων καὶ
ἐν Πλαταιαῖς ποιῆσαι τῆς
Ἀθηνᾶς τὰ ἀγάλματα.

the image is of ivory and gold : they say that Pheidias made it before he made the statues of Athena on the Akropolis of Athens and at Plataea.

τὴν πόλιν] Pellene in Achaia.
ἐν Πλαταιαῖς] V. next No.

122. Paus. ix. 4. 1 Πλαται-
εῦσι δὲ Ἀθηνᾶς ἐπίκλησιν
Ἀρείας ἐστὶν ἱερόν· ᾠκοδομήθη
δὲ ἀπὸ λαφύρων, ἃ τῆς μάχης
σφίσιν Ἀθηναῖοι τῆς ἐν Μαραθῶνι ἀπένειμαν. τὸ μὲν δὴ
ἄγαλμα ξόανόν ἐστιν ἐπί-
χρυσον, πρόσωπον δέ οἱ καὶ
χεῖρες ἄκραι καὶ πόδες λίθου
τοῦ Πεντελησίου εἰσί· μέγεθος
μὲν οὐ πολὺ δή τι ἀποδεῖ τῆς
ἐν ἀκροπόλει χαλκῆς ἣν καὶ
αὐτὴν Ἀθηναῖοι τοῦ Μαραθῶνι
ἀπαρχὴν ἀγῶνος ἀνέθηκαν.
Φειδίας δὲ καὶ Πλαταιεῦσιν
ἦν ὁ τῆς Ἀθηνᾶς τὸ ἄγαλμα
ποιήσας.

The Plataeans have a temple of Athena, surnamed Areia, which was built from the share of the spoils of Marathon assigned to them by the Athenians. The image is of wood gilt, and the face, hands and feet are of Pentelic marble ; in size it is not much smaller than the image of bronze on the Akropolis, which was also dedicated by the Athenians as the firstfruits of their victory at Marathon. It was Pheidias, too, who made the image of Athena for the Plataeans.

123. Paus. ix. 10. 2 πρῶτα
μὲν δὴ λίθου κατὰ τὴν ἔσοδόν
ἐστιν Ἀθηνᾶ καὶ Ἑρμῆς ὀνο-

First of all there stand at the entrance of the temple statues of Athena and

μαζόμενοι Πρόναοι· ποιῆσαι δὲ αὐτὸν Φειδίας ... λέγεται.

Hermes, called the 'Gods before the Shrine': the Hermes is said to be the work of Pheidias.

At Thebes. The temple is the Ismenion.

124. Plin. *N. H.* xxxvi. 15 Et ipsum Phidian tradunt sculpsisse marmorea Ueneremque eius esse Romae in Octauiae operibus eximiae pulchritudinis.

Tradition tells that Pheidias himself also worked in marble, and that there is an Aphrodite by his hand of surpassing beauty in the gallery of Octavia at Rome.

Octauiae operibus] Built by Augustus in the name of his sister Octavia. A colonnade (Porticus Octauiae) enclosed two temples (of Jupiter and Juno) and a public library (Curia Octauiae). It was destroyed by fire under Titus.

125. Demetr. de Eloc. 14 ἡ δὲ τῶν μετὰ ταῦτα ἑρμηνεία τοῖς Φειδίου ἔργοις ἤδη ἔοικεν, ἔχουσά τι καὶ μεγαλεῖον καὶ ἀκριβὲς ἅμα.

The oratory of the school which followed them is like the works of Pheidias; it is at once sublime and precise.

Cp. No. 87.

2. THE PUPILS OF PHEIDIAS.

(a) ALKAMENES.

Date.—He is represented as a *rival* of Pheidias in Pliny's chronological table under Ol. 88 (448 B.C.), by Paus. in his account of the west pediment of Olympia (No. 134), and by Tzetzes, but (more probably) as his *pupil* by Pliny in the alphabetical list (v. No. 135) and in Bk. xxxvi. Putting aside the sculptures at Olympia, the only certain date is that of No. 133 (403 B.C.), which accords with the latter version. Suidas calls him a Lemnian, Tzetzes an islander; but their authority is of little value.

H 2

126. Plin. *N. H.* xxxvi. 16 Alcamenen Atheniensem, quod certum est, docuit (Phidias) in primis nobilem, cuius sunt opera Athenis complura in aedibus sacris, praeclarumque Ueneris extra muros, quae appellatur Ἀφροδίτη ἐν Κήποις. Huic summam manum ipse Phidias imposuisse dicitur.

It is certain that Pheidias was the teacher of Alkamenes the Athenian. an artist of the first rank, whose works are to be found in many of the temples at Athens: by him is also the famous statue of Aphrodite without the walls, called the 'Aphrodite in the Gardens.' Pheidias himself is said to have put the finishing touches to this work.

quod certum est] Should be taken with 'docuit,' not (as by Robert, who is disposed to favour the Lemnian origin of A.) with 'Atheniensem.'

ἐν Κήποις] The gardens on the banks of the Ilissos, to the southeast of the Akropolis.

The type is generally recognized in the so-called Venus Genitrix (*F. W.* 1208). See *Ov.* I⁴. 437.

127. Lucian, Εἰκόνες 6 τὰ μῆλα δὲ καὶ ὅσα τῆς ὄψεως ἀντωπὰ παρ' Ἀλκαμένους καὶ τῆς ἐν Κήποις λήψεται καὶ προσέτι χειρῶν ἄκρα καὶ καρπῶν τὸ εὔρυθμον καὶ δακτύλων τὸ εὐάγωγον ἐς λεπτὸν ἀπολῆγον παρὰ τῆς ἐν Κήποις καὶ ταῦτα.

The cheeks and prominent parts of the face he shall borrow from Alkamenes and the Goddess in the Garden, and furthermore the hands and the symmetry of the wrists and the delicacy of the taper fingers he shall take from the same goddess.

Cp. Nos. 83, 103, 118.

128. Plin. *N. H.* xxxvi. 17 Certauere autem inter

Both pupils competed in representing Aphrodite, and

se ambo discipuli Uenere facienda uicitque Alcamenes non opere sed ciuitatis suffragiis contra peregrinum suo fauentes.

Alkamenes bore the palm, not by the merit of his work, but by the votes of his city, whose people supported their townsman against an alien.

ambo discipuli] The other was Agorakritos of Paros (No. 136). Both were pupils of Pheidias. There is no reason to identify this Aphrodite with ἡ ἐν Κήποις.

129. Paus. ii. 30. 2 'Αλκαμένης δέ, ἐμοὶ δοκεῖν, πρῶτος ἀγάλματα Ἑκάτης τρία ἐποίησε προσεχόμενα ἀλλήλοις, ἣν 'Αθηναῖοι καλοῦσιν Ἐπιπυργιδίαν· ἕστηκε δὲ παρὰ τῆς 'Απτέρου Νίκης τὸν ναόν.

Alkamenes was in my opinion the first to represent Hekate by three figures joined to each other. The Athenians call his statue 'Hekate on the Bastion': it stands beside the temple of Wingless Victory.

προσεχόμενα ἀλλήλοις] Leaning against a pillar, back to back. See Miss Harrison, *Mythology and Monuments*, p. 378.
'Απτέρου Νίκης] Athena Nike, v. No. 82.

130. Paus. i. 20. 3 τοῦ Διονύσου δέ ἐστι πρὸς τῷ θεάτρῳ τὸ ἀρχαιότατον ἱερόν· δύο δέ εἰσιν ἐντὸς τοῦ περιβόλου ναοὶ καὶ Διόνυσοι, ὅ τε Ἐλευθερεὺς καὶ ὃν 'Αλκαμένης ἐποίησεν ἐλέφαντος καὶ χρυσοῦ.

Close to the theatre is the most ancient precinct of Dionysos: within its walls are two temples and two images of Dionysos — one the Dionysos of Eleutherai, the other that which Alkamenes made of ivory and gold.

Represented on coins of Athens, *Num. Comm. CC.* 1–3.

131. Cic. *N. D.* i. 30
Athenis laudamus Uulcanum eum, quem fecit Alcamenes, in quo stante atque uestito leuiter apparet claudicatio non deformis.

We admire the Hephaistos made by Alkamenes at Athens, in whom, though he is standing upright and clothed, lameness is slightly indicated in a manner not unpleasing to the eye.

132. Paus. i. 1. 5 ἔστι δὲ κατὰ τὴν ὁδὸν τὴν ἐς ᾿Αθήνας ἐκ Φαλήρου ναὸς ῞Ηρας οὔτε θύρας ἔχων οὔτε ὄροφον· Μαρδόνιόν φασιν αὐτὸν ἐμπρῆσαι τὸν Γωβρύου. τὸ δὲ ἄγαλμα τὸ νῦν δή, καθὰ λέγουσιν, ᾿Αλκαμένους ἐστὶν ἔργον· οὐκ ἂν τοῦτό γε ὁ Μῆδος εἴη λελωβημένος.

On the way from Phaleron to Athens is a temple of Hera which has neither door nor roof: they say that it was burnt by Mardonios, the son of Gobryas. The image which now stands there is said to be the work of Alkamenes: in that case it certainly could not have been damaged by the Persians.

Μαρδόνιον] In 479 B.C.

Petersen identifies the type with that of Overbeck, *Kunstmyth.* Pl. xv. 20.

133. Paus. ix. 11. 6
Θρασύβουλος δὲ ὁ Λύκου καὶ ᾿Αθηναίων οἱ σὺν αὐτῷ τυραννίδα τὴν τῶν τριάκοντα καταλύσαντες, ὁρμηθεῖσι γάρ σφισιν ἐκ Θηβῶν ἐγένετο ἡ κάθοδος, ᾿Αθηνᾶν καὶ ῾Ηρακλέα κολοσσοὺς ἐπὶ τύπου, λίθου τοῦ

Thrasybulos, the son of Lykos, and the Athenians who joined him in putting an end to the tyranny of the Thirty, having made Thebes the starting-point of their return, dedicated a colossal relief representing Athena

Πεντέλησιν, ἔργα δὲ ᾽Αλκα-   and Herakles in Pentelic
μένους, ἀνέθηκαν ἐς῾Ηράκλειον.   marble, by Alkamenes, in
the shrine of Herakles.

τυραννίδα τὴν τῶν τριάκοντα] 404–403 B. C.
κολοσσοὺς . . . λίθου] The simplest alteration of the corrupt text
κολοσσοῦ ἐπὶ λίθου τύπου. ἐπὶ τύπου is a technical expression = 'in
relief.' Cp. ix. 11. 3 ἐπὶ τύπου γυναικῶν εἰκόνες.

134. Paus. v. 10. 8 τὰ μὲν
δὴ ἔμπροσθεν ἐν τοῖς ἀετοῖς
ἐστὶ Παιωνίου . . . τὰ δὲ ὄπισθεν αὐτῶν ᾽Αλκαμένους ἀνδρὸς ἡλικίαν τε κατὰ Φειδίαν
καὶ δευτερεῖα ἐνεγκαμένου
σοφίας ἐς ποίησιν ἀγαλμάτων.
τὰ δὲ ἐν τοῖς ἀετοῖς ἐστὶν
αὐτῷ Λαπιθῶν ἐν τῷ Πειρίθου
γάμῳ πρὸς Κενταύρους ἡ μάχη.
κατὰ μὲν δὴ τοῦ ἀετοῦ τὸ μέσον
Πειρίθους ἐστί· παρὰ δὲ αὐτὸν
τῇ μὲν Εὐρυτίων ἡρπακὼς τὴν
γυναῖκά ἐστι τοῦ Πειρίθου καὶ
ἀμύνων Καινεὺς τῷ Πειρίθῳ,
τῇ δὲ Θησεὺς ἀμυνόμενος
πελέκει τοὺς Κενταύρους. Κέν-
ταυρος δὲ ὁ μὲν παρθένον, ὁ
δὲ παῖδα ἡρπακώς ἐστιν ὡραῖον.

The pediment sculptures
of the front are by Paionios;
those of the back are by
Alkamenes, a contemporary
of Pheidias, and second only
to him in the sculptor's art.
His pediment - sculptures
represent the battle of the
Lapithai and Centaurs at
the marriage of Peirithous.
In the centre of the pediment is Peirithous: on one
side of him is Eurytion,
who has seized the wife of
Peirithous, and Kaineus,
who is helping Peirithous,
on the other is Theseus
defending himself against
the Centaurs with an axe.
There are two Centaurs,
one of whom has seized
a maiden, the other a beautiful boy.

On the pediment sculptures of Olympia and their restoration
v. Ov. I ⁴. 349 ff., Coll. I. 436 ff. and references there quoted. The
style of the west pediment forbids us to assign it to the pupil of

Pheidias and artist of No. 132 ; we should have to assume an earlier Alkamenes (perhaps the Lemnian of Suidas). But Paus. may have been misled by a baseless tradition. See No. 175 note.

Πειρίθους] The figure is on a larger scale than the rest, and must represent a god, probably Apollo.

τὴν γυναῖκα] Deidamia.

135. Plin. *N. H.* xxxiv. 72 Alcamenes Phidiae discipulus et marmorea fecit et aeneum pentathlum, qui uocatur Ἐγκρινόμενος.

Alkamenes the pupil of Pheidias made statues in marble, and a victor in the five contests in bronze, called 'the Chosen Athlete.'

Klein would correct ἐγχριόμενος ('anointing himself'), and connect with the statue at Munich, *M. d. I.* xi. 7, but this is not probable.

Other works by Alkamenes :—
ARES at Athens (Paus. i. 8. 4).
ASKLEPIOS at Mantineia (Paus. viii. 9. 1).

(b) AGORAKRITOS.

136. Plin. *N. H.* xxxvi. 16 Eiusdem (Phidiae) discipulus fuit Agoracritus Parius et aetate gratus, itaque e suis operibus pleraque nomine eius donasse fertur. Certauere autem inter se ambo discipuli Uenere facienda uicitque Alcamenes . . . Agoracritus ea lege signum suum uendidisse traditur, ne Athenis esset, et appellasse Nemesin; id positum est Rhamnunte pago Atticae, quod Uarro

Agorakritos of Paros was also a pupil of Pheidias, who was attracted by his youthful beauty, and so is said to have allowed his name to appear on several of his own works. Both pupils however entered into competition with representations of Aphrodite, and Alkamenes bore the palm ; Agorakritos accordingly sold his statue, as the story goes, on the condition that it should not remain

omnibus signis praetulit.
Est et in Matris magnae
delubro eadem ciuitate
Agoracriti opus.

at Athens, and called it
Nemesis; it was set up at
Rhamnus, a deme of Attica,
and was preferred by Varro
to all statues. There is
also a work of Agorakritos
in the temple of the Mother
of the Gods in the same
city.

certauere] V. No. 128.
Nemesin] V. infr. No. 137.
Matris magnae] Paus. i. 3. 5 ascribes this statue to Pheidias
himself.

137. Paus. i. 33. 2 (At
Rhamnus) Νεμέσεώς ἐστιν
ἱερόν, ἣ θεῶν μάλιστα ἀνθρώ-
ποις ὑβρισταῖς ἐστιν ἀπαραί-
τητος. δοκεῖ δὲ καὶ τοῖς
ἀποβᾶσιν ἐς Μαραθῶνα τῶν
βαρβάρων ἀπαντῆσαι μήνιμα
ἐκ τῆς θεοῦ ταύτης· κατα-
φρονήσαντες γάρ σφισιν ἐμ-
ποδὼν εἶναι τὰς Ἀθήνας ἑλεῖν,
λίθον Πάριον ὡς ἐπ᾽ ἐξειργασ-
μένοις ἦγον ἐς τροπαίου ποίησιν. τοῦτον Φειδίας τὸν
λίθον εἰργάσατο, ἄγαλμα μὲν
εἶναι Νεμέσεως, τῇ κεφαλῇ δὲ
ἔπεστι τῆς θεοῦ στέφανος ἐλάφους ἔχων καὶ Νίκης ἀγάλματα
οὐ μεγάλα· ταῖς δὲ χερσὶν
ἔχει, τῇ μὲν κλάδον μηλέας,
τῇ δεξιᾷ δὲ φιάλην· Αἰθίοπες

(At Rhamnus) there is
a temple of Nemesis, who
is of all deities the most
implacable enemy of in-
solent men. It would seem
that the barbarians who
landed at Marathon in-
curred the wrath of the
goddess: for thinking in
their pride that Athens lay
as a prize at their feet,
they brought Parian marble
for the erection of a trophy
as though they had accom-
plished their end. This
marble was wrought by
Pheidias into a statue of
Nemesis. On the head of
the goddess rests a crown
bearing stags and small

δὲ ἐπὶ τῇ φιάλῃ πεποίηνται.
. . . 7. πτερὰ δ' ἔχον οὔτε
τοῦτο τὸ ἄγαλμα Νεμέσεως
οὔτε ἄλλο πεποίηται τῶν ἀρχαίων. . . . νῦν δὲ ἤδη δίειμι
ὁπόσα ἐπὶ τῷ βάθρῳ τοῦ ἀγάλματός ἐστιν εἰργασμένα, το-
σόνδε ἐς τὸ σαφὲς προδηλώσας.
Ἑλένη Νέμεσιν μητέρα εἶναι
λέγουσιν, Λήδαν δὲ μαστὸν
ἐπισχεῖν αὐτῇ καὶ θρέψαι·
πατέρα δὲ καὶ οὗτοι καὶ πάντες
κατὰ ταὐτὰ Ἕλληνες Δία καὶ
οὐ Τυνδάρεων εἶναι νομίζουσι.
8. ταῦτα ἀκηκοὼς Φειδίας
πεποίηκε μὲν Ἑλένην ὑπὸ
Λήδας ἀγομένην παρὰ τὴν Νέμεσιν, πεποίηκε δὲ Τυνδάρεών
τε καὶ τοὺς παῖδας καὶ ἄνδρα
σὺν ἵππῳ παρεστηκότα, Ἱππέα
ὄνομα· ἔστι δὲ Ἀγαμέμνων
καὶ Μενέλαος καὶ Πύρρος
ὁ Ἀχιλλέως, πρῶτος οὗτος
Ἑρμιόνην τὴν Ἑλένης γυ-
ναῖκα λαβών. . . . ἐξῆς δὲ ἐπὶ
τῷ βάθρῳ καὶ Ἔποχος καλούμενος καὶ νεανίας ἐστὶν ἕτερος.
ἐς τούτω ἄλλο μὲν ἤκουσα
οὐδέν, ἀδελφοὺς δὲ εἶναι σφᾶς
Οἰνόης, ἀφ' ἧς ἐστὶ τὸ ὄνομα
τῷ δήμῳ.

images of Victory; in her left hand she holds an apple-branch, in her right a bowl, on which Ethiopians are represented. Neither this nor any other ancient statue of Nemesis is represented with wings. Next I will describe in order all the reliefs on the base of the statue, premising for the sake of clearness what follows. They say that Helen was the mother of Nemesis, but that Leda suckled and reared her; and the people of Rhamnus agree with all the Greeks that Zeus and not Tyndareos was her father. Pheidias, having heard this account, has represented Helen being brought by Leda to Nemesis, and also Tyndareos and his sons and a man standing by with a horse, Hippeus by name. Agamemnon also is there and Menelaos and Pyrrhos, the son of Achilles, who was the first to take Hermione, the daughter of Helen, to wife. Next in order on the base comes

a youth named Epochos
and another youth ; of
these I could learn nothing
except that they were
the brothers of Oinoe,
after whom the deme is
called.

καταφρονήσαντες] A Herodotean use. Cp. Hdt. i. 66 καταφρονή-
σαντες Ἀρκάδων κρέσσονες εἶναι.

Φειδίας] Antigonos of Karystos (Introduction, § 1) mentioned
a tablet suspended from the statue with the inscription Ἀγοράκριτος
Πάριος ἐποίησεν. Others (probably Polemon, cp. Wilamowitz,
Antigonos von Karystos, p. 10) retorted that Pheidias had allowed
his favourite to inscribe his name on the work which was really
his own.

ἄγαλμα] Ten cubits in height, according to the Lexicographers.
Fragments have been found at Rhamnus, and are published in
Ath. Mitth. 1890, Pl. xv (Rossbach).

ἐλάφους ἔχων καὶ Νίκης ἀγάλματα] Probably this means that the
early type of the winged Artemis holding a stag in each hand (often
called the ' Persian' Artemis) was used in the decoration of the
circlet. Cp. Dümmler ap. Studniczka, Kyrene, p. 106, n. 102.

τῷ βάθρῳ] Several fragments have been discovered, and are published in Jahrb. 1894, Pl. i-vii (Pallat).

Πύρρος] Neoptolemos.

138. Paus. ix. 34. 1 πρὶν
δὲ ἐς Κορώνειαν ἐξ Ἀλαλκο-
μενῶν ἀφικέσθαι, τῆς Ἰτωνίας
Ἀθηνᾶς ἐστὶ τὸ ἱερόν· καλεῖται
δὲ ἀπὸ Ἰτώνου τοῦ Ἀμφικτύ-
ονος, καὶ ἐς τὸν κοινὸν συνίασιν
ἐνταῦθα οἱ Βοιωτοὶ σύλλογον.
ἐν δὲ τῷ ναῷ χαλκοῦ πεποιημένα Ἀθηνᾶς Ἰτωνίας καὶ Διός
ἐστιν ἀγάλματα· τέχνη δὲ

Before arriving at Koro-
nea from Alalkomenai, the
traveller comes to the
temple of Athena Itonia: it
derives its title from Itonos,
the son of Amphiktyon,
and it is there that the
federal assembly of Boeotia
meets. In the temple are
the statues of Athena

'Αγορακρίτου, μαθητοῦ δὲ καὶ
ἐρωμένου Ψειδίου.

Itonia and Zeus, made of
bronze, the work of Agorakritos, a pupil and favourite
of Pheidias.

Perhaps represented on a gem, Müller-Wieseler, *Denkmäler*,
ii. 226.

(c) KOLOTES.

139. Plin. *N. H.* xxxv.
54 Panaenum, qui clipeum
intus pinxit Elide Mineruae,
quam fecerat Colotes discipulus Phidiae et ei in faciendo Ioue Olympio adiutor.

Panainos, who painted
the inner surface of the
shield of an Athena at
Elis made by Kolotes, the
pupil of Pheidias, and his
assistant in the construction
of the Olympian Zeus.

Mineruae] Paus. vi. 26. 3 says that the statue was attributed to
Pheidias, and that the goddess bore the device of a cock on her
shield. It was of gold and ivory.

140. Paus. v. 20. 1 ἔστι
δὲ ἐνταῦθα . . . τράπεζα, ἐφ᾽
ἧς προτίθενται τοῖς νικῶσιν οἱ
στέφανοι. . . . 2. ἡ τράπεζα δὲ
ἐλέφαντος μὲν πεποίηται καὶ
χρυσοῦ, Κωλώτου δέ ἐστιν
ἔργον. εἶναι δέ φασιν ἐξ Ἡρα-
κλείας τὸν Κωλώτην· οἱ δὲ
πολυπραγμονήσαντες σπουδῇ
τὰ ἐς τοὺς πλαστὰς Πάριον ἀπο-
φαίνουσιν ὄντα αὐτόν, μαθη-
τὴν Πασιτέλους, Πασιτέλην δὲ
αὐτὸν διδαχθῆναι.... ⟨ἔμπροσ-
θεν μέν⟩ . . . καὶ Ἥρα τε καὶ
Ζεὺς καὶ θεῶν Μήτηρ καὶ Ἑρμῆς

Here there is a table,
upon which the garlands
are set out for the victors.
The table is made of ivory
and gold, and is the work
of Kolotes. Kolotes is
said to have been a native
of Herakleia, but those who
have made a special study
of sculptors show him to
be of Parian origin, a pupil
of Pasiteles, who in his turn
was taught by . . . ⟨on the
front⟩ are represented. . . .
and Hera and Zeus and

καὶ ᾿Απόλλων μετὰ ᾿Αρτέμιδος πεποίηται. ὄπισθε δὲ ἡ διά- θεσίς ἐστιν ἡ τοῦ ἀγῶνος. 3. κατὰ δὲ ἑκατέραν πλευράν, τῇ μὲν ᾿Ασκληπιὸς καὶ τῶν ᾿Ασκληπιοῦ θυγατέρων Ὑγίειά ἐστιν, ἔτι δὲ καὶ ῎Αρης καὶ ᾿Αγὼν παρ᾿ αὐτόν, τῇ δὲ Πλού- των καὶ Διόνυσος Περσεφόνη τε καὶ νύμφαι, σφαῖραν αὐτῶν ἡ ἑτέρα φέρουσα· ἐπὶ δὲ ⟨τῇ⟩ κλειδί, ἔχει γὰρ δὴ ὁ Πλούτων κλεῖν, λέγουσιν ἐπ᾿ αὐτῇ τὸν καλούμενον ῎Αδην κεκλεῖσθαί τε ἀπὸ τοῦ Πλούτωνος, καὶ ὡς ἐπάνεισιν οὐδεὶς αὖθις ἐξ αὐτοῦ.

the Mother of the Gods and Hermes and Apollo together with Artemis. On the back is the ordering of the contest ; on one of the sides Asklepios and Hygieia, one of the daughters of Asklepios, as well as Ares and beside him Agon, on the other side Pluto, Diony- sos, Persephone and the Nymphs, one of whom carries a ball ; as to the key which is held by Pluto, they tell the story that the abode called Hades is kept locked by Pluto and that no one will ever return from it.

ἐνταῦθα] In the ὀπισθόδομος of the Heraion at Olympia.

οἱ δὲ πολυπραγμονήσαντες] Perhaps Antigonos or Polemon (Intro- duction, § 1).

αὐτὸν διδαχθῆναι . . .] The name of the master is omitted (αὐτοδι- δαχθῆναι is suggested). The lacuna may have contained the names of another pair of deities, possibly Athena and Herakles. Cp. No. 110.

᾿Αγών] Cp. No. 47 note.

Other works by Kolotes :—
ASKLEPIOS at Kyllene (of ivory) (Strab. viii. 334).
Portraits of 'philosophers' (Plin. N. H. xxxiv. 87).

(d) THE SCULPTURES OF THE PARTHENON.

141. Paus. i. 24. 5 ἐς δὲ τὸν ναόν, ὃν Παρθενῶνα ὀνομά-

The sculptures in the pediment, as it is called,

ζουσιν, ἐς τοῦτον ἐσιοῦσιν over the entrance to the
ὁπόσα ἐν τοῖς καλουμένοις temple known as the Par-
ἀετοῖς κεῖται, πάντα ἐς τὴν thenon, are all concerned
'Αθηνᾶς ἔχει γένεσιν, τὰ δ' with the birth of Athena,
ὄπισθεν ἡ Ποσειδῶνος πρὸς while at the back of the
'Αθηνᾶν ἐστιν ἔρις ὑπὲρ τῆς temple is represented the
γῆς. strife of Athena with Po-
seidon for the land.

See *Ov.* I⁴. 400 ff. and references there given ; also Furtwängler,
Meisterwerke, pp. 223–260, and A. H. Smith, *Brit. Mus. Catalogue
of Greek Sculpture,* pp. 101–132.

3. PRAXIAS AND ANDROSTHENES.

142. Paus. x. 19. 4 τὰ δὲ In the pediment are re-
ἐν τοῖς ἀετοῖς ἔστιν "Αρτεμις presented Artemis, Leto,
καὶ Λητὼ καὶ 'Απόλλων καὶ Apollo and the Muses, the
Μοῦσαι, δύσις τε 'Ηλίου καὶ setting Sun, Dionysos and
Διόνυσός τε καὶ αἱ γυναῖκες the Thyiades ; the earliest
αἱ Θυιάδες· τὰ μὲν δὴ πρῶτα of the figures were made by
αὐτῶν 'Αθηναῖος Πραξίας μα- Praxias of Athens, a pupil
θητὴς Καλάμιδός ἐστιν ⟨ὁ⟩ of Kalamis ; but as a con-
εἰργασμένος· χρόνου δὲ ὡς ὁ siderable time elapsed
ναὸς ἐποιεῖτο ἐγγιγνομένου during the construction of
Πραξίαν μὲν ἔμελλεν ἀπάξειν the temple, Praxias, as his
τὸ χρεών, τὰ δὲ ὑπολειπόμενα destiny was, succumbed to
τοῦ ἐν τοῖς ἀετοῖς κόσμου ἐποί- fate, and the remainder of
ησεν 'Ανδροσθένης, γένος μὲν the pediment-sculptures
καὶ οὗτος 'Αθηναῖος, μαθητὴς were executed by Andro-
δὲ Εὐκάδμου. sthenes, also an Athenian
by birth, but a pupil of
Eukadmos.

From the temple of Apollo at Delphi, built in the early years of
the fifth century B. C. No fragments of the temple-sculptures have
been recovered by the French excavators.

143. Eur. *Ion* 190 ff.

190 ἰδοὺ τάνδ᾽ ἄθρησον,
Λερναῖον ὕδραν ἐναίρει
χρυσέαις ἅρπαις ὁ Διὸς
παῖς·
φίλα, πρόσιδ᾽ ὄσσοις.

ἀντ. ὁρῶ. καὶ πέλας ἄλλος αὐ-
195 τοῦ πανὸν πυρίφλεκτον
αἴ-
ρει τις· ἆρ᾽ ὃς ἐμαῖσι μυ-
θεύεται παρὰ πήναις
ἀσπιστὰς Ἰόλαος, ὃς
κοινοὺς αἰρόμενος πόνους
200 δίῳ παιδὶ συναντλεῖ;

καὶ μὰν τάνδ᾽ ἄθρησον
πτεροῦντος ἔφεδρον ἵπ-
που·
τὰν πῦρ πνέουσαν ἐναίρει
τρισώματον ἀλκάν.

205 παντᾷ τοι βλέφαρον διώ-
κω. σκέψαι κλόνον ἐν τύ-
ποισι
λαΐνοισι Γιγάντων.
ὧδε δερκόμεθ᾽, ὦ φίλαι.
λεύσσεις οὖν ἐπ᾽ Ἐγκε-
λάδῳ
210 γοργῶπιν πάλλουσαν ἴτ-
υν;
λεύσσω Παλλάδ᾽ ἐμὰν
θεόν.

See! behold yon monster! 'Tis the hydra of Lerna, whom the son of Zeus is slaying with his golden scythe. Look, friend, look!

I see. And beside him stands another who uplifts a blazing torch; can it be he whose tale is told beside my loom, the spearman Iolaos, who shares with the son of Zeus his toils and drains the bitter cup at his side?

And oh! behold yon knight bestriding his winged steed; he is slaying the mighty three-bodied form that breathes fire.

My eye turns every way. Behold the rout of Giants carved on the marble wall.

We see it all, good friends. Dost thou then note her who shakes o'er Enkelados her Gorgon shield?

I see Pallas, mine own Goddess.

τί γάρ, κεραυνὸν
ἀμφίπυρον ὄβριμον ἐν
　　Διὸς
ἐκηβόλοισι χερσίν ;
215　ὁρῶ, τὸν δάϊον
Μίμαντα πυρὶ καταιθαλοῖ.

What ? Seest thou the
massy bolt breathing flame
from either point in the far-
darting hands of Zeus ?
Aye; 'tis consuming with
its flame Mimas, his deadly
foe.

καὶ Βρόμιος ἄλλον
ἀπολέμοισι　κισσίνοισι
　　βάκτροις
ἐναίρει Γᾶς τέκνων ὁ Βακ-
　　χεύς.

Bromios too with his ivy-
wand, no warrior's weapon,
is slaying another child of
Earth.

τύποισι] For τείχεσι of the MSS. Hermann emended τύκαισι, which is accepted by most editors. The word does not exist.

The chorus approaches the temple of Apollo at Delphi and describes the metopes. The following are the groups :—(1) Herakles, the Hydra, and Iolaos (vv. 190–200); (2) Bellerophon and the Chimaira (vv. 201–204); (3) Athena and Enkelados (vv. 209–211); (4) Zeus and Mimas (vv. 212–216) ; (5) Dionysos and a Giant (vv. 217–219).

4. LYKIOS.

Date.—(1) L. was the son of Myron, and is called by Polemon ap. Ath. xi. 486 D a *Boeotian* of Eleutherai. Eleutherai became Attic in 460 B. C. or a little later. (2) No. 147 seems to be posterior to 446 B. C. (3) No. 146 may have commemorated a victory gained circ. 431 B. C., v. note. (4) Autolykos was victorious in the pancration in 421 B. C.

144. Plin. *N. H.* xxxiv. 79 Lycius Myronis discipulus fuit, qui fecit dignum praeceptore puerum sufflantem languidos ignes, et Argonautas, ⟨et⟩ Autolycum pancratii uictorem,

Lykios was the pupil of Myron and made a figure of a boy blowing the dying embers of a fire worthy of his teacher, and statues of the Argonauts and a portrait of Autolykos the victor

propter quem Xenophon symposium scripsit ... Lycius et ipse puerum suffitorem.

in the pankration, who is the hero of Xenophon's 'Banquet.' Lykios also represented a boy offering incense.

discipulus] Really his son, v. the following Nos.

puerum sufflantem ... puerum suffitorem] The two may perhaps be identical, Pliny's notes being derived from different sources. Both must be distinguished from No. 145.

Autolycum] The notice is out of its place in the text of Pliny, who attributes the statue to Leochares.

145. Paus. i. 23. 7 καὶ ἄλλα ἐν τῇ 'Αθηναίων ἀκροπόλει θεασάμενος οἶδα, Λυκίου τοῦ Μύρωνος χαλκοῦν παῖδα, ὃς τὸ περιρραντήριον ἔχει.

Other works too I remember to have seen on the Akropolis of Athens, such as the bronze boy of Lykios, the son of Myron, holding the sprinkler of lustral water.

The basin stood in front of the temple of the Brauronian Artemis, the water being used to sprinkle worshippers.

146. Paus. v. 22. 2 (At Olympia) παρὰ δὲ τὸ 'Ιπποδάμιον καλούμενον λίθου τε βάθρον ἐστί, κύκλος ἥμισυς, καὶ ἀγάλματα ἐπ' αὐτῷ Ζεὺς καὶ Θέτις τε καὶ 'Ημέρα ὑπὲρ τῶν τέκνων ἱκετεύουσαι. ταῦτα ἐπὶ μέσῳ τῷ βάθρῳ, οἱ δὲ ἤδη σχῆμα ἀντιτεταγμένων ὅ τε 'Αχιλλεὺς παρέχεται καὶ ὁ Μέμνων ἐπὶ ἑκατέρῳ τοῦ βάθρου τῷ πέρατι ἑκάτερος. ἀνθεστήκασι δὲ καὶ ἄλλος ἄλλῳ κατὰ

(At Olympia) beside the so-called Hippodamion is a semicircular marble base upon which stand figures of Zeus with Thetis and Dawn who are praying for their children. These are in the centre of the base, while Achilles and Memnon, standing one at each end of the base, are already drawn up in the attitude of warriors about to fight.

I

τὰ αὐτά, ἀνὴρ βάρβαρος ἀνδρὶ
Ἕλληνι, Ὀδυσσεὺς μὲν Ἑλένῳ,
ὅτι οὗτοι μάλιστα ἐπὶ σοφίᾳ
δόξαν ἐν ἑκατέρῳ τῷ στρατεύ-
ματι εἰλήφεσαν, Μενελάῳ δὲ
κατὰ τὸ ἔχθος τὸ ἐξ ἀρχῆς
Ἀλέξανδρος, Διομήδει δὲ Αἰν-
είας, καὶ τῷ Τελάμωνος Αἴαντι
Δηίφοβος. 3. ταῦτά ἐστιν
ἔργα μὲν Λυκίου τοῦ Μύρωνος,
Ἀπολλωνιᾶται δὲ ἀνέθηκαν οἱ
ἐν τῷ Ἰονίῳ. καὶ δὴ καὶ ἐλεγεῖον γράμμασίν ἐστιν ἀρ-
χαίοις ὑπὸ τοῦ Διὸς τοῖς ποσί.

μνάματ' Ἀπολλωνίας ἀνακεί-
μεθα, τὰν ἐνὶ πόντῳ
Ἰονίῳ Φοῖβος ᾤκισ' ἀκερσε-
κόμας.
οἳ γᾶς τέρμαθ' ἑλόντες Ἀβαντί-
δος ἐνθάδε ταῦτα
ἔστασαν σὺν θεοῖς ἐκ Θρο-
· νίου δεκάταν.

There are other pairs drawn up in the same manner, a barbarian being pitted against a Greek in each case. There are Odysseus and Helenos — the chiefs most renowned for their cunning in each army, Menelaos and his old enemy Paris. Diomedes and Aineias, Deiphobos and Telamonian Ajax. These are the work of Lykios, the son of Myron, and were dedicated by the people of Apollonia on the Ionian sea. There is also an elegiac inscription engraved in antique characters under the feet of Zeus :—

Here we stand as memorials of Apollonia, founded by Phoibos of the unshorn locks on the Ionian sea, whose people conquered the borders of the Abantes' land, and here by god's grace set up these offerings from the tithe of the spoils of Thronion.

Ἀπολλωνιᾶται] A. was a colony of Corinth on the coast of Epiros, almost opposite Korkyra. The victory over the Abantes of Euboia and capture of Thronion probably took place about 431 B. C.

γράμμασιν . . . ἀρχαίοις] i. e. in the Attic alphabet, replaced by the
Ionic in the archonship of Eukleides (403 B. C.).

147. Δελτ. Ἀρχ. 1889,
p. 179 οἱ ἱππῆς ἀπὸ τῶν
πολεμίων, ἱππαρχούντων Λακεδαιμονίου Ξενοφῶντος Προνά-
που. | Λύκιος ἐποίησεν Ἐλευ-
θερεὺς Μύρωνος.

Dedicated by the knights
from the spoils of the enemy.
The cavalry was com-
manded by Lakedaimonios,
Xenophon and Pronapos.
Lykios of Eleutherai the
son of Myron, made the
statues.

From the base of a group of two horsemen which stood at the
entrance to the Propylaia, referred to by Paus. i. 22. 4. He seems
to have misinterpreted the inscription, as he writes, ' I cannot tell
whether the statues of horsemen represent the sons of Xenophon,
or are merely decorative.' Lakedaimonios may be identified with
the son of Kimon (Thuc. i. 45). The monument seems to have
commemorated the reduction of Euboia after its revolt in 446 B.C.

5. KRESILAS.

Date.—Four inscriptions exist, of which three were found on the
Akropolis of Athens : (1) Löwy 46 Ἑρμόλυκος | Διειτρεφοῦς | ἀπαρχήν. |
Κρησίλας | ἐποίησεν. Dated circ. 450 B. C. See No. 148 note. (2)
Δελτ. Ἀρχ. 1889, p. 36 [Περ]ικλέο(υ)s | Κρησ]ίλας ἐποίει. Date
440–430. See No. 148 note. (3) Löwy 47 [τόνδε Πύρης] ἀνέθηκε
Πολυμνήστου φίλο[s υἱὸς] εὐξάμενος δεκάτην Παλλάδι Τριτογενεῖ |
Κυδωνιήτας Κρησίλας εἰργάσσατο. Repeated in *Anth. Pal.* xiii. 13.
Somewhat later than (2). Besides these (4) Löwy 45, found at
Hermione, Ἀλεξίας Λύωνος ἀνέθη[κε] | τᾷ Δάματρι τᾷ [Χ]θονία[ι] |
Ἑρμιονεύς. | Κρησίλας ἐποίησε Κυδωνιάτ[ας]. Probably rather later
than the Athenian inscriptions.

148. Plin. *N. H.* xxxiv. 74
Cresilas (fecit) uolneratum
deficientem in quo possit

The works of Kresilas
are a man wounded and
dying, in whom the spec-

intelligi quantum restet animae et Amazonem uolneratam et Olympium Periclen dignum cognomine, mirumque in hac arte est quod nobiles uiros nobiliores fecit.

tator can feel how little life is left, and a wounded Amazon, and Perikles the 'Olympian,' worthy of his name. The marvel of this art is, that it has made men of renown yet more renowned.

uolneratum] Paus. i. 23. 3, in describing the Akropolis of Athens, mentions Διτρεφοῦς χαλκοῦς ἀνδριὰς ὀιστοῖς βεβλημένος, 'a bronze portrait of Diïtrephes shot with arrows.' Paus. identifies the subject of the portrait with the Athenian general mentioned in Thuc. vii. 29 (414 B.C.) and viii. 64 (411 B.C.). Ross conjectured that the inscription (1) quoted above belonged to the statue mentioned by Paus., and that this was identical with Pliny's wounded man. The character of the lettering, however, compels us to date the inscription (v. supr.) too early for the Diïtrephes of Paus., so that Furtwängler (*Meisterwerke*, p. 278) is probably right in referring it to an elder Diïtrephes, father of Nikostratos (Thuc. iii. 75, iv. 119, 129). Possibly the statue is represented on a b. f. lekythos figured in Furtw. *op. cit.* p. 280.

quantum restet animae] For 'quantum' = 'how little,' cp. Cic. *Q. Fr.* i. 2. 8 sed haec tibi praecipiens quantum profecerim non ignoro, Hor. *Sat.* ii. 9, 81 in scobe quantus | consistit sumptus?

Amazonem] V. No. 111 note.

Periclen] The busts in the British Museum (*F. W.* 481), in the Vatican, and at Munich are copies of this work. The inscription (supr. No. 2) was found on the Akropolis in 1889.

nobiles] Either 'famous' (the usual sense of the word in Pliny) or, as Prof. Gardner suggests, a translation of γενναῖος, perhaps from an epigram.

Other works :—Inscription (4) belongs to an offering to Demeter Chthonia. *Anth. Pal.* xiii. 13 preserves an inscription from an offering to Pallas Tritogeneia. A 'doryphoros,' ascribed by Pliny to Ktesilaos (best MSS.), probably belongs to Kresilas, since a 'wounded Amazon' is ascribed to the same artist.

6. STRONGYLION.

Date.—The inscription of No. 149 (Löwy 52) reads Χαιρέδημος Εὐαγγέλ[ου ἐ]κ Κοίλης ἀνέθηκεν. | Στρογγυλίων ἐποίησεν, and must have been recently erected when the work was mentioned by Ar. *Av.* 1128 (acted 414 B. C.).

149. Paus. i. 23. 8 ἵππος δὲ ὁ καλούμενος δούριος ἀνάκειται χαλκοῦς . . . λέγεται δὲ ἐς ἐκεῖνον τὸν ἵππον, ὡς τῶν Ἑλλήνων ἔνδον ἔχοι τοὺς ἀρίστους, καὶ δὴ καὶ τοῦ χαλκοῦ τὸ σχῆμά ἐστι κατὰ ταὐτά, καὶ Μενεσθεὺς καὶ Τεῦκρος ὑπερκύπτουσιν ἐξ αὐτοῦ, προσέτι δὲ καὶ οἱ παῖδες οἱ Θησέως.

Another offering consists in a bronze figure of the so-called Wooden Horse. The story of that horse is that it contained the bravest of the Greeks, and the bronze horse is in accordance therewith, for Menestheus and Teukros are leaning out of it, and the sons of Theseus also.

On the Akropolis of Athens.
Schol. Ar. *Av.* 1128 preserves the first five words of the inscription. The whole, including the artist's name, was discovered in 1840 (v. supr.).

150. Paus. i. 40. 2 (At Megara) τῆς δὲ κρήνης οὐ πόρρω ταύτης ἀρχαῖόν ἐστιν ἱερόν . . . ἄγαλμά τε κεῖται χαλκοῦν Ἀρτέμιδος ἐπίκλησιν Σωτείρας . . . τὴν δὲ Ἄρτεμιν . . . Στρογγυλίων ἐποίησε.

(At Megara) not far from this spring is an ancient temple; and in it there is an image of Artemis called 'the Saviour.' This Artemis was made by Strongylion.

Represented on coins of Megara (*Num. Comm.* A. 1).
Artemis 'the Saviour' was so called by the Megarians, because in 479 B. C. she deceived a party of Persians by night and caused them to shoot all their arrows at a rock, so that they fell an easy prey in the morning.

151. Paus. ix. 30. 1 ταῖς Μούσαις δὲ ἀγάλματά ... ἐστι ... τρεῖς μέν εἰσιν ... Κηφισοδότου, Στρογγυλίωνος δὲ ἕτερα τοσαῦτα, ἀνδρὸς βοῦς καὶ ἵππους ἄριστα εἰργασμένου.

There is a group of statues of the Muses. Three are by Kephisodotos, and as many more by Strongylion, an artist whose oxen and horses are of remarkable excellence.

On Mount Helikon.

152. Plin. *N. H.* xxxiv. 82 Strongylion (fecit) Amazonem quam ab excellentia crurum Εὔκνημον appellant, ob id in comitatu Neronis circumlatam. Idem fecit puerum quem amando Brutus Philippensis cognomine suo illustrauit.

Strongylion made an Amazon called 'Εὔκνημος' from the beauty of the legs, and for that reason carried from place to place in Nero's train. By the same artist is the boy on which Brutus, the hero of Philippi, by his admiration shed the lustre of his name.

cognomine suo] The statue is thrice referred to by Martial as 'Bruti puer.'

7. KALLIMACHOS.

Date.—The Erechtheion (v. No. 154) was completed in 408 B. C. Vitruvius (iv. 1. 10) makes K. the inventor of the Corinthian Capital. On the inscription Καλλίμαχος ἐποίει on an archaistic relief (Löwy 500), see Furtwängler, *Meisterwerke*, p. 202 ff.

153. Plin. *N. H.* xxxiv. 92 Ex omnibus autem maxume cognomine insignis est Callimachus semper

Of all artists Kallimachos is the most remarkable for the epithet applied to him. He continually subjected

calumniator sui nec finem habentis diligentiae, ob id 'catatexitechnus' appellatus, memorabili exemplo adhibendi et curae modum; huius sunt saltantes Lacaenae, emendatum opus, sed in quo gratiam omnem diligentia abstulerit.

his own work to the severest criticism and bestowed endless labour upon it, for which reason he was called 'the man who put his art into the crucible,'—a memorable warning that even diligence must have its limit : his dancing maidens of Sparta is a work of flawless precision, but one robbed of all its charm by the excessive labour spent on it.

calumniator sui] Calumnia='pedantic self-criticism,' in the writers of the Silver Age (cp. however Cic. *Fam.* ix. 2. 3). See Quint. x. 1. 115 (Caluum) nimia contra se calumnia uerum sanguinem perdidisse ; also Quint. x. 3. 6, viii. *Prooem.* 3.

catatexitechnus] The significance of the epithet is well illustrated by Dion. Hal. *de ui Demosth.* 51, who says that sculptors and painters do not fritter away their labour on the representation of tiny veins, feathers, down, &c., nor κατατήκειν (lit. melt down) εἰς ταῦτ ι τὰς τέχνας.

saltantes Lacaenae] Probably Karyatides (cp. No. 184), i. e. maidens of Karyae in Laconia, who danced at festivals of Artemis. Perhaps the group of ' Neo-Attic' reliefs treated by Winter (50. *Winckelmannsprogramm*, p. 97 ff.) may serve to illustrate this work.

gratiam] In No. 87 λεπτότης and χάρις are mentioned as characteristic of Kallimachos. The contrast, however, in that passage is with a ' broad treatment.'

·

154. Paus. i. 26. 6 λύχνον δὲ τῇ θεῷ χρυσοῦν Καλλίμαχος ἐποίησεν . . . ὁ δὲ Καλλίμαχος . . . ἀποδέων τῶν πρώτων ἐς

Kallimachos made a golden lamp for the goddess. This Kallimachos, though in art he fell short

αὐτὴν τὴν τέχνην, οὕτω σοφίᾳ πάντων ἐστὶν ἄριστος, ὥστε καὶ λίθους πρῶτος ἐτρύπησε, καὶ ὄνομα ἔθετο κατατηξίτεχνον ἢ θεμένων ἄλλων κατέστησεν ἐφ' αὑτῷ.

of the first rank, so far excelled his rivals in ingenuity that he was the first to bore marble, and gave to himself—or caused others to give him—the name of 'the man who put his art into the crucible.'

τῇ θεῷ] Athena Polias. The lamp hung in the Erechtheion. A golden palm served as a chimney.

πρῶτος ἐτρύπησε] i. e. he introduced the use of the 'running borer.' This was not used in the Parthenon sculptures, according to Puchstein (Arch. Anz. 1890, p. 110).

155. Paus. ix. 2. 7 Πλαται-εῦσι δὲ ναός ἐστιν Ἥρας . . . ἐνταῦθα . . . Ἥρας ἄγαλμα καθήμενον Καλλίμαχος ἐποί-ησε· Νυμφευομένην δὲ τὴν θεὸν . . . ὀνομάζουσιν.

The Plataeans have a temple of Hera. Here there is a seated image of Hera by Kallimachos. They call the goddess 'the Bride.'

8. SOKRATES.

156. Paus. i. 22. 8 κατὰ δὲ τὴν ἔσοδον αὐτὴν ἤδη τὴν ἐς ἀκρόπολιν Ἑρμῆν, ὃν προπύ-λαιον ὀνομάζουσι, καὶ Χάριτας Σωκράτη ποιῆσαι τὸν Σωφρο-νίσκου λέγουσιν.

At the very entrance to the Akropolis stand Hermes —called Hermes of the Gateway—and the Graces, both said to be works of Sokrates the son of Sophroniskos.

Σωκράτη] The philosopher (468–399 B. C.).

From Paus. ix. 36. 3 we learn that they were draped, and from
Schol. Ar. *Nub.* 773 that they were in relief (ἐγγεγλυμμένα τῷ τοίχῳ).
But the work cannot be identified with the original of the archaistic
relief in the Vatican (*A. Z.* 1869, xxii).

9. PYRRHOS.

157. Plin. *N. H.* xxxiv.
80 Pyrrhus (fecit) Hygiam
[et] Mineruam.

Pyrrhos represented Hy-
gieia [and] Athena.

A statue of Athena Hygieia is mentioned by Paus. on the Akropolis near the portrait of Diïtrephes (No. 148 note). The inscrip-
tion, found in 1839 (Löwy 53), reads Ἀθηναῖοι τῇ Ἀθηναίᾳ τῇ Ὑγιείᾳ. |
Πύρρος ἐποίησεν Ἀθηναῖος, and may be dated circ. 420 B.C. Plutarch
(*Perikl.* 13) states that Perikles erected the statue (which was of
bronze) to commemorate the healing of his favourite slave, who had
fallen from the roof of the Propylaia, by a remedy prescribed by
Athena in a dream. (V. next No.) The inscription appears to be
some years later than the building of the Propylaia (437–433 B.C.).

10. STYPPAX.

158. Plin. *N. H.* xxxiv.
81 Styppax Cyprius uno
celebratur signo, splan-
chnopte ; Periclis Olympii
uernula hic fuit exta torrens
ignemque oris pleni spiritu
accendens.

Styppax of Kypros owes
his fame to a single statue,
the ‘ roaster of entrails ’ :
this represented a slave of
Perikles the Olympian,
roasting entrails and kindling a fire with a blast
from his swollen cheeks.

From Plin. *N. H.* xxii. 44 we learn that the slave was identical
with the one mentioned in the note to the last No., and that his
statue was of bronze.

11. THE SCULPTURES OF THE ERECHTHEION.

159. *C.I.A.* i. 324 cd = Löwy 526.

... τὸν τὸ δ]όρυ ἔχοντα . . . . .   ⊠Δ

Φυρόμα|[χος Κ]ηφισιεὺς τὸν νεανίσκο[ν τὸ]ν
παρὰ τὸν θώρακα . . . .   ⊠Δ

Πραχ|[σίας] ἐμ Μελίτῃ οἰκῶν τὸν ʹ|ίππο]ν
καὶ τὸν ὀπισθοφανῆ τ|[ὸν πα]ρα-
κρούοντα . . . .   ΗΔΔ

'Αντιφάν|[ης ἐκ] Κεραμέων τὸ ἄρμα καὶ τ|[ὸν
νε]ανίσκον καὶ τὼ ἵππω τὼ | [ζευγ]νυ-
μένω . . . .   ΗΗΔΔΔΔ

Φυρόμαχ|[ος Κη]φισιεὺς τὸν ἄγοντα τὸν
ἵππον . . . .   ⊠Δ

Μυννίων 'Αγρυλῆ|[σι] οἰκῶν τὸν ἵππον καὶ
τὸν | [ἄ]νδρα τὸν ἐπικρούοντα. καὶ | [τὴ]ν
στήλην ὕστερον προσέθηκε . . . .   ΗΔΔΓⱵⱵ

Σῶκλος 'Αλωπεκῆ|[σι] οἰκῶν τὸν τὸν χαλινὸν
ἔ|[χο]ντα . . . .   ⊠Δ

Φυρόμαχος Κηφισιε|[ὺς] τὸν ἄνδρς τὸν ἐπὶ
τῆς βα|[κτ]ηρίας εἰστηκότα, τὸν παρὰ
[τὸ]ν βωμόν . . . .   ⊠Δ

ʹΙασος Κολλυτε|[ὺς] τὴγ γυναῖκα, ἧ ἡ παῖς
προσ|[πέ]πτωκε . . . .   ⊠ΔΔΔ

κεφάλαιον ἀ|[γα]λματοποϊκοῦ . . . .   ΧΧΧΗΗΗΔΓ

λῆ|[μμ]α . . . . . .   ΧΧΧ(Χ)ΗΗΗⱵⱵ

ἀνάλωμα τὸ α|[ὐτ]όν.

· · · · · · ·

...τὸν γρ]άφοντα νεα[νίσ]κον | [καὶ τὸν πρ]ο-
[σεστ]ῶτα αὐ[τ]ῷ . . . .   Η|[ΔΔ]

... ἐν Κολλυτῷ οἰκ[ῶν ... κ]αὶ τὴν ἄμαξαν
πλ[ὴν | τοῖν ἡμιόν]οιν . . . . .   ⊠ΔΔΔ

'Αγαθάν|[ωρ 'Αλωπεκῆσι] οἰκῶν τὸ γύνα|-
[ιον τὸ πρὸς τῇ ἀμ]άξῃ καὶ τ|[ὼ ἡμιόνω]   Η⊠ΔΔΔ

Dr.

To . . . for the man holding a spear 60

To Phyromachos of Kephisia for the youth beside
the breastplate 60

To Praxias, resident at Melite, for the horse and the
man seen behind it who is turning it 120

To Antiphanes of Kerameis, for the chariot and the
youth and the pair of horses being yoked . . 240

To Phyromachos of Kephisia, for the man leading
the horse 60

To Mynnion, resident at Agryle, for the horse and
the man striking it. He afterwards added the
pillar 127

To Soklos, resident at Alopeke, for the man holding
the bridle 60

To Phyromachos of Kephisia, for the man leaning
upon his staff beside the altar 60

To Iason of Kollytos, for the woman at whose feet
the child has fallen 80

Total expenditure on sculpture . . 3315
Received, 4302 dr. 1 ob.
Disbursed, the same sum.

To . . . for the young man writing and the man who
is standing beside him 120

To . . . resident at Kollytos, for . . . and the chariot
(but not the pair of mules) 80

To Agathanor, resident at Alopeke, for the woman
beside the chariot and the pair of mules . . . 180

X (χίλιοι) = 1000, H (Hεκατόν) = 100, Δ (δέκα) = 10, Γ (πέντε) = 5, Ѩ (5 × 10) = 50, Ͱ = 1 drachma, Ι = 1 obol.

From the accounts of expenditure on the building of the Erechtheion (407 B. C.). The names are those of the workmen, who executed the individual figures at sixty drachmas each. The composition was no doubt the work of a first-class artist, who furnished models (τύποι), and was paid at a higher rate. See No. 221'. One drachma = about 10*d*. or a franc. Artists whose name is followed by that of their deme are Attic citizens, those described as 'resident at . . .' are aliens. Attempts to reconstruct the scene, and to identify some of the figures with existing fragments (Brunn-Bruckmann 31–33) have been made by Bergk, *Zeitschrift für Alterthumswissenschaft*, 1845, p. 987 ff., and Stephani, *A. d. I.* 1843, p. 286 ff. On the fragments see *F. W.* 812–820.

[πα]ρακρούοντα] Since ἀνακρούειν = to 'pull up' a horse with the bridle (Xen. *de Eq.* 11. 33) παρακρούειν may mean to 'turn' the animal.

§ 2. THE ARGIVE SCHOOL.

1. POLYKLEITOS.

Date.—(1) The inscription from the base of the portrait of Kyniskos (v. infr.) (Löwy 50) may be dated circ. 440 B. C., and the Amazon (No. 117), if really contemporary with that of Pheidias, would belong to the same time. The inscriptions from the portraits of Pythokles (Löwy 91) and Xenokles (Löwy 90), whose alphabet shows increasing Ionic influence, are generally attributed to the younger P., but Furtw. thinks that they may date from the Peloponnesian war (*Meisterwerke*, p. 415). (2) Plat. *Protag.* 311 C makes Polykleitos a contemporary of Pheidias, and in the same dialogue, 328 C, represents his sons as contemporary with those of Perikles. (3) The Hera at Argos (No. 161) is posterior to 423 B. C., when the temple was built; hence Pliny's date, Ol. 90 = 420 B. C. (4) The memorials of the Spartan victory at Aigospotamoi (405 B. C.) were for the most part executed by the pupils of Polykleitos;

but the tripod at Amyklai (No. 160) was his own work, unless we assign it to the younger P. (The works assigned with probability to the latter artist are placed last, Nos. 165, 166.)

160. Plin. *N. H.* xxxiv. 55 Polyclitus Sicyonius Ageladae discipulus diadumenum fecit molliter iuuenem centum talentis nobilitatum ; idem et doryphorum uiriliter puerum fecit, quem Κανόνα artifices uocant lineamenta artis ex eo petentes ueluti a lege quadam, solusque hominum artem ipsam fecisse artis opere iudicatur. Fecit et destringentem se et nudum telo incessentem, duosque pueros item nudos talis ludentes qui uocantur ἀστραγαλίζοντες et sunt in Titi Imperatoris atrio—hoc opere nullum absolutius plerique iudicant—item Mercurium qui fuit Lysimacheae, Herculem qui Romae, ἀγητῆρα arma sumentem, Artemona qui περιφορητός appellatus est. Hic consummasse hanc scientiam iudicatur et toreuticen sic erudisse ut Phidias aperuisse. Proprium eius est uno crure ut

Polykleitos of Sikyon was a pupil of Ageladas ; his works were :—a youth with boyish forms binding his hair, famous for its price, 100 talents ; also a boy of manly form bearing a lance, called 'the Canon' by artists, who draw from it the rudiments of art as from a code (so that Polykleitos is held to be the only man who has embodied art itself in a work of art) ; also a man scraping himself and a nude figure hurling a javelin, and two boys, also nude, playing with knucklebones, which are called 'the Dice-players' and stand in the hall of the Imperator Titus, considered by many to be the most faultless work of sculpture—also a Hermes which was at Lysimacheia, a Herakles at Rome, a captain putting on his armour, and a portrait of Artemon called 'the Man

insisterent signa excogitasse, quadrata tamen esse ea tradit Uarro et paene ad exemplum.

in the Litter.' He is held to have brought the bronze-caster's art to perfection and to have expounded sculpture, as Pheidias revealed it. Peculiar to him is the device by which his statues step forward with one leg. Varro, however, states that they are squarely built and seem almost to be made on a uniform pattern.

Sicyonius] P. describes himself as 'Αργεῖος on the base of the portrait of Pythokles, and this is corroborated by Plato and Pausanias. Naukydes (v. infr.) was also an Argive. Daidalos, Kanachos, and Alypos (v. infr.) show that the school afterwards transferred itself to Sikyon, which was the home of Lysippos. Possibly therefore Pliny's version is a kind of anachronism (Furtw. *Meisterwerke*, p. 416 f.), unless P. was a Sikyonian by birth who gained the citizenship of Argos.

Ageladae discipulus] Chronologically impossible, v. supr. p. 33.

diadumenum] A copy found at Vaison is in the British Museum (*Catalogue of Greek Sculpture*, p. 266). See *F. W.* 508.

molliter iuuenem . . . uiriliter puerum] The antithesis may be Pliny's own, or borrowed from an epigram.

doryphorum . . . quem κανόνα uocant] MSS. insert et before quem, but it has been omitted in accordance with No. 163 note. The best copy (from Pompeii) is at Naples (*F. W.* 503).

destringentem se] A translation of ἀποξυόμενον—an athlete scraping himself with the strigil after anointing.

telo incessentem] The MSS. read 'talo,' but this can only be retained if with Benndorf we regard the phrase as a mistranslation of ἀστραγάλῳ ἐπικείμενος, supposing that Pliny rendered ἐπικείμενος 'standing upon' by 'incessens,' 'pursuing.' A large basis in the form of a knucklebone was found at Olympia, and Benndorf believes that it supported a statue of Καιρός ('Opportunity') here referred to. But it is better to accept Benndorf's alternative suggestion 'telo'; on the meaning see Wölfflin, *Archiv für lateinische Lexikographie*, 1894, p. 105 ff., who quotes Ov. *Met.* xiv. 402 saeuisque parant incessere telis and Plin. *N. H.* xxxvii. 111 fundis e longinquo incessunt.

Titi Imperatoris] Titus received the title Imperator in 72 A. D.

ἀγητῆρα] A Dorian title (cp. πεντηκοντήρ, ἁρμοστήρ at Sparta). The word is not to be regarded as an attribute of Herakles (Urlichs, *Wochenschrift für klassische Philologie*, 1894, Sp. 1299).

Artemona] An engineer employed by Perikles at the siege of Samos (440 B. C.). Being lame he was carried about (περιφορητός) in a litter.

hanc scientiam] The art of bronze-casting.

uno crure] The typical attitude of Polykleitan statues is that in which the figure is *coming to rest* on one leg (*uno crure*, not *uni cruri* ' resting its weight on one leg ').

quadrata] As compared with the more slender figures of Lysippos. V. Introduction, § 2.

ad exemplum] 'unum' is inserted in the inferior MSS. But the same sense may be obtained by laying stress on 'exemplum,' almost = a lay figure (Gk. κατὰ τὸ παράδειγμα).

---

161. Paus. ii. 17. 4 (At Argos) τὸ δὲ ἄγαλμα τῆς "Ηρας ἐπὶ θρόνου κάθηται μεγέθει μέγα, χρυσοῦ μὲν καὶ ἐλέφαντος, Πολυκλείτου δὲ ἔργον· ἔπεστι δέ οἱ στέφανος Χάριτας ἔχων καὶ "Ωρας ἐπειργασμένας, καὶ τῶν χειρῶν τῇ μὲν ἔχει καρπὸν ῥοιᾶς, τῇ δὲ σκῆπτρον. . . . κόκκυγα δὲ ἐπὶ τῷ σκήπτρῳ καθῆσθαί φασι, λέγοντες τὸν Δία, ὅτε ἤρα παρθένου τῆς "Ηρας, ἐς τοῦτον τὸν ὄρνιθα ἀλλαγῆ-

(At Argos) the image of Hera is colossal in size, seated upon a throne: it is made of gold and ivory, and is the work of Polykleitos; on her head is a crown adorned with Graces and Seasons; in one hand she holds the fruit of the pomegranate, in the other a sceptre. They say that a cuckoo is perched on the sceptre. and tell the story that Zeus, when he loved

ναι, τὴν δὲ ἅτε παίγνιον θηρ-
ᾶσαι.

the maiden Hera, took the
form of that bird, and was
pursued and taken by her
as a plaything.

The base was laid bare by the American excavators in 1892.
The statue is represented on coins of Argos (Overbeck, *Kunstmyth.* iii, Münztafel iii. 1, 2). A passage of Tertullian (*de Cor. Mil.* 7),
of doubtful authority, seems to imply that Hera wore a garland of
vine-leaves, and that a tiger's skin was spread over her footstool,
in allusion to Dionysos and Herakles.

162. Paus. iii. 18. 7 ἐν
'Αμύκλαις ... τρίποδες χαλκοῖ
... 8. ... 'Αρίστανδρος δὲ
Πάριος καὶ Πολύκλειτος 'Αργεῖος, ὁ μὲν γυναῖκα ἐποίησεν ἔχουσαν λύραν, Σπάρτην
δῆθεν, Πολύκλειτος δὲ 'Αφρο-
δίτην παρὰ 'Αμυκλαίῳ καλουμένην. οὗτοι δὲ οἱ τρίποδες
μεγέθει τε ὑπὲρ τοὺς ἄλλους
εἰσὶ καὶ ἀπὸ τῆς νίκης τῆς ἐν
Αἰγὸς ποταμοῖς ἀνετέθησαν.

At Amyklai there are
bronze tripods. (To support
these) Aristandros of Paros
made a figure of a woman
holding a lyre, which is
called 'Sparta,' and Polykleitos of Argos an Aphrodite called 'the Aphrodite
of Amyklai.' These tripods
are larger than the others
and were dedicated from
the spoils of the victory at
Aigospotamoi.

τρίποδες] The earlier and smaller tripods were used by Gitiadas
(No. 37) and Kallon of Aegina (No. 53). Aristandros may have
been the father of Skopas (infr. Part II. § 1. 2 (a)).
τῆς νίκης τῆς ἐν Α. π.] 405 B.C.

163. Galen, de plac. Hipp.
et Plat. 5 τὸ δὲ κάλλος οὐκ
ἐν τῇ τῶν στοιχείων, ἀλλ' ἐν
τῇ τῶν μορίων συμμετρίᾳ συν-
ίστασθαι νομίζει (Χρύσιππος),

Chrysippos holds beauty
to consist in the proportions
not of the elements but of
the parts, that is to say, of
finger to finger and of all

δακτύλου πρὸς δάκτυλον δηλο-
νότι καὶ συμπάντων αὐτῶν
πρός τε μετακάρπιον καὶ καρ-
πόν, καὶ τούτων πρὸς πῆχυν,
καὶ πήχεως πρὸς βραχίονα καὶ
πάντων πρὸς πάντα καθάπερ
ἐν τῷ Πολυκλείτου κανόνι
γέγραπται. πάσας γὰρ ἐκδιδά-
ξας ἡμᾶς ἐν ἐκείνῳ τῷ συγ-
γράμματι τὰς συμμετρίας τοῦ
σώματος ὁ Πολύκλειτος, ἔργῳ
τὸν λόγον ἐξεβεβαίωσε, δημι-
ουργήσας ἀνδριάντα κατὰ τὰ
τοῦ λόγου προστάγματα, καὶ
καλέσας δὴ καὶ αὐτὸν τὸν ἀνδριάντα, καθάπερ καὶ τὸ σύγ-
γραμμα κανόνα.

the fingers to the palm and wrist, and of these to the forearm, and of the forearm to the upper arm, and of all the parts to each other, as they are set forth in the Canon of Polykleitos. For Polykleitos, when he had taught us all the proportions of the human figure by means of that treatise, confirmed his theory by a practical illustration and made a statue according to the dictates of the theory, and called the statue, like the treatise, his ' Canon.'

The identity of this 'Canon' with the doryphoros is shown by the anecdote told of Lysippos, who used to say that the doryphoros of Polykleitos was his master (Cic. *Brut.* 86. 296) and by Quint. (v. 12. 21) who states that sculptors took it as their model. An expression is quoted from the theoretical treatise by Philon περὶ βελοποιϊκῶν iv. 2 τὸ γὰρ εὖ παρὰ μικρὸν διὰ πολλῶν ἀριθμῶν ἔφη γίγνεσθαι— 'Beauty, he said, was produced from a small unit through a long chain of numbers.' The system given by Vitruv. iii. 1 does not agree with the statues of Polykleitos. Kalkmann (53. *Winckelmannsprogramm*) connects it with the canon of Euphranor (No. 230) on very slight grounds.

164. Plut. Quaest. Conu. ii. 3. 2 Πολύκλειτος ὁ πλάστης εἶπε χαλεπώτατον εἶναι τὸ ἔργον, ὅταν ἐν ὄνυχι ὁ πηλὸς γίνηται.

Polykleitos the sculptor said that the work was most difficult, when the clay came under the nail.

K

ὅταν ἐν ὄνυχι κ.τ.λ.] If these words are to be taken literally they may be interpreted, (1) of the nail of the artist, with which he works over the surface of the finished model; (2) of the nail of the model itself, which is the last detail to be finished. But this would require ἐν τοῖς ὄνυξι. It is possible that the phrase (which was a proverbial one, cp. the use of ἐξονυχίζειν Ar. *Fr.* 230 Bgk. and Dion. Hal. *de ui Demosth.* 13 ὁ τοῦ Δημοσθένους λόγος ... τὸν Λυσιακὸν χαρακτῆρα ἐκμέμακται εἰς ὄνυχα) is used without any literal implication.

Other works by Polykleitos :—
The AMAZON (v. No. 117).
HERAKLES and the Hydra (Cic. *de Or.* ii. 16. 70).
The KANEPHOROI (Cic. *Verr.* iii. 4. 5).
Portraits of Olympic victors :—
KYNISKOS of Mantineia, victor in the boys' boxing-match (Paus. vi. 4. 11); the inscription Löwy 50.

Works ascribed to the younger Polykleitos (v. infr. p. 192) :—

165. Paus. ii. 20. 1 (At Argos) ἄγαλμά ἐστι καθήμενον Διὸς Μειλιχίου, λίθου λευκοῦ, Πολυκλείτου δὲ ἔργον.

(At Argos) there is a seated image of Zeus the Merciful in white marble, the work of Polykleitos.

Stated by Paus. to have been set up in expiation of a massacre in 418 B. C., in which case it would be a work of the elder P. But the material (marble) is not that employed by him, and the massacre may have been the 'σκυταλισμός' in 370 B. C. (Diod. xv. 58).

166. Paus. ii. 24. 5 ᾠκοδόμηται δὲ ἐπὶ κορυφῇ τοῦ ὄρους Ἀρτέμιδος Ὀρθίας ἱερόν, καὶ ἀγάλματα Ἀπόλλωνος καὶ Λητοῦς καὶ Ἀρτέμιδος πεποίηται λευκοῦ λίθου. Πολυκλείτου δέ φασιν εἶναι ἔργα.

On the summit of the mountain stands a temple of Artemis Orthia, in which are images of Apollo, Leto and Artemis of white marble. These are said to be the work of Polykleitos.

τοῦ ὄρους] Mount Lykone in Arkadia. Ascribed to the younger P. on the ground of the material.

Portraits of Olympic victors : —

ARISTION of Epidauros, victor in the boys' boxing-match (Paus. vi. 13. 6). Inscription Löwy 92.

THERSILOCHOS of Korkyra, victor in the boxing-match (Paus. vi. 13. 6). Coupled by Paus. with the last.

ANTIPATROS of Miletos, victorious in the boys' boxing-match in the time of Dionysios I (probably 388 B.C.) (Paus. vi. 2. 6).

(PYTHOKLES of Elis, victor in the five contests (Paus. vi. 7. 10). Inscription Löwy 91.)

(XENOKLES of Mainalos, victor in the boys' wrestling-match (Paus. vi. 9. 2). Inscription Löwy 90.)

The case of the two last-named is doubtful. V. supr. ad init.; and Furtwängler, *loc. cit.*

2. THE FAMILY AND SCHOOL OF POLYKLEITOS.

(a) THE FAMILY OF PATROKLES.

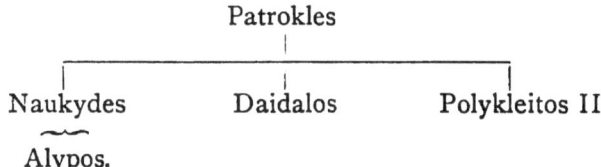

Naukydes and Daidalos describe themselves as sons of Patrokles in their inscriptions (Löwy 86, 88). A Polykleitos, brother of Naukydes, is mentioned by Pausanias (No. 173), who (though Robert believes him to be the elder P.), must be in reality the younger artist of the name ; on whom see Part iv. § 2. 1 (b). The relationship of the elder Polykleitos to the other members of the family must remain uncertain. He may have been the brother of Patrokles.

Date.—Patrokles was employed (v. No. 172) on the Spartan memorial of Aigospotamoi (405 B.C.). Pliny dates him 400 B.C. Naukydes seems to have worked with the elder Polykleitos at Argos (No. 170), and his inscriptions (Löwy 86, 87, see especially note on the latter inscription) show that he was at work in the early years of the fourth century. His younger brothers belong to the next period. His pupil Alypos, however, was employed on the memorial of Aigospotamoi (No. 172).

167. Plin. *N. H.* xxxiv.
91 Athletas autem et armatos et uenatores sacrificantesque (fecit) . . . Patrocles.

Patrokles made statues
of athletes, warriors, hunters,
and sacrificers.

P.'s place is with the artists of the second grade, who are classi-
fied according to their subjects (Introduction, § 1).

168. Plin. *N. H.* xxxiv.
80 Naucydes Mercurio et
discobolo et immolante
ariem censetur.

The fame of Naukydes
rests on his Hermes, his
quoit - thrower, and his
figure sacrificing a ram.

The last named is usually identified with a figure standing in the
precinct of Athena Ergane on the Akropolis of Athens, described
by Paus. in the following No.

169. Paus. i. 24. 2 κεῖται
δὲ καὶ Φρίξος ὁ Ἀθάμαντος
ἐξενηνεγμένος ἐς Κόλχους ὑπὸ
τοῦ κριοῦ. θύσας δὲ αὐτὸν
ὅτῳ δὴ θεῷ, ὡς δὲ εἰκάσαι τῷ
Λαφυστίῳ καλουμένῳ, παρὰ
Ὀρχομενίοις, τοὺς μηροὺς κατὰ
νόμον ἐκτεμὼν τὸν Ἑλλήνων,
ἐς αὐτοὺς καιομένους ὁρᾷ.

There stands also Phrixos,
the son of Athamas, who
was borne to Kolchis by
the ram. He has sacrificed
the animal to some god,
probably to him who is
called Laphystios at Orchomenos, and having cut out
the thigh-pieces after the
Greek fashion, is watching
them as they are consumed
by the flames.

Zeus Laphystios was worshipped on Mount Laphystion in Boeotia
and at Halos in Achaia Phthiotis, where human sacrifices, of which
that of Phrixos and Helle (for whom the ram with the golden fleece
was substituted) was the prototype, were offered in historical times
(Hdt. vii. 197).

170. Paus. ii. 17. 5 λέγεται δὲ παρεστηκέναι τῇ Ἥρᾳ τέχνη Ναυκύδους ἄγαλμα Ἥβης, ἐλέφαντος καὶ τοῦτο καὶ χρυσοῦ.

It is said that beside the Hera there stands an image of Hebe, the work of Naukydes. This is also of ivory and gold.

The Hera is that of Polykleitos at Argos (No. 161). Both figures are represented on bronze coins of Argos (Overbeck, *Kunstmyth.* iii, Münztafel iii. 1).

171. Paus. ii. 22. 7 (At Argos) τοῦ δὲ ἱεροῦ τῆς Εἰλειθυίας πέραν ἐστὶν Ἑκάτης ναός, Σκόπα δὲ τὸ ἄγαλμα ἔργον. τοῦτο μὲν λίθου, τὰ δ᾽ ἀπαντικρὺ χαλκᾶ, Ἑκάτης καὶ ταῦτα ἀγάλματα, τὸ μὲν Πολύκλειτος ἐποίησε, τὸ δὲ ἀδελφὸς Πολυκλείτου Ναυκύδης* Μόθωνος*.

(At Argos) beyond the temple of Eileithuia is a temple of Hekate, and the image is the work of Skopas. This is of marble, and the bronze figures which stand opposite to it also represent Hekate. One was made by Polykleitos, the other by Naukydes, the brother of Polykleitos*, and son of Mothon*.

Μόθωνος] The text is corrupt, since the inscription quoted above shows that Naukydes was the son of Patrokles. Klein suggests μαθητής ; but this would involve a lacuna for the teacher's name.

Other works :—
A portrait of the poetess Erinna (Tatian, *c. Graec.* 52).
Athlete statues :—
BAUKIS of Troizen, victorious in wrestling (Paus. vi. 8. 4).
CHEIMON, victorious in wrestling (Paus. vi. 9. 3).
EUKLES of Rhodes, grandson of Diagoras, victorious in wrestling (Paus. vi. 6. 2). Inscription Löwy 86.
Portraits by Alypos, pupil of Naukydes :—
SYMMACHOS of Elis, victorious in boxing (Paus. vi. 1. 3).
NEOLAIDAS of Pheneos in Arkadia, victorious in the boys' boxing-match (id. *ib.*).

ARCHIDAMOS of Elis, victorious in the boys' boxing-match (Paus. vi. 1. 3).

EUTHYMENES of Mainalos in Arkadia, victorious in the boys' wrestling-match (Paus. vi. 8. 5).

(b) THE SCHOOL OF POLYKLEITOS.

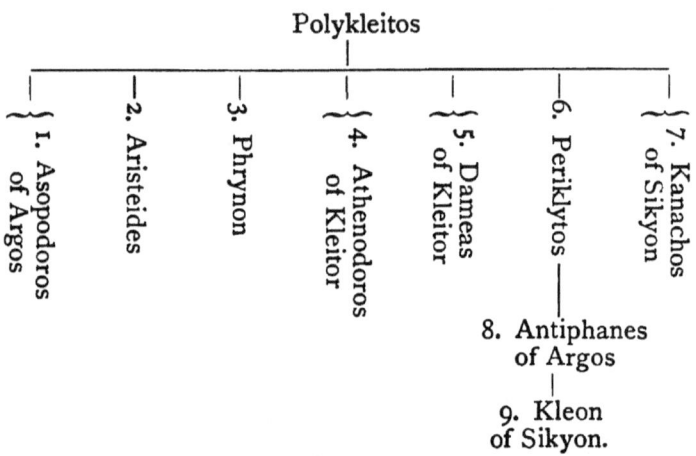

Polykleitos

1. Asopodoros of Argos
2. Aristeides
3. Phrynon
4. Athenodoros of Kleitor
5. Dameas of Kleitor
6. Periklytos
7. Kanachos of Sikyon

8. Antiphanes of Argos

9. Kleon of Sikyon.

The first five names are from Pliny's list in the chronological table; Alexis, a pupil of the younger Polykleitos, and Dinon (wanting in best MS.) have been omitted. The rest are from Pausanias.

Date.—Nos. 4, 5, 7, 8 were engaged on the memorial of Aigospotamoi (405 B. C.), No. 8 also on a memorial of an Argive success against Sparta in 414 B. C. (No. 173).

172. Paus. x. 9. 7 Λακεδαιμονίων δὲ . . . ἀναθήματά ἐστιν ἀπ' 'Αθηναίων Διόσκουροι καὶ Ζεὺς καὶ 'Απόλλων τε καὶ ''Αρτεμις, ἐπὶ δὲ αὐτοῖς Ποσειδῶν τε καὶ Λύσανδρος ὁ 'Αριστοκρίτου στεφανούμενος ὑπὸ τοῦ Ποσειδῶνος, ''Αβας τε, ὃς τῷ Λυσάνδρῳ τότε ἐμαντεύετο, καὶ ''Ερμων ὁ τὴν ναῦν

The offerings of the Spartans from the spoils of the Athenians consist of figures of the Dioskouroi, Zeus, Apollo and Artemis, beside Poseidon and Lysander, the son of Aristokritos, on whose head Poseidon is placing a garland, and Abas who acted as diviner to Lysander

τὴν Λυσάνδρου τὴν στρατηγίδα κυβερνῶν. 8. τοῦτον μὲν δὴ τὸν "Ερμωνα Θεόκοσμος ποιήσειν ἔμελλεν ὁ Μεγαρεὺς ἅτε ὑπὸ τῶν Μεγαρέων ἐγγραφέντα ἐς τὴν πολιτείαν· οἱ δὲ Διόσκουροι Ἀντιφάνους εἰσὶν Ἀργείου, καὶ ὁ μάντις τέχνη Πίσωνος ἐκ Καλαυρείας τῆς Τροιζηνίας. Ἀθηνόδωρος δὲ καὶ Δαμέας, ὁ μὲν τὴν Ἄρτεμίν τε καὶ Ποσειδῶνα εἰργάσατο, ἔτι δὲ τὸν Λύσανδρον, Ἀθηνόδωρος δὲ τὸν Ἀπόλλωνα ἐποίησε καὶ τὸν Δία· οὗτοι δὲ Ἀρκάδες εἰσιν ἐκ Κλείτορος. 9. ἀνάκεινται δὲ καὶ ὄπισθεν τῶν κατειλεγμένων ὅσοι συγκατειργάσαντο τῷ Λυσάνδρῳ τὰ ἐν Αἰγὸς ποταμοῖς ἢ αὐτῶν Σπαρτιατῶν ἢ ἀπὸ τῶν συμμαχησάντων· εἰσὶ δὲ οἵδε, Ἀρακὸς μὲν καὶ Ἐριάνθης, ὁ μὲν αὐτῶν ἐκ Λακεδαίμονος, ὁ δὲ Ἐριάνθης Βοιώτιος * * * ὑπὲρ τοῦ Μίμαντος, ἐντεῦθεν μὲν Ἀστυκράτης, Χῖοι δὲ Κηφισοκλῆς καὶ Ἑρμόφαντός τε καὶ Ἱκέσιος, Τίμαρχος δὲ καὶ Διαγόρας Ῥόδιοι, Κνίδιος δὲ Θεόδαμος, ἐκ δὲ Ἐφέσου Κιμμέριος, καὶ Μιλήσιος Αἰαντίδης. 10. τούτους μὲν δὴ ἐποίησε Τίσ-

on the occasion of the victory, and Hermon who was the helmsman of Lysander's flag-ship. This Hermon was destined to be portrayed by Theokosmos of Megara, because he had been enrolled as a citizen of Megara, the Dioskouroi are by Antiphanes of Argos, and the diviner is the work of Pison of Kalaureia, a possession of Troizen. Dameas made the Artemis and the Poseidon, besides the portrait of Lysander, while Athenodoros made the Apollo and the Zeus: both Athenodoros and Dameas were Arkadians from Kleitor. Behind the figures already enumerated are other offerings, the portraits of all who assisted Lysander at the victory of Aigospotamoi, whether Spartans or allies. These are the following:—Arakos, a Spartan, and Erianthes, a Boeotian * * * beyond Mimas, next is Astykrates and Kephisokles, Hermophantos and Hikesios of

ανδρος, τοὺς δὲ ἐφεξῆς Ἄλυπος
Σικυώνιος, Θεόπομπον Μύνδιον
καὶ Κλεομήδην Σάμιον καὶ ἐξ
Εὐβοίας Ἀριστοκλέα τε Καρύ-
στιον καὶ Αὐτόνομον Ἐρετριέα
καὶ Ἀριστόφαντον Κορίνθιον
καὶ Ἀπολλόδωρον Τροιζήνιον
καὶ ἐξ Ἐπιδαύρου Δίωνα τῆς ἐν
τῇ Ἀργολίδι. ἐχόμενοι δὲ τούτων Ἀξιόνικός ἐστιν Ἀχαιὸς
ἐκ Πελλήνης, ἐκ δὲ Ἑρμιόνης
Θέκρης, καὶ Φωκεύς τε Πυρ-
ρίας καὶ Κώμων Μεγαρεὺς καὶ
Ἀγασιμένης Σικυώνιος, ἐκ δὲ
Ἀμβρακίας καὶ Κορίνθου τε
καὶ Λευκάδος Τηλυκράτης καὶ
Πυθόδοτος Κορίνθιος καὶ Ἀμ-
βρακιώτης Εὐαιτίδας· τελευ-
ταῖοι δὲ Ἐπικυρίδας καὶ Ἐτεό-
νικος οἱ Λακεδαιμόνιοι. Πατρο-
κλέους δὲ καὶ Κανάχου φασὶν
ἔργα.

Chios, Timarchos and Dia-
goras of Rhodes, Theoda-
mos of Knidos, Kimmerios
of Ephesos and Aiantides
of Miletos. These figures
were made by Tisandros,
and those which follow by
Alypos of Sikyon. These
are Theopompos of Myndos
and Kleomedes of Samos
and two Euboeans—Aris-
tokles of Karystos and
Autonomos of Eretria, and
Aristophantos of Corinth
and Apollodoros of Troizen
and Dion of Epidauros in
Argolis. Next to these
come Axionikos an Achaean
of Pellene and Theseus of
Hermione and Pyrrhias the
Phokian and Komon the
Megarian and Agasimenes
the Sikyonian, while Am-
bracia, Corinth and Leukas
are represented by Tely-
krates and Pythodotos the
Corinthian and Euantidas
of Ambrakia. Last of all
come the Spartans, Epi-
kyridas and Eteonikos:
these are said to be the
work of Patrokles and Ka-
nachos.

Θεόκοσμος] v. No. 178.

ὑπὲρ τοῦ Μίμαντος] The lacuna which precedes these words may perhaps have contained ⟨ (ὁ δεῖνα) ἐξ Ἐρυθρῶν τῶν⟩. Erythrai 'beyond Cape Mimas' (i.e. in Ionia) is to be distinguished from the town of the same name in Boeotia.

173. Paus. x. 9. 12 τὸν δὲ ὑπὲρ τῆς καλουμένης Θυρέας Λακεδαιμονίων ἀγῶνα καὶ Ἀργείων, Σίβυλλα μὲν καὶ τοῦτον προεθέσπισεν, ὡς συμβήσοιτο ἐξ ἴσου ταῖς πόλεσιν. Ἀργεῖοι δὲ ἀξιοῦντες ἐσχηκέναι πλέον ἐν τῷ ἔργῳ χαλκοῦν ἵππον, τὸν δούρειον δῆθεν, ἀπέστειλαν ἐς Δελφούς· τὸ δὲ ἔργον Ἀντιφάνους ἐστὶν Ἀργείου.

The Sibyl also foretold that in the battle fought between the Spartans and Argives for the possession of the district called Thyrea, neither side should gain the victory. The Argives however claimed the advantage in the fight and sent to Delphi a bronze horse representing the Wooden Horse of Troy: this was the work of Antiphanes of Argos.

The battle was fought in 414 B.C. (Thuc. vi. 95). This favours the earlier date for No. 238, on which Antiphanes was engaged (q. v.).

Other works by pupils of Polykleitos :—
ARISTIDES, chariot-groups (Plin. *N. H.* xxxiv. 72).
KANACHOS, portrait of Bykelos of Sikyon, victorious in boxing at Olympia (Paus. vi. 13. 7).

(c) THE SCULPTURES OF THE HERAION AT ARGOS.

174. Paus. ii. 17. 3 ἀρχιτέκτονα μὲν δὴ γενέσθαι τοῦ ναοῦ λέγουσιν Εὐπόλεμον Ἀργεῖον ... ὁπόσα δὲ ὑπὲρ τοὺς

Eupolemos of Argos is said to have been the architect ... The subjects which fill the spaces above the

κίονάς ἐστιν εἰργασμένα, τὰ
μὲν ἐς τὴν Διὸς γένεσιν καὶ
Θεῶν καὶ Γιγάντων μάχην
ἔχει, τὰ δὲ ἐς τὸν πρὸς
Τροίαν πόλεμον καὶ Ἰλίου τὴν
ἅλωσιν.

columns are taken partly
from the legends of the
birth of Zeus and the battle
of the Gods and Giants,
partly from the story of
the Trojan war and the fall
of Ilion.

The temple was restored after its destruction by fire in 423 B. C.
The site has been recently excavated by the American School at
Athens, and fragments of the metopes discovered. See Waldstein,
Excavations at the Heraion of Argos, 1892, who however (p. 18)
appears to take Paus.' words to be a description of the pediment-
sculptures. This would be τὰ ἐν τοῖς ἀετοῖς in the language of Paus.,
while τὰ ὑπὲρ τοὺς κίονας unmistakably refers to metopes.

§ 3. OTHER ARTISTS.

1. PAIONIOS OF MENDE.

Date.—Dependent on that assigned to the Nike at Olympia
(Nos. 175, 176), on which see commentary.

175. Paus. v. 26. 1 Μεσ-
σηνίαν δὲ τῶν Δωριέων οἱ
Ναύπακτόν ποτε παρὰ Ἀθη-
ναίων λαβόντες ἄγαλμα ἐν
Ὀλυμπίᾳ Νίκης ἐπὶ τῷ κίονι
ἀνέθεσαν. τοῦτο ἔστιν ἔργον
μὲν Μενδαίου Παιωνίου πεποίηται δὲ ἀπὸ ἀνδρῶν πολεμίων
ὅτε Ἀκαρνᾶσι καὶ Οἰνιάδαις,
ἐμοὶ δοκεῖν, ἐπολέμησαν. Μεσσήνιοι δὲ αὐτοὶ λέγουσι, τὸ

The Dorian Messenians
who formerly received Nau-
paktos from the Athenians
dedicated at Olympia a
statue of Victory on a pillar.
This was the work of Pai-
onios of Mende, and was
set up from spoils taken from
the enemy when the Mes-
senians were at war with
the Akarnanians and the

ἀνάθημά σφισιν ἀπὸ τοῦ ἔργου τοῦ ἐν τῇ Σφακτηρίᾳ νήσῳ μετὰ ᾿Αθηναίων, καὶ οὐκ ἐπιγράψαι τὸ ὄνομα τῶν πολεμίων σφᾶς τῷ ἀπὸ Λακεδαιμονίων δείματι, ἐπεὶ Οἰνιαδῶν γε καὶ ᾿Ακαρνάνων οὐδένα ἔχειν φόβον.

people of Oiniadai. Such at least is my view: but the Messenians themselves assert that the statue is a memorial of the engagement on the island of Sphakteria in which they fought beside the Athenians, and that they did not inscribe the name of the enemy on the monument for fear of the Spartans, while they had no fear of the Akarnanians or the people of Oiniadai.

ποτε] Probably in 460 B.C. V. note on No. 42.

ἐμοὶ δοκεῖν] Paus.' view is improbable, because the Messenians were forced to beat a retreat by night from Oiniadai, which they left empty-handed (Paus. iv. 25. 9, 10). The expedition took place in 452 B.C.

τῷ ἀπὸ Λακεδαιμονίων δείματι] This would be operative so long as Elis remained the ally of Sparta. The engagement at Sphakteria took place in 424 B.C., the rupture between Elis and Sparta in 420 B.C. The date of the Victory therefore probably lies between these years.

178. Löwy, *I. G. B.* 49
Μεσσάνιοι καὶ Ναυπάκτιοι ἀνέθεν Διὶ | ᾿Ολυμπίῳ δεκάταν ἀπὸ τῶν πολεμίων | Παιώνιος ἐποίησε Μενδαῖος | καὶ τἀκρωτήρια ποιῶν ἐπὶ τὸν ναὸν ἐνίκα.

The Messenians and Naupaktians dedicated to Olympian Zeus as a tithe of the spoil of their enemies. Paionios of Mende made the statue and was a successful competitor in the construction of the gable-figures for the temple.

From the original of No. 175, preserved in the Museum at Olympia. See *F. W.* 496, 497. The later of the dates given on No. 175 is supported by the style.

τἀκρωτήρια] Figures of Victory in gilded bronze, which stood on the extremities of the gable (Paus. v. 10. 4). It is impossible to give to this word the sense of 'pediment-sculptures,' i. e. ἐναέτια (*C. I. A.* iv. 297 b, Kavvadias, *Fouilles d'Épidaure*, 241, 98, &c.). See next No.

177. Paus. v. 10. 6 τὰ δὲ ἐν τοῖς ἀετοῖς, ἔστιν ἔμπροσθεν Πέλοπος ἡ πρὸς Οἰνόμαον τῶν ἵππων ἅμιλλα ἔτι μέλλουσα, καὶ τὸ ἔργον τοῦ δρόμου παρὰ ἀμφοτέρων ἐν παρασκευῇ. Διὸς δὲ ἀγάλματος κατὰ μέσον πεποιημένου μάλιστα τὸν ἀετόν ἐστιν Οἰνόμαος ἐν δεξιᾷ τοῦ Διὸς ἐπικείμενος κράνος τῇ κεφαλῇ, παρὰ δὲ αὐτὸν γυνὴ Στερόπη, θυγατέρων καὶ αὕτη τῶν Ἄτλαντος. Μυρτίλος δέ, ὃς ἤλαυνε τῷ Οἰνομάῳ τὸ ἅρμα, κάθηται πρὸ τῶν ἵππων· οἱ δέ εἰσιν ἀριθμὸν οἱ ἵπποι τέσσαρες. μετὰ δὲ αὐτόν εἰσιν ἄνδρες δύο. ὀνόματα μέν σφισιν οὐκ ἔστι, θεραπεύειν δὲ ἄρα τοὺς ἵππους καὶ τούτοις προσετέτακτο ὑπὸ τοῦ Οἰνομάου. 7. πρὸς αὐτῷ δὲ κατάκειται τῷ πέρατι Κλάδεος· ἔχει δὲ καὶ ἐς τὰ ἄλλα παρ' Ἠλείων τιμὰς ποταμῶν μάλιστα μετά γε Ἀλφειόν. τὰ δὲ ἐς ἀρισ-

The sculptures of the front pediment represent the moment before the chariot-race of Pelops with Oinomaos, and the preparations for the contest on both sides. Just in the centre of the pediment is an image of Zeus, and on the right of Zeus is Oinomaos with a helmet on his head, and beside him stands his wife Sterope, who was also one of the daughters of Atlas. And Myrtilos who drove the chariot of Oinomaos is seated in front of the team; this consists of four horses. After him come two men; they have no names, but were doubtless also told off by Oinomaos to tend the horses. Close to the end of the pediment reclines Kladeos, who in various ways enjoys higher honours

τερὰ ἀπὸ τοῦ Διὸς ὁ Πέλοψ
καὶ Ἱπποδάμεια καὶ ὅ τε ἡνίοχός ἐστι τοῦ Πέλοπος καὶ
ἵπποι, δύο τε ἄνδρες, ἱπποκόμοι
δὴ καὶ οὗτοι τῷ Πέλοπι. καὶ
αὖθις ὁ ἀετὸς κάτεισιν ἐς
στενόν, καὶ κατὰ τοῦτο 'Αλ-
φειὸς ἐπ' αὐτοῦ πεποίηται. τῷ
δὲ ἀνδρὶ ὃς ἡνιοχεῖ τῷ Πέλοπι
λόγῳ μὲν τῷ Τροιζηνίων ἐστὶν
ὄνομα Σφαῖρος, ὁ δὲ ἐξηγητὴς
ἔφασκεν ὁ ἐν Ὀλυμπίᾳ Κίλλαν
εἶναι. 8. τὰ μὲν δὴ ἔμπροσθεν
ἐν τοῖς ἀετοῖς ἐστὶ Παιωνίου,
γένος ἐκ Μένδης τῆς Θρᾳκίας.

in Elis than any river except Alpheios. On the left of Zeus are Pelops and Hippodameia and the charioteer of Pelops and his team, and two men, doubtless also grooms employed by Pelops. Here again the lines of the pediment converge, and at this point Alpheios is represented. The charioteer of Pelops is called Sphairos in the Troizenian account, but the guide at Olympia asserted that his name was Killas. The sculptures of the front pediment are the work of Paionios, a native of Mende in Thrace.

On the east pediment of Olympia, v. *Ov.* I⁴. 309 ff., *Coll.* I. 436 ff.

ἀγάλματος] Paus. seems to think that the figure of Zeus in the centre represents a statue. This may have been due to the fact that Zeus takes no part in the action, and has no attention directed to him by the other figures.

ἐν δεξιᾷ τοῦ Διός] The two last words are absent from many MSS. Paus. refers in all such cases to *the spectator's* right or left.

ἄνδρες δύο] A mistake of Pausanias. The figures are those of an old man and a maiden.

Κλάδεος] Furtwängler and others reject this explanation (as well as Alpheios) on the ground that personifications of rivers are a product of the Hellenistic age, and regard the figures as those of spectators, but Treu justly points out that the river-gods Selinus

and Hypsas appear in human form on contemporary coins of Selinus (Head, *Historia Numorum*, Fig. 91, Gardner, *Types of Greek Coins*, Pl. ii. 16).

Παιωνίου] If the attribution of the west pediment to Alkamenes (No. 134) is improbable, that of the east pediment to Paionios is impossible, owing to the difference of style between the pediment-sculptures and the Victory. The account given to Pausanias by his guides may have arisen from a misinterpretation of the inscription of the Victory (No. 175), ἀκρωτήρια being translated 'pediment-sculptures.' An unsuccessful competitor was invented in the person of Alkamenes.

2. THEOKOSMOS OF MEGARA.

Date.—His statue of Zeus at Megara (No. 178) was incomplete on the outbreak of the Peloponnesian war (432 B.C.). He was employed in the construction of the Spartan memorial of Aigospotamoi (405 B.C.) (No. 172). His son Kallikles made a portrait of Diagoras of Rhodes, the famous περιοδονίκης, and his grandson Apellas (Paus. vi. 1. 6, cp. Plin. *N. H.* xxxiv. 56), a portrait of Kyniska, daughter of Archidamos, king of Sparta (inscription Löwy 99, dated circ. 370 B.C.).

178. Paus. i. 40. 4 (At Megara) ἐς τὸ τοῦ Διὸς τέμενος ἐσελθοῦσι καλούμενον Ὀλυμπιεῖον ναός ἐστι θεᾶς ἄξιος· τὸ δὲ ἄγαλμα οὐκ ἐξειργάσθη τοῦ Διός, ἐπιλαβόντος τοῦ Πελοποννησίων πολέμου πρὸς Ἀθηναίους, ἐν ᾧ καὶ ναυσὶν ἀνὰ πᾶν ἔτος καὶ στρατῷ φθείροντες Μεγαρεῦσιν Ἀθηναῖοι τὴν χώραν ἐκάκωσαν . . . τῷ δὲ ἀγάλματι τοῦ Διὸς πρόσωπον ἐλέφαντος καὶ χρυσοῦ, τὰ δὲ λοιπὰ πηλοῦ τέ

(At Megara) at the entrance to the precinct of Zeus called the Olympieion is a remarkable temple: the image of Zeus however was never completed, because the war between the Peloponnesians and Athenians, in the course of which the latter devastated the territory of Megara every year with their fleet and army, interrupted its construction. This image of Zeus has a

ἐστι καὶ γύψου· ποιῆσαι δὲ αὐτὸ Θεόκοσμον λέγουσιν ἐπιχώριον, συνεργάσασθαι δέ οἱ Φειδίαν. ὑπὲρ δὲ τῆς κεφαλῆς τοῦ Διός· εἰσιν Ὧραι καὶ Μοῖραι· . . . ὄπισθε δὲ τοῦ ναοῦ κεῖται ξύλα ἡμίεργα· ταῦτα ἔμελλεν ὁ Θεόκοσμος ἐλέφαντι καὶ χρυσῷ κοσμήσας τὸ ἄγαλμα ἐκτελέσειν τοῦ Διός.

face of ivory and gold, but the other parts are of clay and plaster ; they say that it was the work of Theokosmos, a native of Megara, and that Pheidias assisted him in its construction. Above the head of Zeus are figures of Seasons and Fates ; and behind the temple lie half-wrought blocks of wood. These Theokosmos was about to adorn with ivory and gold in order to complete the image of Zeus.

3. NIKODAMOS OF MAINALOS.

Date.—Androsthenes (v. infr.) was victorious in Ol. 90 (=420 B.C.). The inscription from the portrait of Damoxenidas (v. infr.) belongs to the fourth century.

179. Paus. v. 25. 7 ἐπὶ δὲ τοῦ αὐτοῦ τείχους . . . καὶ Ἡρακλέους δύο εἰσὶν ἀνδριάντες γυμνοί, παῖδες ἡλικίαν. τὸν δὲ—⟨τὸν⟩ ἐν Νεμέᾳ τοξεύοντι ἔοικε λέοντα—τοῦτον μὲν δὴ τόν τε Ἡρακλέα καὶ ὁμοῦ τῷ Ἡρακλεῖ τὸν λέοντα Ταραντῖνος ἀνέθηκεν Ἱπποτίων, Νικοδάμου δέ ἐστι Μαιναλίου τέχνη.

On the same wall are two nude figures representing Herakles as a boy. One of these appears to be shooting with arrows the lion of Nemea. This group—both the Herakles and the lion— was dedicated by Hippotion of Tarentum, and is the work of Nikodamos of Mainalos.

Other works (all at Olympia) :—

ATHENA, wearing aegis and helmet (Paus. v. 26. 6).

Athlete statues :—

Androsthenes of Mainalos, victor in the pankration, Ol. 90 (=420 B. C.) (Paus. vi. 6. 1).

Damoxenidas of Mainalos, victor in boxing (Paus. vi. 6. 3). Inscription Löwy 98.

Antiochos of Lepreon, victor in the pankration (Paus. vi. 3. 9).

4. TELEPHANES OF PHOKIS.

180. Plin. *N. H.* xxxiv. 68 Artifices qui compositis uoluminibus condidere haec miris laudibus celebrant Telephanen Phocaeum ignotum alias, quoniam Thessaliae habitauerit et ibi opera eius latuerint, alioqui suffragiis ipsorum aequatur Polyclito Myroni Pythagorae. Laudant eius Larisam et Spintharum pentathlum et Apollinem ; alii non hanc ignobilitatis fuisse causam, sed quod se regum Xerxis atque Darii officinis dediderit existimant.

The artists who have composed set treatises on this subject bestow extraordinary praise on Telephanes the Phokian, who is otherwise unknown, since he lived in Thessaly and his works remained unnoticed in that country, but is placed by their own testimony on a footing of equality with Polykleitos, Myron and Pythagoras. They praise his Larisa, his portrait of Spintharos, a victor in the five contests, and his Apollo. Others assert that this was not the cause of his lack of fame, but rather the fact that he devoted his talents to the service of Xerxes and Darius.

Phocaeum] Probably 'of Phokis,' possibly 'of Phokaia.'

artifices] Perhaps Xenokrates and Antigonos (v. Introduction, § 1). The selection of the names—Polykleitos, Myron, and Pythagoras—seems to suggest that he had a place in the series of bronze-casters of whom Pliny quotes criticisms (Introduction, § 2).

The names of Persian kings are given at random (Xerxes 485–465 B.C., Darius 424–405 B.C.).

5. THE METOPES OF OLYMPIA.

181. Paus. v. 10. 9 ἔστι δὲ ἐν Ὀλυμπίᾳ καὶ Ἡρακλέους τὰ πολλὰ τῶν ἔργων. ὑπὲρ μὲν τοῦ ναοῦ πεποίηται τῶν θυρῶν ἡ ἐξ Ἀρκαδίας ἄγρα τοῦ ὑός, καὶ τὰ πρὸς Διομήδην τὸν Θρᾷκα καὶ ἐν Ἐρυθείᾳ πρὸς Γηρυόνην, καὶ Ἄτλαντός τε τὸ φόρημα ἐκδέχεσθαι μέλλων καὶ τῆς κόπρου καθαίρων τὴν γῆν ἐστιν Ἠλείοις. ὑπὲρ δὲ τοῦ ὀπισθοδόμου τῶν θυρῶν τοῦ ζωστῆρος τὴν Ἀμαζόνα ἐστὶν ἀφαιρούμενος, καὶ τὰ ἐς τὴν ἔλαφον καὶ τὸν ἐν Κνωσῷ ταῦρον, καὶ ὄρνιθας τὰς ἐπὶ Στυμφήλῳ καὶ ἐς ὕδραν τε καὶ τὸν ἐν τῇ γῇ Ἀργείᾳ λέοντα.

Most of the labours of Herakles are represented at Olympia. Above the door of the temple is the hunt of the Arkadian boar and the fight with Diomedes the Thracian and with Geryon at Erytheia, and Herakles about to receive Atlas' burden and the same hero clearing the land of dung for the Eleans. Over the back door of the temple is Herakles stripping the Amazon of her belt and the hunting of the stag and of the bull of Knossos, and the birds of Stymphalos, and the hydra, and the lion in the land of Argos.

Fragments of all these metopes, and of a twelfth belonging to the west front, and representing Kerberos, have been discovered at Olympia (*Ov.* I⁴. 332 ff., *Coll.* I. 429 ff.).

Ἄτλαντος ... μέλλων] Paus. has inverted the order of the names. Herakles is in reality represented as upholding the heavenly globe, while Atlas approaches with the apples of the Hesperides.

PART IV.

SCULPTURE IN
THE FOURTH CENTURY.

Nos. 182–260.

§ 1. THE ATTIC SCHOOL.

1. THE FAMILY OF KEPHISODOTOS.

(a) Kephisodotos the Elder.

Date.—Since the younger K. was the son of Praxiteles, it is inferred that the elder was his father. He may however have been his elder brother, since Pliny dates him Ol. 102 = 372 B. C., and the cult of Eirene (No. 184) was introduced at Athens in 375 B. C. His sister was the wife of Phokion (402-317 B. C.).

182. Plin. *N. H.* xxxiv. 87 Cephisodoti duo fuere ; prioris est Mercurius Liberum patrem in infantia nutriens; fecit et contionantem manu elata, persona in incerto est.

There were two sculptors named Kephisodotos ; by the earlier is a Hermes nursing the infant Dionysos. He also represented an orator addressing his audience with uplifted arm ; the name however is uncertain.

183. Plin. *N. H.* xxxiv. 74 Cephisodotus (fecit) Mineruam mirabilem in portu Atheniensium et aram ad templum Iouis Seruatoris in eodem portu, cui pauca comparantur.

Kephisodotos was the sculptor of a remarkable statue of Athena in the harbour of Athens, and an altar in the temple of Zeus the Saviour in the same harbour, which has few rivals.

Paus. i. i. 3 describes the precinct of Zeus (Soter) and Athena (Soteira) at the Piraeus, and mentions two statues of bronze, one of Zeus, with sceptre and Victory, the other of Athena, with spear. These are generally identified with the works referred to by Pliny.

184. Paus. ix. 16. 1 Θηβαίοις δὲ . . . Τύχης ἐστὶν ἱερόν· φέρει μὲν δὴ Πλοῦτον παῖδα· ὡς δὲ Θηβαῖοι λέγουσι, χεῖρας μὲν τοῦ ἀγάλματος καὶ πρόσωπον Ξενοφῶν εἰργάσατο Ἀθηναῖος, Καλλιστόνικος δὲ τὰ λοιπὰ ἐπιχώριος. σοφὸν μὲν δὴ καὶ τούτοις τὸ βούλευμα ἐσθεῖναι Πλοῦτον ἐς τὰς χεῖρας ἅτε μητρὶ ἢ τροφῷ τῇ Τύχῃ· σοφὸν δὲ οὐχ ἧσσον Κηφισοδότου· καὶ γὰρ οὗτος τῆς Εἰρήνης τὸ ἄγαλμα Ἀθηναίοις Πλοῦτον ἔχουσαν πεποίηκεν.

At Thebes there is a sanctuary of Fortune: and the goddess bears in her arms the child Wealth. The Thebans allege that the hands and face of the statue were made by Xenophon of Athens, and the rest of the figure by Kallistonikos, a native of Thebes. It was an ingenious device of theirs to place Wealth in the arms of Fortune, as his mother or nurse; and no less ingenious was that of Kephisodotos, for he made for the Athenians an image of Peace bearing the child Wealth in her arms.

From Paus. i. 8. 2 we learn that the statue of Peace and Wealth stood beside the statue of the Eponymi on the Areopagus. It is reproduced on coins of Athens, *Num. Comm. DD.* ix, x, and the so-called Leukothea in the Glyptothek at Munich (*F. W.* 1210) is a copy.

185. Paus. ix. 30. 1 ταῖς Μούσαις δὲ ἀγάλματα μὲν πρῶτά ἐστι Κηφισοδότου τέχνη πάσαις. προελθόντι δὲ οὐ πολύ, τρεῖς μέν εἰσιν αὖθις Κηφισοδότου.

The first group of statues of the Muses are all the work of Kephisodotos. A little farther on is another group, of which three again are by Kephisodotos.

On Mount Helikon. The remaining Muses of the second group were by Strongylion (No. 151) and Olympiosthenes.

(b) PRAXITELES.

Date.—Plin. gives Ol. 104 (364 B.C.), and this is the only recorded date, except for the doubtful statements of Vitruvius (vii. Praef. 12), that he was employed on the Mausoleion (353 B.C.) and of Strabo (xiv. 641) that he made an altar for the temple of Artemis at Ephesos (after the fire of 356 B.C.). As the date of his sons in Pliny's table (Ol. 121 = 296 B.C.) seems to be too late (v. infr. (c)), his career may perhaps be placed circ. 370–330 B.C. The only inscription (Löwy 76 from Leuktra) falls towards the close of this period, and belongs to a portrait. On the various dates assigned to the Hermes of Olympia see No. 193 note.

186. Plin. *N. H.* xxxvi. 20 Praxitelis aetatem inter statuarios diximus, qui marmoris gloria superauit etiam semet. Opera eius sunt Athenis in Ceramico, sed ante omnia est non solum Praxitelis uerum in toto orbe terrarum Uenus quam ut uiderent multi nauigauerunt Cnidum. Duas fecerat simulque uendebat, alteram uelata specie, quam ob id praetulerunt quorum condicio erat Coi, cum eodem pretio detulisset, seuerum id ac pudicum arbitrantes ; reiectam Cnidii emerunt immensa differentia famae. 21. Uoluit eam a Cnidiis postea emercari

In my account of the bronze-casters I have mentioned the date of Praxiteles, who surpassed even himself by the fame of his work in marble. His works may be seen at Athens in the Potter's Quarter, but the Aphrodite, to see which many have sailed to Knidos, is the finest statue not only by Praxiteles, but in the whole world. He had made and was offering for sale two figures of Aphrodite, one whose form was draped, and which was therefore preferred by the people of Kos, to whom the choice of either figure was offered at the same price, as

rex Nicomedes, totum aes alienum, quod erat ingens, ciuitatis dissoluturum se promittens ; omnia perpeti maluere, nec immerito ; illo enim signo Praxiteles nobilitauit Cnidum. Aedicula eius tota aperitur, ut conspici possit undique effigies dea fauente ipsa, ut creditur, facta ; nec minor ex quacumque parte admiratio est. . . . 22. Sunt in Cnido et alia signa marmorea illustrium artificum, Liber Pater Bryaxidis et alter Scopae et Minerua nec maius aliud Ueneris Praxiteliae specimen, quam quod inter haec sola memoratur. Eiusdem est et Cupido objectus a Cicerone Verri, ille propter quem Thespiae uisebantur, nunc in Octauiae scholis positus. 23. Eiusdem et alter nudus in Pario colonia Propontidis, par Ueneri Cnidiae nobilitate. . . . Romae Praxitelis opera sunt Flora Triptolemus Ceres in hortis Seruilianis, Boni Euentus et Bonae Fortunae simulacra

the more chaste and severe, while the other which they rejected was bought by the Knidians, and became immeasurably more celebrated. King Nikomedes wished to buy it from the Knidians, and offered to discharge the whole debt of the city, which was enormous : but they preferred to undergo the worst, and justly so, for by that statue Praxiteles made Knidos famous. The shrine which contains it is quite open, so that the image, made, as is believed, under the direct inspiration of the goddess, can be seen from all sides : and from all sides it is equally admired. There are in Knidos other statues by artists of the first rank— a Dionysos of Bryaxis, another Dionysos and an Athena by Skopas — and there is no greater testimony to the Aphrodite of Praxiteles than the fact that amongst all these it is the only one thought worthy of mention. By Praxiteles also is the Eros which

in Capitolio, item Maena-
des et quas Thyiadas
uocant et Caryatides et
Sileni, in Pollionis Asinii
monumentis et Apollo et
Neptunus.

Cicero cast in the teeth of
Verres, which formerly drew
travellers to Thespiai, and
now stands in the gallery
of Octavia, also another
nude Eros in the colony of
Parion on the Propontis,
whose fame equals that of
the Knidian Aphrodite.
The works of Praxiteles
preserved at Rome are :—
Flora, Triptolemos and
Demeter in the gardens of
Servilius, figures of Good
Luck and Good Fortune on
the Capitol, where are also
Maenads and Thyiades, as
they are called, Karyatids,
and Sileni; lastly Apollo
and Poseidon in the gallery
of Asinius Pollio.

inter statuarios] See No. 189.

Uenus] See Nos. 187, 188. Athenaios says that Phryne (No. 196) served as a model, while Clement of Alexandria tells the same story of Kratina. The statue is represented on coins of Knidos (*Ov.* II⁴. Fig. 156). On the existing copies v. *F. W.* 1215. A fine head is published in *Antike Denkmäler* i. 41.

Nicomedes] N. III, king of Bithynia, 90–74 B. C. The debt was due to the forced contribution levied by Sulla in 84 B. C.

Bryaxidis ... Scopae] See No. 2 (a), (b).

Cupido] Paus. ix. 27. 3 tells us that it was of Pentelic marble. It was transferred to Rome by Gaius, restored to Thespiai by Claudius, and finally transported to Rome by Nero, where it was destroyed by fire in 80 A. D. Cicero mentions it in *Verr.* iv. 2. 4 and iv. 60. 135, while inveighing against Verres for robbing Heius of Messana of another Eros by Praxiteles. The statue was presented by P. to Phryne, and dedicated by her in her native town (Ath. xiii. 591 B). Thespiai was dismantled by the Thebans in 37¾ B.C., and (apparently) not restored until after Chaironeia, so that Phryne must have been born before the former year, and must have dedicated the Eros while the town was still subject to Thebes.

alter nudus in Pario] Represented on coins of Parion (*Ov.* II⁴. Fig. 152).

Flora] The figure doubtless represented Kore (Persephone), and was mistaken for Flora because holding a garland to crown Triptolemos, whose departure was represented by the group.

Boni Euentus et Bonae Fortunae] Ἀγαθὸς δαίμων and Ἀγαθὴ Τύχη.

Thyiadas] Attic maidens, who joined in the orgies of Dionysos on Parnassos.

Caryatides] Spartan maidens of Karyai in Lakonia, who danced at festivals of Artemis. See No. 153 note.

---

187. Lucian, Εἰκόνες 6 καὶ μὴν ἤδη σοι ὁρᾶν παρέχει γιγνομένην τὴν εἰκόνα ὧδε συναρμόζων, τῆς ἐκ Κνίδου ἠκούσης μόνον τὴν κεφαλὴν λαβών ... τὰ μὲν ἀμφὶ τὴν κόμην καὶ μέτωπον ὀφρύων τε τὸ εὔγραμμον ἐάσει ἔχειν ὥσπερ ὁ Πραξιτέλης ἐποίησε, καὶ τῶν ὀφθαλμῶν δὲ τὸ ὑγρὸν ἅμα τῷ φαιδρῷ καὶ κεχαρισμένῳ, καὶ τοῦτο διαφυλάξει κατὰ τὸ Πραξιτέλει δοκοῦν.

Now he will allow you to see the growth of the figure as he constructs it piece by piece, taking the head only from the goddess of Knidos. The hair and forehead and the finely-pencilled eyebrows he will allow her to keep as Praxiteles made them, and in the melting gaze of the eyes with their bright and joyous expression he will also preserve the spirit of Praxiteles.

Cp. Nos. 83, 103, 118.

---

188. Lucian, Ἔρωτες 13 ἡ μὲν οὖν θεὸς ἐν μέσῳ καθί-

The goddess stands in the midst of her shrine, and

δρυται . . . ὑπερήφανον καὶ σεσηρότι γέλωτι μικρὸν ὑπομειδιῶσα.

a disdainful smile plays gently over her parted lips.

From a description of the shrine at Knidos mentioned in No. 186.

σεσηρότι] The word is properly applied to the grin of a dog, and hence to a smile in which the lips are parted and the teeth appear. Cp. Theokr. vii. 19 σεσαρὼς | ὄμματι μειδιόωντι.

189. Plin. *N. H.* xxxiv. 69 Praxiteles quoque marmore felicior, ideo et clarior fuit, fecit tamen et ex aere pulcherrima opera, Proserpinae raptum, item catagusam, et Liberum patrem ebriolatum nobilemque una Satyrum quem Graeci περιβοητόν cognominant, et signa quae ante Felicitatis aedem fuere Ueneremque quae et ipsa aedis incendio cremata est Claudii principatu marmoreae illi suae per terras inclutae parem item stephanusam, pseliumenen, canephoram, 70. Harmodium et Aristogitonem tyrannicidas, quos a Xerxe Persarum rege captos uicta Perside Atheniensibus remisit Magnus Alexander. Fecit et puberem Apollinem subrepenti lacertae cominus sagitta insidian-

Praxiteles too, though he was more prolific and therefore more famous as a sculptor in marble, produced works of great beauty in bronze—the rape of Persephone and also her restoration, as well as Dionysos merry with wine, and with him the celebrated Satyr called by the Greeks 'the World - famed,' and the statues which stood before the temple of Good Fortune, and the Aphrodite which, like them, was destroyed by fire when the temple was burnt in the reign of Claudius, a statue as fine as her world-famous peer in marble; also a woman with a garland, another putting on her bracelets, and a third bearing a basket, and Harmodios and Aristogiton the slayers of

tem, quem σαυροκτόνον uo-
cant. Spectantur et duo
signa eius diuersos adfectus
exprimentia, flentis ma-
tronae et meretricis gau-
dentis ; hanc putant Phrynen fuisse deprehenduntque
in ea amorem artificis et
mercedem in uoltu mere-
tricis.   Habet simulacrum
et benignitas eius. Calamidis enim quadrigae aurigam suum imposuit, ne
melior in equorum effigie
defecisse in homine crederetur.

the tyrant, which were
captured by Xerxes, king
of Persia, and restored to
the Athenians by Alex-
ander the Great after the
conquest of Persia.   He
also represented Apollo as
a boy lying in wait for the
lizard which steals up to
him and ready to strike with
his arrow at close quarters
(known as the Lizard-
slayer). Two of his statues
also which portray opposite
emotions are notable sights;
they are the Weeping Ma-
tron and the Rejoicing
Harlot ; the latter is supposed to represent Phryne,
and one may detect in it
the passion of the artist
and his reward depicted in
the countenance of the harlot.   There is also a statue
which bears witness to his
kindness. For he placed
a charioteer of his own
on a four-horse chariot of
Kalamis, lest the artist who
excelled in representing
horses, should be thought
to have failed in his treatment of the human frame.

catagusam] κατάγουσαν. Either (1) Hekate '*bringing back*' Persephone from Hades ; or (2) 'the spinning-girl.'

ebriolatum] Suggested by Milani for 'Ebrietatem' of MSS. (=Μέθη).

signa . . . fuere] Cic. *Verr.* iv. 2. 4 and Plin. *N. H.* xxxvi. 39 call these 'Thespiades,' and the first-named writer mentions that they were brought by L. Mummius from Thespiai. Probably they represented the Muses. Cp. Varro, *L. L.* vi. 2 Thespiades deae, Musae, a Thespiis Boeotiae oppido.

stephanusam] στεφάνουσαν. Possibly Nike holding a garland.

pseliumenen] ψελιουμένην. ψέλιον = bracelet.

canephoram] So Urlichs for 'ephoram' of the best MS. Another MS. reads 'oporam' = ὀπώραν (Autumn).

Harmodium et Aristogitonem] Erroneously ascribed to Praxiteles by Pliny. See No. 64 note.

Apollinem] On existing copies see *F. W.* 1214.

duo signa] Not necessarily grouped. The description may have been borrowed by Pliny from an epigram.

Phrynen] See No. 196.

Habet simulacrum, &c.] See No. 88. Attributed, but not with certainty, to the elder Praxiteles.

190. Paus. viii. 9. 1 τὸ δὲ ἕτερον Λητοῦς ἐστὶν ἱερὸν καὶ τῶν παίδων· Πραξιτέλης δὲ τὰ ἀγάλματα εἰργάσατο τρίτῃ μετὰ ᾿Αλκαμένην ὕστερον γενεᾷ· τούτων πεποιημένα ἐστὶν ἐπὶ τῷ βάθρῳ Μοῦσαι καὶ Μαρσύας αὐλῶν.

The other is a temple of Leto and her children ; Praxiteles made their statues in the third generation after Alkamenes. On the base which supports them are represented the Muses and Marsyas playing the flute.

At Mantineia. Three slabs from the base were discovered in 1887, and published in *Bull. Corr. Hell.* 1888, i–iii. See *Ov.* II⁴. 61 f. Figs. 160, 161. As *all* the Muses were (probably) represented, we must read Μοῦσαι for Μοῦσα in the text of Paus.

191. Paus. i. 23. 7 καὶ ᾿Αρτέμιδος ἱερόν ἐστι Βραυρωνίας,

There is also a temple of Artemis Brauronia ; the

Πραξιτέλους μὲν τέχνη τὸ ἄγαλμα.

image is the work of Praxiteles.

The inscriptions with inventories of treasure from the Akropolis mention *two* statues in the temple—(1) τὸ ἕδος τὸ ἀρχαῖον: (2) τὸ ἄγαλμα τὸ ὀρθόν. The latter must be that of Praxiteles, and since the first is also called τὸ λίθινον ἕδος, it seems to follow that the latter was of bronze or some other material, not marble. Robert supposes, but without sufficient reason, that it was of gold and ivory, and the work of the elder Praxiteles. Studniczka identifies it with the original of the 'Artemis of Gabii' in the Louvre (Brunn-Bruckmann 59). It was clothed in actual garments.

192. Paus. x. 37. 1 τῆς πόλεως δὲ ἐν δεξιᾷ, δύο μάλιστα προελθόντι ἀπ' αὐτῆς σταδίους, πέτρα τέ ἐστιν ὑψηλή, μοῖρα ὄρους ἡ πέτρα, καὶ ἱερὸν ἐπ' αὐτῆς πεποιημένον ἐστὶν 'Αρτέμιδος· ἔργων τῶν Πραξιτέλους, δᾷδα ἔχουσα ἐν τῇ δεξιᾷ καὶ ὑπὲρ τῶν ὤμων φαρέτραν, παρὰ δὲ αὐτὴν κύων ἐν ἀριστερᾷ, μέγεθος δὲ ὑπὲρ τὴν μεγίστην γυναῖκα τὸ ἄγαλμα.

On the right of the city, and about two stades distant from it, stands a high rock, a fragment of a mountain, and upon it is built a temple of Artemis: the statue is the work of Praxiteles; it holds a torch in the right hand and a quiver hangs from the shoulder; beside it, on the left, is a dog; and it is taller than the tallest woman.

At Antikyra, on the coins of which city the statue is represented, *Num. Comm. A.* xiv.

193. Paus. v. 17. 3 χρόνῳ δὲ ὕστερον καὶ ἄλλα ἀνέθεσαν ἐς τὸ 'Ηραῖον, 'Ερμῆν λίθου, Διόνυσον δὲ φέρει νήπιον, τέχνῃ δέ ἐστι Πραξιτέλους.

In later times other offerings were dedicated in the Heraion. Amongst these was a Hermes of marble, bearing the infant Dionysos, the work of Praxiteles.

At Olympia ; discovered May 8, 1877. See *F. W.* 1212.

S. Reinach (*Rev. Arch.* 1888, p. 1 ff.) conjectures that the work was symbolic of a peace concluded in 363 B. C. between Elis (represented by Dionysos, Paus. vi. 26. 1) and Arkadia (represented by Hermes), while Furtw. *Meisterwerke*, p. 531, refers it to an alliance between the oligarchs of Elis and Arkadia in 343 B.C. (Diod. xvi. 63).

194. Paus. ii. 21. 8 (At Argos) τὸ δὲ ἱερὸν τῆς Λητοῦς ἐστὶ μὲν οὐ μακρὰν τοῦ τροπαίου, τέχνη δὲ τὸ ἄγαλμα Πραξιτέλους. 9. τὴν δὲ εἰκόνα παρὰ τῇ θεῷ τῆς παρθένου Χλῶριν ὀνομάζουσι Νιόβης μὲν θυγατέρα εἶναι λέγοντες, Μελίβοιαν δὲ καλεῖσθαι τὸ ἐξ ἀρχῆς.

(At Argos) the temple of Leto is not far from the trophy ; the image is the work of Praxiteles, and the figure of a maiden standing by the goddess they call Chloris, asserting that she was the daughter of Niobe, originally called Meliboia.

Represented on coins of Argos, *Num. Comm. K.* xxxvi–xxxviii.

195. Paus. i. 20. 1 ἔστι δὲ ὁδὸς ἀπὸ τοῦ Πρυτανείου καλουμένη Τρίποδες· ἀφ' οὗ καλοῦσι τὸ χωρίον, ναοὶ ὅσον ἐς τοῦτο μεγάλοι καί σφισιν ἐφεστήκασι τρίποδες, χαλκοῖ μὲν, μνήμης δὲ ἄξια μάλιστα περιέχοντες εἰργασμένα. Σάτυρος γάρ ἐστιν, ἐφ' ᾧ Πραξιτέλην λέγεται φρονῆσαι μέγα.

There is a street leading from the Prytaneion called the Street of Tripods ; the place takes its name from the shrines large enough to support tripods, which stand upon them. These are of bronze, but they contain very remarkable works of art, amongst which is a Satyr, of which Praxiteles is said to have been extremely proud.

ὅσον] Robert's correction for MSS. θεῶν.

The story ran that Phryne exacted from Praxiteles a promise to give her his most beautiful work, and entrapped him into declaring his own preference by a false report that most of the works in his studio had been destroyed by fire. He coupled this Satyr in his inquiries with the Eros, which she chose and dedicated at Thespiai.

196. Paus. x. 15. 1 Φρύνης δὲ εἰκόνα ἐπίχρυσον Πραξιτέλης μὲν εἰργάσατο ἐραστὴς καὶ οὗτος· ἀνάθημα δὲ αὐτῆς Φρύνης ἐστὶν ἡ εἰκών.

A gilded portrait statue of Phryne was made by Praxiteles, who was also her lover ; and the portrait was dedicated by Phryne herself.

At Delphi. Athenaios (xiii. 591 B) tells us on the authority of Alketas, who wrote a guide to Delphi, that this statue stood between those of Archidamos, king of Sparta, and Philip of Macedon, and bore the inscription Φρύνη Ἐπικλέους Θεσπική.

197. Paus. i. 43. 6 (At Megara) μετὰ δὲ τοῦ Διονύσου τὸ ἱερόν ἐστιν Ἀφροδίτης ναός. ... Πειθὼ δὲ καὶ ἑτέρα θεός, ἣν Παρήγορον ὀνομάζουσιν, ἔργα Πραξιτέλους, Σκόπα δὲ Ἔρως καὶ Ἵμερος καὶ Πόθος· εἴδη διάφορά ἐστι κατὰ ταὐτὰ τοῖς ὀνόμασι καὶ τὰ ἔργα σφισί.

(At Megara) Next to the shrine of Dionysos is a temple of Aphrodite. In it are Persuasion, and another divinity, whom they call Consolation, works of Praxiteles, and Eros, Yearning and Desire by Skopas. The forms of the three differ as their names, and also their functions, differ.

εἴδη] Overbeck's correction for MSS. εἰ δή, '*if indeed* their functions differ as their names do.'

198. Diod. xxvi. Fr. ad init. Πραξιτέλης, ὁ καταμίξας ἄκρως τοῖς λιθίνοις ἔργοις τὰ τῆς ψυχῆς πάθη.

Praxiteles, who with consummate art informed his marble figures with the passions of the soul.

Other works :—

APOLLO, LETO, and ARTEMIS at Megara (Paus. i. 44. 2). Represented on coins of Megara, *Num. Comm. A.* x.

HERA, ATHENA, and HEBE at Mantineia (Paus. viii. 9. 3).

The TWELVE GODS in the temple of Artemis the Saviour, at Megara (Paus. i. 40. 3). Cp. No. 150. Sometimes attributed to the elder Praxiteles on account of the association with Strongylion.

DIONYSOS at Elis (Paus. vi. 26. 1). Represented on coins of Elis, *Num. Comm.* p. 74.

TYCHE at Megara (Paus. i. 43. 6). Represented on coins of Megara, *Num. Comm. A.* xiv.

TROPHONIOS at Lebadeia, similar in type to Asklepios (Paus. ix. 39. 4).

SATYR in the temple of Dionysos at Megara (Paus. i. 43. 5).

APHRODITE and PHRYNE at Thespiai (Paus. ix. 27. 5).

APHRODITE at Alexandria in Karia (Steph. Byz. s.v. 'Αλεξανδρεία)

WARRIOR with HORSE on a tomb at Athens (Paus. i. 2. 3).

DANAE, the Nymphs, and Pan (*Anth. Pal.* vi. 317, *Plan.* iv. 262).

Strabo (xiv. 641) mentions P. as the artist of the altar in the temple of Artemis at Ephesos, while Vitruvius (vii. Praef. 12) enumerates him amongst the sculptors of the Mausoleion. Kallistratos describes an Eros (*Stat.* 3), a Dionysos (*Stat.* 8), and a Diadumenos (*Stat.* 11), professedly by Praxiteles, in rhetorical style.

Works of doubtful origin :—

199. Plin. *N. H.* xxxvi. 28 Par haesitatio est in templo Apollinis Sosiani, Niobae liberos morientis Scopas an Praxiteles fecerit, item Janus pater in suo templo dicatus ab Augusto ex Aegypto aduectus utrius manus sit, iam quidem et auro occultatus. Similiter in curia Octauia quaeritur de

The same doubt arises as to whether Skopas or Praxiteles made the group of Niobe's children meeting their death in the temple of Apollo Sosianus ; and again, to which of these artists is to be attributed the Janus brought from Egypt, and dedicated by Augustus in his own temple,

Cupidine fulmen tenente; which is now coated with id demum affirmatur, Alcibiaden esse, principem forma in ea aetate.

which is now coated with gold. The same question is debated with reference to the Eros holding a thunderbolt in the Council-chamber of Octavia; all that is positively asserted is that the figure represents Alkibiades, the reigning beauty of that time.

Apollinis Sosiani] C. Sosius, a legatus of Antony, commanded in Syria 38 B. C., and was pardoned by Augustus after Actium. He built a temple to Apollo on the Palatine.

Niobae liberos morientis] On the existing copies of this group see *Ov.* II⁴. Book iii. ch. 4, and *F. W.* 1247–1259.

Janus pater] This was no doubt a double-faced bust of Hermes which served as the Roman Janus.

Alcibiaden] The popular tradition, involving a chronological error of half a century.

Works attributed to the elder Praxiteles :—

200. Paus. i. 2. 4 ἐσελ-θόντων δὲ ἐς τὴν πόλιν οἰκο-δόμημα ἐς παρασκευήν ἐστι τῶν πομπῶν ... καὶ πλησίον ναός ἐστι Δήμητρος· ἀγάλματα δὲ αὐτή τε καὶ ἡ παῖς καὶ δᾷδα ἔχων Ἴακχος· γέγραπται δὲ ἐπὶ τῷ τοίχῳ γράμμασιν Ἀττι-κοῖς ἔργα εἶναι Πραξιτέλους.

At the entrance of the city is a building where the processions are arranged, and near it is a temple of Demeter; in this are statues of Demeter herself and her daughter, and Iacchos holding a torch; and on the wall is an inscription in the Attic alphabet stating that they are the work of Praxiteles.

ἐσελθόντων] By the Dipylon gate of Athens.

γράμμασιν 'Αττικοῖς] Superseded by the Ionic alphabet in 403 B. C. Unless we attribute the work to the elder Praxiteles we must suppose with Köhler that the inscription was re-engraved in the Attic alphabet under Hadrian, when such antiquarian revivals were not uncommon, or with Löschcke, that as the inscription was on the wall it had no real connection with the group.

201. Paus. ix. 2. 7 Πλαταιεῦσι δὲ ναός ἐστιν "Ηρας, θέας ἄξιος μεγέθει τε καὶ ἐς τῶν ἀγαλμάτων τὸν κόσμον. ἐσελθοῦσι μὲν 'Ρέα τὸν πέτραν κατειλημένον σπαργάνοις, οἷα δὴ τὸν παῖδα ὃν ἔτεκε, Κρόνῳ κομίζουσά ἐστι· τὴν δὲ "Ηραν Τελείαν καλοῦσι. πεποίηται δὲ ὀρθὸν μεγέθει ἄγαλμα μέγα· λίθου δὲ ἀμφότερα τοῦ Πεντελησίου, Πραξιτέλους δέ ἐστιν ἔργα.

The Plataeans have a temple of Hera, remarkable both for its size and for the statues which adorn it. At the entrance is Rhea, bearing to Kronos the rock rolled up in swaddling clothes, as though it were the child which she bore. Hera they call 'the Goddess of Wedlock'; she is represented by a colossal standing figure. Both are of Pentelic marble and are the work of Praxiteles.

The temple of Hera was erected 42⅞ B. C. (Thuc. iii. 68).

202. Paus. ix. 11. 6 Θηβαίοις δὲ τὰ ἐν τοῖς ἀετοῖς Πραξιτέλης ἐποίησε τὰ πολλὰ τῶν δώδεκα καλουμένων ἄθλων· καί σφισι τὰ ἐς τὰς ὄρνιθας ἐνδεῖ τὰς ἐπὶ Στυμφήλῳ, καὶ ὡς ἐκάθηρεν 'Ηρακλῆς τὴν 'Ηλείαν χώραν ἀντὶ τούτων δὲ ἡ πρὸς 'Ανταῖον πάλη πεποίηται.

The pediment-sculptures were made for the Thebans by Praxiteles, and represent most of the Twelve Labours of Herakles, as they are called ; the hunting of the birds of Stymphalos, and the cleansing of the land of Elis are wanting, and in their place is the wrestling-match of Antaios.

M 2

Without a parallel among the works of the great Praxiteles, and possibly to be connected with the Athena and Herakles of Alkamenes, dedicated in the same temple 403 B.C. (No. 133).

For the connexion of Praxiteles (perhaps the elder) and Kalamis see No. 189 ad fin.

(c) THE SONS OF PRAXITELES.

(Kephisodotos the younger and Timarchos.)

Date.—Three inscriptions (Löwy 108–110), one from the portrait of Menander (L. 108), one from that of a priestess of Athena Polias (L. 109), and one from a pair of portraits at Megara (L. 110), may be dated at the close of the fourth century. Lycurgos (No. 205) died 323 B.C., Menander in 291 B.C., Myro flourished circ. 284 B.C. Two further inscriptions (Löwy 111, 112, from portraits) of Kephisodotos only seem rather earlier, showing K. to be the elder brother.

203. Plin. *N. H.* xxxvi. 24 Praxitelis filius Cephisodotus et artis heres fuit. Cuius laudatum est Pergami symplegma nobile digitis corpori uerius quam marmori impressis. Romae eius opera sunt Latona in Palatii delubro, Uenus in Pollionis Asinii monumentis et intra Octauiae porticus in Iunonis aede Aesculapius ac Diana.

Kephisodotos was the son of Praxiteles and the heir of his talent. Much praise has been bestowed on his famous group of interlaced figures at Pergamon, where the pressure of the fingers seems to be exerted on flesh rather than marble. His works preserved at Rome are a Leto in the temple on the Palatine, an Aphrodite in the gallery of Asinius Pollio, and an Asklepios and Artemis in the temple of Juno within the colonnade of Octavia.

symplegma] Formerly supposed to mean a group of wrestlers, but almost certainly of an erotic character.

204. Paus. viii. 30. 10
ταύτης τῆς στοᾶς ἐστιν ἐγγυ-
τάτω ὡς πρὸς ἥλιον ἀνίσχοντα
ἱερὸν Σωτῆρος ἐπίκλησιν Διός·
κεκόσμηται δὲ πέριξ κίοσι.
καθεζομένῳ δὲ τῷ Διὶ ἐν θρόνῳ
παρεστήκασιν τῇ μὲν ἡ Μεγάλη
Πόλις, ἐν ἀριστερᾷ δὲ 'Αρτέμιδος Σωτείρας ἄγαλμα· ταῦτα
μὲν λίθου τοῦ Πεντελησίου
'Αθηναῖοι Κηφισόδοτος καὶ
Ξενοφῶν εἰργάσαντο.

Close to the portico on the Eastern side is a temple of Zeus called the Saviour, which is surrounded by a colonnade. Zeus is seated on a throne, and beside him stand on the right Megalo-polis, and on the left an image of Artemis the Saviour. These are of Pentelic marble, and are the work of the Athenians Kephisodotos and Xenophon.

At Megalopolis. The precinct of Zeus Soter, discovered by the English excavators, is dated by Dörpfeld considerably later than the foundation of the city (371 B.C.). The work must therefore belong to the younger K. The statue is represented on coins of Megalopolis, *Num. Comm.* V. 1.

205. Plut. Uita x. Or.
Lycurg. 38 καὶ εἰκόνες ξυλίναι
τοῦ τε Λυκούργου καὶ τῶν υἱῶν
αὐτοῦ "Αβρωνος Λυκούργου,
Λυκόφρονος, ἃς εἰργάσαντο
Τίμαρχος καὶ Κηφισόδοτος οἱ
Πραξιτέλους παῖδες.

There are wooden por-trait statues of Lykurgos and his sons, Habron, Lykurgos and Lykophron, made by Kephisodotos and Timarchos, the sons of Praxiteles.

Other works (1) by Kephisodotos only :—
Portraits of the poetesses MYRO and ANYTE (Tatian *c. Graec.* 52).
    ,,   'philosophers' (Plin. *N. H.* xxxiv. 87).
(2) By Kephisodotos and Timarchos :—
ENYO in the temple of Ares at Athens (Paus. i. 8. 4).
KADMOS of Thebes (Paus. ix. 12. 4).

Portrait of Menander (Löwy 108).

Not to be identified with the statue of Menander in the Vatican (*F. W.* 1622), which must have matched that of Poseidippos, (whose plays were not performed in M.'s lifetime), and is moreover too large for the inscribed base.

2. SKOPAS AND THE SCULPTORS OF THE MAUSOLEION.

(a) SKOPAS.

Date.—S. *may* have been the son of Aristandros of Paros (v. No. 162), employed on a memorial of Aigospotamoi (405 B. C.). He was employed on the restoration of the temple of Athena Alea at Tegea (destroyed by fire 394 B. C.) and on the Mausoleion (begun about 353 B.C.).

206. Plin. *N. H.* xxxvi. 25 Scopae laus cum his certat. Is fecit Uenerem et Pothon qui Samothrace sanctissimis caerimoniis coluntur, item Apollinem Palatinum, Uestam sedentem laudatam in Seruilianis hortis duosque campteras circa eam, quorum pares in Asinii monumentis sunt, ubi et canephoros eiusdem. Sed in maxuma dignatione delubro Cn. Domitii in Circo Flaminio Neptunus ipse et Thetis atque Achilles, Nereides supra delphinos et cete aut hippocampos sedentes, item

The fame of Skopas rivals that of these artists. His works are Aphrodite and Desire at Samothrace, to which the most reverent worship is paid, the Apollo of the Palatine, and the famous seated Hestia in the gardens of Servilius between two pillars: a precisely similar pair may be seen in the gallery of Asinius Pollio, where is also the basket-bearer of Skopas. But the highest reputation is enjoyed by his group in the temple of Cn. Domitius in the Flaminian Circus, representing Poseidon him-

Tritones chorusque Phorci et pistrices ac multa alia marina, omnia eiusdem manu, praeclarum opus, etiam si totius uitae fuisset. Nunc uero praeter supra dicta quaeque nescimus Mars etiamnum est sedens colossiaeus eiusdem manu in templo Bruti Gallaeci apud circum eundem, praeterea Uenus in eodem loco nuda Praxiteliam illam antecedens et quemcunque alium locum nobilitatura.

self, Thetis, Achilles, Nereids seated on dolphins, huge fish or sea-horses, also Tritons and the rout of Phorkys and sea monsters and many other creatures of the sea, all by the same hand; a group which would have been remarkable had it been the work of a lifetime. As it is, beside those above mentioned and others of which we know not, there is by the hand of the same artist a colossal seated figure of Ares in the temple of Brutus Gallaecus close to the same circus, besides a nude Aphrodite in the same place which surpasses the famous Aphrodite of Praxiteles and would make any other spot famous.

his] Praxiteles and the younger Kephisodotos.

Apollinem Palatinum] The great temple of Apollo on the Palatine was built by Augustus 36–28 B.C. to commemorate the victory of Actium. In the *Curiosum Urbis Romae* it is called 'Aedes Apollinis Rhamnusii,' which shows that the Apollo was brought from Rhamnus in Attica. The statue is represented on coins of Nero (Overbeck, *Kunstmyth.*, Apollon, Münztafel v. 47, 48, 50, 51); there is a copy in the Vatican (Helbig, *Führer* 267). Cp. Prop. ii. 31. 6 Pythius in longa carmina ueste sonat.

campteras] καμπτῆρας, Lat. metae, the pillars at the turning-points in the race-course. Von Jan corrects 'lampteras,' 'candelabra.'

Neptunus ipse] Cn. Domitius Ahenobarbus built a temple to Neptune in the Circus Flaminius circ. 35-32 B.C. As he held the post of legatus pr. pr. in Bithynia 40-35 B.C. he may have brought the work from his province, where there was a famous temple of Poseidon at Astakos (Olbia). The subject of the work described by Pliny is the progress of Achilles to the Isles of the Blest.

Bruti] D. Junius Brutus Gallaecus erected a temple to Mars after his triumph over the Gallaeci and Lusitani in 132 B.C.

207. Paus. viii. 45. 4

Τεγεάταις δὲ ᾿Αθηνᾶς τῆς ᾿Αλέας τὸ ἱερὸν τὸ ἀρχαῖον ἐποίησεν ῎Αλεος· χρόνῳ δὲ ὕστερον κατεσκευάσαντο οἱ Τεγεᾶται τῇ θεῷ ναὸν μέγαν τε καὶ θέας ἄξιον. ἐκεῖνο μὲν δὴ πῦρ ἠφάνισεν ἐπινεμηθὲν ἐξαίφνης, Διοφάντου παρ᾿ ᾿Αθηναίοις ἄρχοντος, δευτέρῳ δὲ ἔτει τῆς ἕκτης καὶ ἐνενηκοστῆς ᾿Ολυμπιάδος.... 5. ὁ δὲ ναὸς ὁ ἐφ᾿ ἡμῶν πολὺ δή τι τῶν ναῶν, ὅσοι Πελοποννησίοις εἰσίν, ἐς κατασκευὴν προέχει τὴν ἄλλην καὶ ἐς μέγεθος. ὁ μὲν δὴ πρῶτός ἐστιν αὐτῷ κόσμος τῶν κιόνων Δώριος, ὁ δὲ ἐπὶ τούτῳ Κορίνθιος· ἑστήκασι δὲ καὶ ἐκτὸς τοῦ ναοῦ κίονες ἐργασίας τῆς ᾿Ιώνων. ἀρχιτέκτονα δὲ ἐπυνθανόμην Σκόπαν αὐτοῦ γενέσθαι τὸν Πάριον, ὃς καὶ ἀγάλματα πολλαχοῦ τῆς ἀρχαίας ῾Ελλάδος, τὰ δὲ καὶ περὶ

The old temple of Athena Alea at Tegea was built by Aleos; in later times the Tegeans caused a large and remarkable temple to be erected to the goddess. The previous building was suddenly attacked by fire and destroyed in the archonship of Diophantos at Athens and the second year of the ninety-sixth Olympiad (395 B.C.). The temple which is standing at the present day is far superior to the other temples in the Peloponnese in size and magnificence. The first order of columns is Doric, the next Corinthian; and outside the temple stand columns of the Ionic order. I was told that the architect was Skopas of Paros, who was the sculptor of many

'Ιωνίαν τε καὶ Καρίαν ἐποίησε.
τὰ δὲ ἐν τοῖς ἀετοῖς ἐστιν ἔμπροσθεν ἡ θήρα τοῦ ὑὸς τοῦ
Καλυδωνίου· πεποιημένου δὲ
κατὰ μέσον μάλιστα τοῦ ὑὸς
τῇ μέν ἐστιν 'Αταλάντη καὶ
Μελέαγρος καὶ Θησεὺς Τελα-
μών τε καὶ Πηλεὺς καὶ Πολύ-
δεύκης καὶ 'Ιόλαος ὃς τὰ
πλεῖστα 'Ηρακλεῖ συνέκαμνε
τῶν ἔργων, καὶ Θεστίου παῖδες,
ἀδελφοὶ δὲ 'Αλθαίας, Πρόθους
καὶ Κομήτης. 7. κατὰ δὲ τοῦ
ὑὸς τὰ ἕτερα 'Αγκαῖον ἔχοντα
ἤδη τραύματα καὶ ἀφέντα τὸν
πέλεκυν ἀνέχων ἐστιν Ἔποχος·
παρὰ δὲ αὐτὸν Κάστωρ καὶ
'Αμφιάραος ὁ 'Οϊκλέους ἐπὶ δὲ
αὐτοῖς Ἱππόθους ὁ Κερκύονος
τοῦ 'Αγαμήδους τοῦ Στυμ-
φήλου· τελευταῖος δέ ἐστιν
εἰργασμένος Πειρίθους. τὰ δὲ
ὄπισθεν πεποιημένα ἐν τοῖς
ἀετοῖς Τηλέφου πρὸς 'Αχιλλέα
ἐστὶν ἐν Καΐκου πεδίῳ μάχη.
. . . 47. 1. τῷ δὲ ἀγάλματι
τῆς 'Αθηνᾶς τῇ μὲν 'Ασκληπιός,
τῇ δὲ Ὑγίεια παρεστῶσά ἐστι
λίθου τοῦ Πεντελησίου, Σκόπα
δὲ ἔργα Παρίου.

statues in different parts of Greece proper, and also in Ionia and Karia. In the front pediment is represented the chase of the Kalydonian boar; the boar is placed almost exactly in the centre, and on the one side are Atalanta, Meleagros, Theseus, Telamon, Peleus, Polydeukes and Iolaos, who assisted Herakles in most of his labours, and the sons of Thestios and brothers of Althaia, Prothous and Kometes. On the other side of the boar is Epochos supporting Ankaios, who is already wounded and has dropped his axe, and beside him are Kastor and Amphiaraos, the son of Oïkles, and beyond them Hippothous the son of Kerkyon the son of Agamedes the son of Stymphalos; while Peirithous comes last of all. The sculptures of the back pediment represent the battle of Telephos against Achilles in the plain of the Kaïkos. . . . Beside the image of Athena stands on the one side Asklepios, on the other Hygieia. Both are of Pentelic marble, and are the work of Skopas of Paros.

Ἄλεος] An Arkadian hero, the mythical founder of Tegea.

τὰ δὲ ἐν τοῖς ἀετοῖς] Fragments of these sculptures were discovered in 1879, of which the most important are two male heads and the ead of the boar. See *Ov.* II⁴. p. 28, and references there given.

208. Schol. Aeschin Timarch. 747 R τρεῖς ἦσαν αὗται αἱ λεγόμεναι Σεμναὶ Θεαὶ ἢ Εὐμενίδες ἢ Ἐρινύες· ὧν τὰς μὲν δύο ἑκατέρωθεν Σκόπας ὁ Πάριος ἐποίησεν ἐκ τοῦ λυχνίτου λίθου, τὴν δὲ μέσην Κάλαμις.

These were the three deities called 'the Awful Goddesses' or the Eumenides or the Erinyes: two of them (one at each side) were made by Skopas of Paros of Parian marble, while the central figure was by Kalamis.

Paus. i. 28. 6 says that these figures had no attributes such as the snakes, &c. described by Aischylos.

λυχνίτου λίθου] Plin. *N. H.* xxxvi. 14 informs us, on the authority of Varro, that the name λυχνίτης was given to Parian marble because it was hewn by lamp-light in the quarries of Paros. Lepsius thinks that the name is derived from the transparency of the lower and finer strata.

209. Strab. xiii. 604 ἐν δὲ τῇ Χρύσῃ ταύτῃ καὶ τὸ τοῦ Σμινθέως Ἀπόλλωνός ἐστιν ἱερόν, καὶ τὸ σύμβολον τὸ τὴν ἐτυμότητα τοῦ ὀνόματος σῶζον,

In this town of Chryse is the temple of Apollo Smintheus, and the symbol which preserves the derivation of his name, i. e. the

· ὁ μῦς, ὑπόκειται τῷ πόδι τοῦ
ξοάνου· Σκόπα δ᾽ ἐστὶν ἔργα
τοῦ Παρίου.

mouse, lies at the foot of
the statue.   They are the
work of Skopas of Paros.

Χρύσῃ] Afterwards known as Alexandria Troas, on certain coins
of which city the statue appears to be represented (Baumeister,
Denkmäler, Fig. 1742).

210. Strab. xiv. 640 ὄντων
δ᾽ ἐν τῷ τόπῳ πλειόνων ναῶν,
τῶν μὲν ἀρχαίων τῶν δὲ ὕστερον γενομένων, ἐν μὲν τοῖς
ἀρχαίοις ἀρχαῖά ἐστι ξόανα,
ἐν δὲ τοῖς ὕστερον Σκόπα ἔργα·
ἡ μὲν Λητὼ σκῆπτρον ἔχουσα,
ἡ δ᾽ Ὀρτυγία παρέστηκεν ἑκατέρᾳ τῇ χειρὶ παιδίον ἔχουσα.

There are several temples
in the place, some of earlier
and some of later date.   In
the earlier temples are early
statues, in those of later date
works of Skopas.   There is
Leto holding a sceptre, and
beside her stands Ortygia
with a child on each arm.

τῷ τόπῳ] The grove Ortygia near Ephesos.
Ὀρτυγία] The nurse of Apollo and Artemis, here represented as
infants.

211. Paus. vi. 25. 1 κρηπὶς
δὲ ἐντὸς τοῦ τεμένους πεποίηται, καὶ ἐπὶ τῇ κρηπῖδι ἄγαλμα
Ἀφροδίτης χαλκοῦν ἐπὶ τράγῳ
κάθηται χαλκῷ. Σκόπα τοῦτο
ἔργον, Ἀφροδίτην δὲ Πάνδημον
ὀνομάζουσι.

Within the precinct is
a base, and on the base
a bronze figure of Aphro-
dite seated on a bronze goat.
This is the work of Skopas,
and is called Aphrodite
Pandemos.

τοῦ τεμένους] The precinct of Aphrodite at Elis, which contained
the Aphrodite Urania of Pheidias (No. 116).   The statue is perhaps
represented on coins of Elis (*Ov.* II⁴. Fig. 137).

212. Plin. *N. H.* xxxiv.
95 Uniuerso templo longi-

The length of the whole
temple is 425 ft., and the

tudo est ccccxxv pedum, latitudo ccxxv, columnae cxxvii a singulis regibus factae lx pedum altitudine ex iis xxxvi caelatae, una a Scopa.

breadth 225 ft. It contains 127 columns, each furnished by a king, 60 ft. in height: of these 36 are decorated with reliefs, which in one case are the work of Skopas.

templo] That of Artemis at Ephesos, restored after the destruction by fire of the old temple in 356 B.C. See Newton, *Essays on Art and Archaeology*, p. 210 ff.

caelatae, una a Scopa] The reliefs in most cases decorated the lowest drum only, above which was an Ionic shaft of the usual type. Hence Curtius and others read 'imo scapo'='on the lowest drum.' The date of the building, however, and the style of the existing fragments (*F. W.* 1242, 1243) make it quite possible to retain the MS. reading.

Other works :—

ASKLEPIOS (beardless) and HYGIEIA at Gortys in Arkadia (Paus. viii. 28. 1).

HEKATE at Argos (No. 171).

HERAKLES at Sikyon (Paus. ii. 10. 1). Possibly represented on coins of Sikyon (*Num. Comm. H.* xi.)

ATHENE Pronaia at Thebes (cf. No. 123).

ARTEMIS Eukleia at Thebes (Paus. ix. 17. 1).

DIONYSOS and ATHENA at Knidos (No. 186).

EROS, HIMEROS and POTHOS at Megara (No. 197).

A BACCHANTE, described at length by Kallistr. *Stat.* 2 ; cp. *Anth. Pal.* ix. 774.

(b) LEOCHARES.

Date.—Six inscriptions (Löwy 77–82) mostly fragmentary, and in some cases possibly the work of a much later Leochares (Löwy 320, 321), have been found at Athens. The most complete may be dated circ. 350 B.C. Another inscription from a series of portraits executed by Leochares and Sthennis (v. § 3 (b)) in common (Löwy 83) is somewhat later (temp. Alexander).

213. Plin. *N. H.* xxxiv. 79 Leochares (fecit) aquilam sentientem quid rapiat in Ganymede et cui ferat parcentemque unguibus etiam per uestem puero, Iouemque illum Tonantem in Capitolio ante cuncta laudabilem Apollinem diadematum, [Lyciscum mangonem, puerum subdolae et fucatae uernilitatis].

Leochares represented the eagle which feels what a treasure it is stealing in Ganymede, and to whom it is bearing him, and using its talons gently, though the boy's garment protects him. He also made the famous statue of Zeus the Thunderer on the Capitol, a work of unequalled excellence, and Apollo wearing a fillet, [and Lykiskos the slave-dealer, and a boy in whom all the craft and cunning of the slave are embodied.]

aquilam . . . Ganymede] Probably reproduced in a group in the Vatican, *F. W.* 1246.

Lyciscum mangonem] This is the reading of the best MS., but as the passage occurs in the alphabetical list of the sculptors, it is very probable that we should accept the reading of other MSS. 'Lyciscus Langonem.' Lyciscus will then be another artist (identified by Klein with Lykios, Part II. § 1. 4), and Lango the name of the boy. Martial (ix. 51. 5) couples a statue of that name ('Langona uiuum') with the 'boy of Brutus' (No. 152).

214. Paus. v. 20. 9 ἔστι δὲ ἐντὸς τοῦ Ἄλτεως ... οἴκημα περιφερὲς ὀνομαζόμενον Φιλιππεῖον. ἐπὶ κορυφῇ δέ ἐστι τοῦ Φιλιππείου μήκων χαλκῆ σύνδεσμος ταῖς δοκοῖς. 10. τοῦτο τὸ οἴκημά ἐστι μὲν κατὰ τὴν ἔξοδον τὴν κατὰ τὸ

Within the Altis is a circular building called the Philippeion. On the summit of the Philippeion is a bronze poppy-head which holds the rafters together. This building stands close to the egress by the Pry-

Πρυτανεῖον ἐν ἀριστερᾷ, πεποίηται δὲ ὀπτῆς πλίνθου,
κίονες δὲ περὶ αὐτὸ ἑστήκασι.
Φιλίππῳ δὲ ἐποιήθη μετὰ τὸ
ἐν Χαιρωνείᾳ τὴν Ἑλλάδα
ὀλισθεῖν. κεῖνται δὲ αὐτόθι
Φίλιππός τε καὶ Ἀλέξανδρος,
σὺν δὲ αὐτοῖς Ἀμύντας ὁ
Φιλίππου πατήρ. ἔργα δέ
ἐστι καὶ ταῦτα Λεωχάρους
ἐλέφαντος καὶ χρυσοῦ, καθὰ
καὶ τῆς Ὀλυμπιάδος καὶ Εὐρυ-
δίκης εἰσὶν αἱ εἰκόνες.

taneion on the left hand. It
is made of baked bricks, and
is surrounded by columns.
It was built for Philip after
the ruin of Greece at Chaironeia. In it stand portraits
of Philip and Alexander,
together with Amyntas the
father of Philip. These are
of ivory and gold and are
the work of Leochares, as
arc also the portraits of
Olympias and Eurydike.

The foundations of this building have been discovered at Olympia, and show that all the figures were standing (*A. Z.* 1882,
67 sqq.).

215. Plut. Uita x. Or.
Isocr. 27 ἀνάκειται δ' αὐτοῦ
καὶ ἐν Ἐλευσῖνι εἰκὼν χαλκῆ
ἔμπροσθεν τοῦ προστῴου, ὑπὸ
Τιμοθέου τοῦ Κόνωνος, καὶ
ἐπιγέγραπται
Τιμόθεος φιλίας τε χάριν, ξεν-
ίην τε προτιμῶν
Ἰσοκράτους εἰκὼ τήνδ' ἀνέθηκε
θεαῖς.

Λεωχάρους ἔργον.

A bronze portrait of him
stands at Eleusis in front
of the porch; it was dedicated by Timotheos the
son of Konon, and bears
the following inscription:—
Timotheos, for friend-
ship's sake and in honour
of hospitality, dedicated
this portrait of Isokrates
to the Goddesses.
The work of Leochares.

216. Uitruu. ii. 8. 11 (At
Halikarnassos) In summa
arce media Martis fanum
habens statuam colossi quam

(At Halikarnassos) in
the centre of the summit of
the citadel stands a temple
of Ares, containing a colossal

ἀκρόλιθον dicunt, nobili manu Leocharis factam. Hanc autem statuam alii Leocharis, alii Timothei putant esse.

statue of the kind termed an 'acrolith,' the handiwork of the famous Leochares. This statue, however, is supposed by some to be the work of Leochares, by others to be that of Timotheos.

ἀκρόλιθον] A statue of which the head and extremities only were of marble, the rest being of wood, gilded or otherwise decorated. Cp. No. 122. On Timotheos see (d).

Other works :—
ZEUS on the Akropolis of Athens (Paus. i. 24. 4). Possibly represented on coins of Athens (Ov. II⁴. Fig. 165).
ZEUS and DEMOS at the Piraeus (Paus. i. 1. 3).

(c) BRYAXIS.

Date.—An inscription found at Athens (Δελτ. 'Αρχ. 1891, 34 ff., 55 ff.) from a base with figures of horsemen in low relief (Bull. Corr. Hell. 1892, Pl. vii) reads Βρύαξις ἐπόησεν, and may be dated circ. 353 B.C. Seleukos Nikator (No. 217) became king of Syria in 312 B.C., but the portrait may be of earlier date.

217. Plin. N. H. xxxiv. 73 Bryaxis Aesculapium et Seleucum fecit.

Bryaxis represented Asklepios and Seleukos.

218. Liban. Orat. 61 καί μοι πρὸ τῶν ὀμμάτων ἵστησιν ὁ λογισμὸς τὸν τύπον ... τὴν φιάλην, τὴν κίθαριν, τὸν ποδήρη χιτῶνα ... ἁπαλότητα δέρρης ἐν λίθῳ, ζωστῆρα περὶ τῷ στήθει, συνάγοντα χιτῶνα χρυσοῦν, ὡς αὐτοῦ τὰ μὲν ἐφι-

Imagination brings before my eyes that form, the bowl, the lyre, the tunic reaching to the feet, the delicacy of the neck in the marble, the girdle about the bosom which holds the golden tunic together, so that some parts fit

ζάνειν τὰ δὲ ὑπανίστασθαι . . .   closely and others hang loose.
ἐῴκει ᾄδοντι μέλος.   He seemed as one that sang.

From a description of the Apollo at Daphne near Antioch, described
as a work of Bryaxis by Cedren., *Hist. Comp.* 306 B; from Theodoret,
Hist. Eccl. iii. 11, we learn that it was of wood, gilt. It is represented on coins of Antiochos Epiphanes (*Ov.* II⁴. Fig. 167). See
Büttner-Wobst, *Historische Studien Förstemann gewidmet*, 1894.

Other works :—
ASKLEPIOS and HYGIEIA at Megara (Paus. i. 40. 6).
DIONYSOS at Knidos (No. 186).
ZEUS and APOLLO with lions at Patara (Clem. Al. *Protr.* iv. 47).
Clement also gives the name of Pheidias as the reputed artist of
these figures.
Five colossal statues of Gods at Rhodes (Plin. *N. H.* xxxiv. 42).
PASIPHAE (Tatian, *c. Graec.* 54).
Clem. Al. (*Protr.* iv. 48) quotes Athenodoros to the effect that
the statue of Sarapis in the Sarapeion at Alexandria (perhaps
set up by Ptolemy Soter) was the work of 'another Bryaxis, not
the Athenian.' See Michaelis, *J. H. S.*, 1885, 289 ff.

(d) TIMOTHEOS.

Date.—Kavvadias places the inscription of Epidauros (No. 221)
in the earliest years of the fourth century on account of the incon-
sistencies in the use of the Ionic alphabet; but Foucart and Gurlitt
have shown that 375 B.C. is the more probable date. Timotheos
was at work on the Mausoleion 353 B.C., and must have been
a well-known sculptor when the temple at Epidauros was built.

219. Plin. *N. H.* xxxvi. 32 Timothei manu Diana Romae est in Palatio Apollinis delubro, cui signo caput reposuit Auianius Euander.

The Artemis in the temple of Apollo on the Palatine at Rome is the work of Timotheos; the head of this statue was restored by Avianius Evander.

C. Auianius Euander] A Greek sculptor brought by Antonius
to Alexandria and by Augustus to Rome after Actium. Cp. Cic.
Fam. vii. 23. 1, xiii. 2. 1.

220. Paus. ii. 32. 4 τοῦ δὲ Ἀσκληπιοῦ τὸ ἄγαλμα ἐποίησε μὲν Τιμόθεος, Τροιζήνιοι δὲ οὐκ Ἀσκληπιόν, ἀλλὰ εἰκόνα Ἱππολύτου φασὶν εἶναι.

The image of Asklepios was made by Timotheos; the Troizenians, however, assert that it represents not Asklepios but Hippolytos.

At Troizen. Plin. *N. H.* xxxiv. 91 also classes Timotheos among the artists who made statues of 'athletes, warriors, hunters, and sacrificers.' (Cp. No. 167.)

221. Kavvadias, Fouilles d'Épidaure, 241. 36 Τιμόθεος ἕλετο τύπ|ος ἐργάσα[σ]θαι καὶ παρέχεν ⊟⊟⊟⊟⊟⊟⊟⊟ ἔγγυος Πυθοκλῆς. . . l. 90 Τιμόθεος ἕλε[το ἀκρω]τ[ήρ]ια ἐπὶ τὸν ἅτερον αἰετὸν [Χ]Χ⊟⊟ == ἔγγυος Πυθοκλῆς.

Timotheos contracted to construct and furnish models for 900 drachmae; his security was Pythokles... He also contracted to furnish akroteria for one of the gables for 2240 dr. His security was Pythokles.

From the inscription recording the expenses incurred in building the temple of Asklepios at Epidauros, discovered in 1885. On the symbols v. No. 159 note. —stands for ten drachmae, ⊟ for H.

ἕλετο, παρέχεν] = εἵλετο, παρέχειν : τύπος = τύπους.

τύπος] Models, no doubt, for the pediment sculptures. The extant remains of these are published by Kavvadias, *op. cit.* Pl. viii. and xi.

ἀκρωτήρια] The figures which stood upon the two gable-ends and the four corners of the temple. Those of the other gable were the work of one Theotimos, who received the same sum (l. 97). The mounted Nereides, Kavv. *op. cit.* Pl. xi. 16, 17, probably represent the two *side* ἀκρωτήρια of the west pediment. Winter (*Ath. Mitth.* 1894, 160) points out the close resemblance of one to the group of Leda and the Swan in the Capitol (Helbig, *Führer* 454) which he attributes to Timotheos.

(e) THE MAUSOLEION.

222. Plin. *N. H.* xxxvi. 30 Scopas habuit aemulos

The rivals and contemporaries of Skopas were

N

eadem aetate Bryaxim et Timotheum et Leocharen, de quibus simul dicendum est quoniam pariter caelauere Mausoleum. Sepulcrum hoc est ab uxore Artemisia factum Mausolo Cariae regulo, qui obiit Olympiadis CVII anno secundo. Opus id ut esset inter septem miracula hi maxime fecere artifices. Patet ab austro et septentrione ⟨centenos⟩ sexagenos ternos pedes, breuius a frontibus, tota circumitu pedes CCCCXXXX, attollitur in altitudinem XXV cubitis, cingitur columnis XXXVI. Πτερόν uocauere circumitum. Ab oriente caelauit Scopas, a septentrione Bryaxis, a meridie Timotheus, ab occasu Leochares, priusque quam peragerent regina obiit. Non tamen recesserunt nisi absoluto iam, id gloriae ipsorum artisque monumentum iudicantes, hodieque certant manus. Accessit et quintus artifex. Namque supra πτερόν pyramis altitudine inferiorem

Bryaxis, Timotheos, and Leochares, who must be treated in a group since they were jointly employed on the sculptures of the Mausoleion. This building is the tomb erected by Artemisia, his widow, for Mausolos, prince of Karia, who died in the second year of the 107th Olympiad (351 B.C.). That this work is among the Seven Wonders is due mainly to the above-named artists. Its frontage on the north and south sides measures 163 feet, while the façades are shorter; the total circumference is 440 feet, the height twenty-five cubits; it is surrounded by thirty-six columns. This colonnade is called the 'Pteron.' The sculptures of the east side are by Skopas, those of the north by Bryaxis, those of the south by Timotheos, and those of the west by Leochares. The queen died before the building was complete; but the artists did not abandon the work

aequat, uiginti quattuor gradibus in metae cacumen se contrahens. In summo est quadriga marmorea quam fecit Pythis. Haec adiecta CXXXX pedum altitudine totum opus includit.

until it was finished, considering that it would redound to their own glory, and be a standing proof of their genius ; and to this day they vie with one another in their handiwork. They were joined by a fifth artist. For above the colonnade is a pyramid equal to the lower structure in height, with a flight of twenty-four steps tapering to a point. On the apex stands a four-horse chariot in marble, the work of Pythis. This addition completes the building, which rises to the height of 140 feet.

On the Mausoleion see *Ov.* II⁴. 100 ff., *F. W.* 1221–1239.

caelauere] Not ' worked in relief,' but in the broad sense ' sculptural,' a Latin equivalent for τορευτική in the broad sense (Nos. 119, 160).

Mausolo] The date of his death, according to Diod. xvi. 36, was 353 B.C. He reigned twenty-four years.

⟨centenos⟩] Omitted in MSS., but necessary if the total of 440 ft. be correct.

xxv cubitis] So best MSS. Various alterations have been made in order to account for the total height of 140 ft. Trendelenburg thinks that Pliny's total is incorrect, and that the height was in reality only fifty cubits = 75 ft. No architectural remains of a high substructure have been discovered.

ab oriente ... Leochares] Brunn (*Sitzungsberichte der bayr. Akad.* 1882, p. 114 ff.) has endeavoured to assign to each sculptor his share in the reliefs preserved. But it is doubtful whether the work of four hands can be distinguished, and the slabs which B. attributes to Bryaxis appear to belong to the east front, and therefore to Skopas.

inferiorem] Sc. altitudinem, which should perhaps be read. It would be more natural to supply 'pyramidem'; and it is suggested that the 'pteron' may have rested on a pyramidal substructure.

quadriga marmorea] Supposed to have contained the colossal portraits of Mausolos and Artemisia in the British Museum. But see P. Gardner, *J. H. S.* xiii. p. 188 ff.

3. OTHER ARTISTS.

(a) SILANION.

Date.—(i) His portrait of Plato (No. 224) was dedicated by Mithradates, who died 363 B. C. (ii) Apollodoros (No. 223) was a pupil of Sokrates (died 399 B. C.), and according to Plat. *Symp.* 137 C was a boy in 416 B. C. On the other hand, Pliny's date (Ol. 113 = 328 B. C.) is supported by the fact that (iii) Satyros (v. infr.) seems to be identical with the athlete victorious at the Amphiaraia at Oropos (*I. G. S.* 414), which were reorganized 32⅔ (Delamarre, *Revue de Philologie*, 1894, 162 ff.). Plin. *N. H.* xxxiv. 51 mentions that he had no teacher, but one pupil, Zeuxiades. Z. made a portrait of the orator Hypereides, who died 322 B. C. (Löwy 483).

223. Plin. *N. H.* xxxiv. 51 Silanion Apollodorum fudit, fictorem et ipsum, sed inter cunctos diligentissimum artis et iniquom sui iudicem, crebro perfecta signa frangentem, dum satiari cupiditate artis non quit, ideoque Insanum cognominatum; hoc in eo expressit nec hominem ex aere fecit sed iracundiam;

Silanion cast in bronze a portrait of Apollodoros, who was also a sculptor and the most painstaking of his craft, as well as a severe critic of his own work, who often broke in pieces finished statues, in his insatiable longing for ideal perfection, and was therefore called 'the Madman': this trait Silanion depicted

et Achillem nobilem idem epistaten exercentem athletas.

in his portrait, and cast in bronze not a man but Rage personified. He also made a famous statue of Achilles and a trainer exercising his athletes.

fictorem] Plin. *N. H.* xxxiv. 86 enumerates him amongst the sculptors who executed portraits of 'philosophers.'

sed] Not adversative, but intensive. Cp. Juv. v. 147 boletus domino, sed qualem Claudius edit, with Mayor's note.

nec hominem ... sed iracundiam] Not necessarily borrowed, as Jahn supposed, from an epigram, since the turn of expression is a common one in Latin. Cp. Cic. *Att.* vii. 136 non hominem sed scopas solutas, Petron. 43 discordia non homo, and (in the language of criticism) Quint. x. 1. 112 (Cicero) non iam hominis nomen sed eloquentiae habeatur, i. e. Cicero was called 'non homo sed eloquentia.'

224. Diog. Laert. iii. 25 ἐν δὲ τῷ πρώτῳ τῶν ἀπομνη-μονευμάτων Φαβωρίνου φέρε-ται, ὅτι Μιθραδάτης ὁ Πέρσης ἀνδριάντα Πλάτωνος ἀνέθετο εἰς τὴν Ἀκαδημίαν καὶ ἐπέ-γραψε· Μιθραδάτης ὁ Ῥοδο-βάτου Πέρσης Μούσαις εἰκόνα ἀνέθετο Πλάτωνος, ἣν Σιλα-νίων ἐποίησε.

In the first book of the Anecdotes of Favorinus it is recorded that Mithradates the Persian dedicated a portrait of Plato in the Academy with the following inscription :—Mithradates the Persian, the son of Rhodobates, dedicated to the Muses a portrait of Plato, made by Silanion.

Probably reproduced by the bust in the Vatican, *Jahrb.* 1886, Pl. vi. 2.

225. Plut. Quaest. Conu. v. 1. 2 τὴν πεπλασμένην

We look with pleasure and admiration on the statue

'Ιοκάστην, ἧς φασὶν εἰς τὸ   of Iokaste, in whose counten-
πρόσωπον ἀργύρου τι συμμῖξαι   ance the artist is said to have
τὸν τεχνίτην, ὅπως ἐκλιπόντος   mixed some silver, in order
ἀνθρώπου καὶ μαραινομένου   that the bronze might re-
λάβῃ περιφάνειαν ὁ χαλκός,   ceive the appearance of a
ἡδόμεθα καὶ θαυμάζομεν.   human being passing away
                                 in death.

From Plut. *de aud. poet.* iii. 30 we learn that this was a work
of Silanion.

Other works :—
THESEUS at Athens (Plut. *Thes.* 4).
SAPPHO taken from the Prytaneion at Syracuse by Verres (Cic.
Verr. iv. 57. 126). Probably reproduced by the bust in the Villa
Albani (*Jahrb.* 1890, Pl. iii).
KORINNA (Tatian, *c. Graec.* 54).
Athlete-statues at Olympia :—
SATYROS of Elis (v. supr.), twice victorious in boxing (Paus.
vi. 4. 5).
TELESTAS the Messenian, victorious in the boys' boxing-match
(Paus. vi. 14. 4).
DAMARETAS the Messenian, victorious in the boys' boxing-match
(Paus. vi. 14. 11).
Silanion was also the author of a work on proportions (Vitruv.
vii. Praef. 12).

(b) STHENNIS OF OLYNTHOS.

Date.—Olynthos was destroyed 348 B.C., after which date he
may have received Athenian citizenship. He was employed with
Leochares on the portrait-group already mentioned (2 (b)) (Löwy
83), and dated circ. 320 B.C. In an inscription from Oropos (Löwy
103 a) he describes himself as ᾿Αθηναῖος, which points to a date
later than 318 B.C., when Oropos became independent of Athens.
(Before this date Attic artists use their demotic names.) Pliny
dates him Ol. 113 (328 B.C.).

226. Plin. *N. H.* xxxiv.   Sthennis made statues of
90 Sthennis Cererem, Io-   Demeter, Zeus, and Athena

uem, Mineruam fecit, qui
sunt Romae in Concordiae
templo, idem flentis matro-
nas et adorantis sacrifican-
tisque.

which stand in the temple
of Concord at Rome ; also
weeping matrons, and figures
engaged in prayer and sacri-
fice.

227. Strab. xii. 5. 46 δὶs
... ἑάλω (Σινώπη) ... ὕστερον ... ὑπὸ Λευκόλλου ...
καὶ ... ὁ Λεύκολλος ... ἦρε
... τὸν Αὐτόλυκον, Σθέννιδος
ἔργον, ὃν ἐκεῖνοι οἰκιστὴν ἐνό-
μιζον καὶ ἐτίμων ὡς θεόν.

Sinope was twice cap-
tured, the second time by
Lucullus, who carried off a
statue by Sthennis repre-
senting Autolykos, whom
the inhabitants regarded as
the founder of the city and
revered as a god.

Lucullus captured Sinope in the Second Mithridatic war
(72 B. C.).

Athlete-statues at Olympia :—
PYTTALOS of Elis, victorious in the boys' boxing-match (Paus.
vi. 16. 8).
CHOIRILOS of Elis, victorious in the boys' boxing-match (Paus.
vi. 17. 5).

(c) EUPHRANOR OF THE ISTHMOS.

Date.—Pliny dates him Ol. 104 = 364 B. C. His portraits of
Alexander and Philip (No. 228) must be dated previous to the
death of the latter (336 B. C.). The inscriptions of his son Sostratos
(Löwy 105, 106) (whom Plin. N. H. xxxiv. 51 dates Ol. 113 = 328
B. C.) belong to the end of the fourth or beginning of the third
century.

228. Plin. N. H. xxxiv.
77 Euphranoris Alexander
Paris est in quo laudatur
quod omnia simul intelli-

By Euphranor is a
statue of Alexander (Paris).
This work is specially admired, because the eye can

guntur, iudex dearum, amator Helenae et tamen Achillis interfector. Huius est Minerua Romae quae dicitur Catuliana, infra Capitolium a Q. Lutatio dicata, et simulacrum Boni Euentus, dextra pateram, sinistra spicam ac papauera tenens, item Latona puerpera Apollinem et Dianam infantis sustinens in aede Concordiae. Fecit et quadrigas bigasque et cliduchon eximia forma, et Uirtutem et Graeciam, utrasque colossaeas, mulierem admirantem et adorantem, item Alexandrum et Philippum in quadrigis.

detect in it at once the judge of the Goddesses, the lover of Helen, and at the same time the slayer of Achilles. By the same artist is the Athena at Rome called 'the Minerva of Catulus,' dedicated by Q. Lutatius below the Capitol, and a figure of Good Luck holding a bowl in the right hand and an ear of corn and a poppy in the left, also Leto holding in her arms the new-born infants Apollo and Artemis (in the temple of Concord). He also represented chariots with four and two horses, and a priestess of surpassing beauty, and Valour and Hellas, both of colossal size, a woman in an attitude of wonder and adoration, also Alexander and Philip in four-horse chariots.

in quo laudatur] Probably borrowed by Pliny from an epigram.

Q. Lutatio] Q. Lutatius Catulus dedicated the temple of Jupiter Capitolinus (restored after its destruction by fire in 83 B. C.) in 78 B. C.

Boni Euentus] To judge by the attributes, this statue originally represented Triptolemos, not Ἀγαθὸς Δαίμων, as the 'Bonus Euentus' of Praxiteles (No. 186). It may be represented on various imperial coins and gems. See Furtwängler, *Meisterwerke*, p. 281, Fig. iii, note 2.

Latona puerpera] Commonly identified with a group appearing on several coins of Ephesos and other cities in Asia Minor, and reproduced in a statue in the Torlonia gallery at Rome (*Ov.* II⁴. Fig. 172); but see Reisch, *Festgruss aus Innsbruck an die Philologenversammlung in Wien*, 1893.

cliduchon] κλειδοῦχον. The temple-key was the mark of the priestess. Cp. No. 119 note.

229. Dion Chrys. 37. 43
τί γὰρ ἐκώλυε μέγαν εἶναι τὸν ἀνδριάντα; τί γὰρ ἀρτίπουν, ὥσπερ τὸν Εὐφράνορος "Ηφαιστον;

What was there to prevent the portrait from being tall? What was there to prevent it from being firm on its feet, like the Hephaistos of Euphranor?

τὸν ἀνδριάντα] A portrait of Agesilaos, king of Sparta.

It is possible that Dion Chrysostom has substituted the name of Euphranor for that of Alkamenes (v. No. 131).

230. Plin. *N. H.* xxxv. 128 Eminuit longe ante omnis Euphranor Isthmius Olympiade CIIII, idem qui inter fictores dictus est nobis. Fecit et colossos et marmorea et typos sculpsit, docilis ac laboriosus ante omnis et in quocunque genere excellens ac sibi aequalis. Hic primus uidetur expressisse dignitates heroum et usurpasse symmetriam, sed fuit in uniuersitate corporum exilior et capitibus articulisque grandior. 129 Uolumina

In the 104th Olympiad (364 B.C.) Euphranor of the Isthmos far outshone his rivals. He has already been mentioned amongst the sculptors, and made colossal statues, works in marble, and reliefs. He was an eager and painstaking student, who maintained a constant level of excellence in every department. He is considered to have been the first to represent heroes in their full majesty, and to master the science of pro-

quoque composuit de sym-
metria et coloribus.

portion; his bodies, how-
ever, were too slender, and
his heads and limbs too
large. He also wrote works
on proportions and colour-
ing.

This account refers primarily to Euphranor as a painter, but the
criticisms may no doubt be regarded as applicable to his sculptures.

expressisse dignitates heroum] The reference may be to his
painting of Theseus, of which he said that 'the Theseus of Parrhasius was fed on roses, but his own on beef' (Plin. *N. H.* xxxv.
129).

Other works :—
APOLLO Patroos at the Piraeus (Paus. i. 3. 3).
DIONYSOS, of which a copy stood on the Aventine at Rome
(Löwy 495).

(d) THRASYMEDES OF PAROS.

Date.—The inscription of Epidauros (No. 232) may be dated
circ. 375 B.C. See note on Timotheos (2 (d)).

231. Paus. ii. 27. 2 (At
Epidauros) τοῦ δὲ 'Ασκλη-
πιοῦ τὸ ἄγαλμα μεγέθει μὲν
τοῦ 'Αθήνησιν 'Ολυμπίου Διὸς
ἥμισυ ἀποδεῖ, πεποίηται δὲ
ἐλέφαντος καὶ χρυσοῦ· μηνύει
δὲ ἐπίγραμμα τὸν εἰργασμένον
εἶναι Θρασυμήδην 'Αριγνώτου
Πάριον. κάθηται δὲ ἐπὶ θρόνου
βακτηρίαν κρατῶν, τὴν δὲ ἑτέραν τῶν χειρῶν ὑπὲρ κεφαλῆς
ἔχει τοῦ δράκοντος, καί οἱ καὶ

(At Epidauros) the image
of Asklepios is smaller by
one half than the Olympian
Zeus at Athens, and is made
of ivory and gold; the inscription states that it is the
work of Thrasymedes the
son of Arignotos of Paros.
The God is seated upon a
throne and holds a staff in
one hand, while he extends
the other above the ser-

κύων παρακατακείμενος πε- | pent's head. A dog is also
ποίηται. τῷ θρόνῳ δὲ ἡρώων | represented lying at his feet.
ἐπειργασμένα Ἀργείων ἐστὶν | On the throne are repre-
ἔργα, Βελλεροφόντου τὸ ἐς τὴν | sented in relief the exploits
Χίμαιραν καὶ Περσεὺς ἀφελὼν | of Argive heroes, viz. the con-
τὴν Μεδούσης κεφαλήν. | test of Bellerophon with the
Chimaira, and Perseus, who
has decapitated Medusa.

τοῦ Ἀθήνησιν Ὀλυμπίου Διός] Dedicated by Hadrian.

The statue is represented on coins of Epidauros (*Num. Comm.* liii). According to Cic. *N. D.* iii. 34. 83 Dionysios I of Syracuse ordered the golden beard to be removed on the ground that it was unseemly that Asklepios should be bearded while his father Apollo was beardless. The reliefs published by Kavvadias, Ἐφ. Ἀρχ. 1894, Pl. i (the first also Brunn-Bruckmann 3), though not *direct* copies, may serve to give an impression of the style of the original.

232. Kavvadias, Fouilles d'Épidaure 241. 45 Θρασυ|-μήδης ἕλετο τὰν ὀροφὰν τὰν ὑπένερθε καὶ τὸ θύρωμα τὸ ἔνδοι καὶ | διὰ στύλων ἐργά-σασθαι XXXXXXXXX888 88888 ἔνγυος Πυθοκλῆ[ς]| Θεοφείδης Ἀγέμων.

Thrasymedes contracted to execute the roof above and the inner doorway as well as that between the columns for 9800 drachmae. His securities were Pytho-kles, Theopheides, and Agemon.

On the inscription see No. 221.

τὸ θύρωμα τὸ ἔνδοι] The door of the cella, also called μέγα θύρωμα. In its construction ivory was used of the value of 3070 dr. (l. 65), and (apparently) golden nails of considerable value (l. 105 ff.).

διὰ στύλων] i. e. τὸ διὰ στύλων θύρωμα. The outer door between the columns of the πρόδομος. See Kavvadias, Pl. i A.

The wood employed in the construction of the doors was that of the pine, box, and lotus (l. 45).

(f) POLYEUKTOS.

233. Plut. Uit. x. Or. Dem. 44 αἰτήσας τε γραμματεῖον (Δημοσθένης) ἔγραψεν ... τὸ ἐπὶ τῆς εἰκόνος αὐτοῦ ἐλεγεῖον ἐπιγεγραμμένον ὑπὸ τῶν Ἀθηναίων ὕστερον·

εἴπερ ἴσην ῥώμην γνώμῃ,
  Δημόσθενες, ἔσχες
οὔποτ᾿ ἂν Ἑλλήνων ἦρξεν
  Ἄρης Μακεδών.

45. κεῖται δὲ ἡ εἰκὼν πλησίον τοῦ περισχοινίσματος καὶ τοῦ βωμοῦ τῶν Δώδεκα Θεῶν, ὑπὸ Πολυεύκτου πεποιημένη.

(Demosthenes) asked for a tablet and wrote the elegiac couplet, which the Athenians afterwards inscribed upon his portrait. It runs as follows:—

Hadst thou, Demosthenes, had might as strong as thy resolve, the war-god of Macedon had never subdued the Greeks.

The portrait stands near the enclosure and the altar of the Twelve Gods, and is the work of Polyeuktos.

We learn from Plut. *Dem.* 31 that the statue had clasped hands (ἕστηκε τοὺς δακτύλους συνέχων δι᾿ ἀλλήλων). It cannot, therefore, be directly reproduced by the statues at Knole (Michaelis, *Ancient Marbles*, p. 417) and in the Vatican (*F. W.* 1312) which hold a roll in their hands. They may, however, be mediately derived from the original of Polyeuktos.

(g) DEMETRIOS.

Date.—Two inscriptions from the Akropolis (Löwy 62, 63) belong to the first half of the fourth century (the first about 380 B. C.). On a third v. No. 234 note.

234. Plin. *N. H.* xxxiv. 76 Demetrius Lysimachen (fecit) quae sacerdos Mineruae fuit lxiiii annis, idem et Mineruam quae musica

The works of Demetrius are a portrait of Lysimache, who was for 64 years priestess of Athena, an Athena called 'the Musical,'

appellatur — dracones in Gorgone eius ad ictus citharae tinnitu resonant— idem equitem Simonem qui primus de equitate scripsit.

because the snakes of her aegis tinkle in response to the notes of a lyre, and a portrait of the knight Simon, who was the first to write a treatise on horse-manship.

Lysimachen] According to Paus. i. 27. 4 the statue stood close to the Erechtheion, and was about a cubit in height. An inscription from the Akropolis (Löwy 64) has been held to belong to this work, since the second line reads [? ἐξή]κοντα δ' ἔτη [κ]αὶ τέσσαρ[α] Ἀθάνᾳ : but the breadth of the foot-print (20 cm.) is too great for a height of one cubit.

musica] So inferior MSS. ; the best has 'myetica.'

Simonem] An Athenian cavalry officer, mentioned in Ar. *Eq.* 242.

235. Lucian, Philops. 18
οὐχ ἑώρακας, ἔφη, εἰσιὼν ἐν τῇ αὐλῇ ἑστηκότα πάγκαλον ἀνδριάντα, Δημητρίου ἔργον τοῦ ἀνθρωποποιοῦ; . . . εἴ τινα παρὰ τὸ ὕδωρ τὸ ἐπιρρέον εἶδες προγάστορα, φαλαντίαν, ἡμίγυμνον τὴν ἀναβολήν, ἠνεμωμένον τοῦ πώγωνος τὰς τρίχας ἐνίας, ἐπίσημον τὰς φλέβας, αὐτοανθρώπῳ ὅμοιον, ἐκεῖνον λέγω, Πέλλιχος ὁ Κορίνθιος στρατηγὸς εἶναι δοκεῖ.

Have you not seen, said he, as you came in a beautiful portrait-statue standing in the court, the work of Demetrios the maker of men? If you have seen beside the running water a figure with a fat paunch and a bald head, wearing a cloak which leaves him half exposed, with some of the hairs of his head flowing in the wind, and prominent veins, like the very man himself, that is the one I mean. It is supposed to represent Pellichos the Co-rinthian general.

On the context v. Introduction, § 1. In § 20 Lucian calls the artist Demetrios of Alopeke, a deme of Attika, and speaks of him as οὐ θεοποιός τις, ἀλλ' ἀνθρωποποιός—'a maker not of gods but of men.'

Πέλλιχος] A Corinthian of this name is mentioned by Thuc. i. 29.

§ 2. THE SCHOOL OF SIKYON.

1. THE YOUNGER SONS OF PATROKLES.

(a) DAIDALOS.

Date.—Two inscriptions (Löwy 88, 89) exist. The original of the first is lost, but the second (from Olympia) must be dated early in the fourth century. The victory commemorated by No. 239 was won in 400 B.C. Eupolemos (v. infr.) was victorious in 396, Aristodemos (v. infr.) in 388. The victory commemorated by No. 238 was probably won in 369 B.C., unless the reference was to mythical times, when the monument might be as early as 392 B.C.

236. Plin. *N. H.* xxxiv. 76 Daedalus et ipse inter fictores laudatus duo pueros destringentes se fecit.

Daidalos, who is also mentioned with praise among the sculptors in marble, represented two boys scraping themselves.

fictores] Here used in the narrower sense of 'sculptor in marble,' opp. statuarius, 'worker in bronze.'

destringentes se] ἀποξυομένους, athletes scraping the ointment from their bodies with the strigil. See Lysippos, No. 241.

237. Plin. *N. H.* xxxvi. 35 Uenerem lauantem se Daedalus (fecit).

Daidalos represented Aphrodite in the bath.

In the temple of Juppiter in the 'porticus Octauiae'; perhaps the original of the numerous statues of Aphrodite crouching in the bath. But see *F. W.* 1467, who attributes the work to a later Daidalos, a Bithynian artist of the third century.

238. Paus. x. 8. 5 ἐφεξῆς δὲ Τεγεατῶν ἀναθήματα ἀπὸ Λακεδαιμονίων ᾿Απόλλων ἐστὶ καὶ Νίκη, καὶ οἱ ἐπιχώριοι τῶν ἡρώων, Καλλιστώ τε ἡ Λυκάονος καὶ ᾿Αρκὰς ὁ ἐπώνυμος τῆς γῆς, καὶ οἱ τοῦ ᾿Αρκάδος παῖδες, Ἕλατος καὶ ᾿Αφείδας καὶ ᾿Αζάν, ἐπὶ δὲ αὐτοῖς Τρίφυλος . . . ἀνάκειται δὲ καὶ Ἕρασος ὁ Τριφύλου παῖς. 6. οἱ δὲ εἰργασμένοι τὰ ἀγάλματα Παυσανίας ἐστὶν ᾿Απολλωνιάτης, οὗτος μὲν τόν τε ᾿Απόλλωνα καὶ Καλλιστώ, τὴν δὲ Νίκην καὶ τοῦ ᾿Αρκάδος τὴν εἰκόνα ὁ Σικυώνιος Δαίδαλος· ᾿Αντιφάνης δὲ ᾿Αργεῖος καὶ Σαμόλας ᾿Αρκάς, οὗτος μὲν τὸν Τρίφυλον καὶ ᾿Αζᾶνα, Ἕλατον δὲ καὶ ᾿Αφείδαντά τε καὶ Ἕρασον ὁ ᾿Αργεῖος. ταῦτα μὲν δὴ οἱ Τεγεᾶται ἔπεμψαν ἐς Δελφούς, Λακεδαιμονίους, ὅτε ἐπὶ σφᾶς ἐστρατεύσαντο, αἰχμαλώτους ἑλόντες.

Next in order come the offerings dedicated by Tegeans from the spoils of the Spartans. These consist in figures of Apollo, Victory and the native heroes of Arkadia, Kallisto the daughter of Lykaon, and Arkas who gave his name to the country, and the sons of Arkas, Elatos and Apheidas and Azan, and after them Triphylos. There is also a statue of Erasos the son of Triphylos. The figures were the work of (1) Pausanias of Apollonia, who made the Apollo and Kallisto, (2) Daidalos of Sikyon, who made the Victory and the figure of Arkas, (3) Antiphanes of Argos, and (4) Samolas the Arkadian, the latter of whom made the figures of Triphylos and Azan, and the former those of Elatos and Apheidas and Erasos. These offerings were sent by the Tegeans to Delphi, when they had made prisoners of the Spartans who invaded them.

At Delphi. Referred by Brunn to 369 B. C., when Sparta suffered severe reverses at the hands of the Arkadians (Diod. xv. 62). But the closing words appear to refer to the legend recorded by Hdt. i. 65, which falls in the mythical period.

Pausanias and Samolas are otherwise unknown, on Antiphanes v. Nos. 172, 173 note. His pupil Kleon was the artist of several athlete-statues at Olympia, amongst which were two of the earliest 'Ζᾶνες' or small bronze statues of Zeus set up from the proceeds of fines. Paus. dates them Ol. 96 = 388 B. C. One of the bases exists (Löwy 95). The base of another portrait (Kritodamos, Paus. vi. 8. 5) (Löwy 96) may be dated circ. 350 B. C.

239. Paus. vi. 2. 8 ἐν δὲ τῇ Ἄλτει παρὰ τὸν τοῦ Τιμοσθένους ἀνδριάντα ἀνάκειται Τίμων καὶ ὁ παῖς τοῦ Τίμωνος Αἴσυπος, παιδίον ἐπὶ ἵππῳ καθήμενον. ἔστι γὰρ δὴ καὶ ἡ νίκη τῷ παιδὶ ἵππου κέλητος· ὁ Τίμων δ' ἐπὶ ἅρματι ἀνηγορεύθη. τῷ δὲ Τίμωνι εἰργάσατο καὶ τῷ παιδὶ τὰς εἰκόνας Δαίδαλος Σικυώνιος ὃς καὶ ἐπὶ τῇ Λακωνικῇ νίκῃ τὸ ἐν τῇ Ἄλτει τρόπαιον ἐποίησεν Ἠλείοις.

In the Altis, beside the statue of Timosthenes stand portraits of Timon and his son Aisypos, represented as a boy mounted on a horse. The reason is that the son's victory was won with a race-horse, while Timon was proclaimed victor with his chariot. The portraits of Timon and his son were the work of Daidalos of Sikyon, who also made the trophy set up by the Eleans in the Altis to commemorate their victory over Sparta.

The victory took place in 400 B. C. when Agis invaded Elis, but was dislodged from Olympia, which he had occupied (Paus. v. 4. 8).

(b) POLYKLEITOS THE YOUNGER.

Date.—(1) He was a pupil of his elder brother Naukydes (No. 171 and Paus. vi. 6. 2), who (Part III. § 2. 2 (a)) worked at the close of the fifth and beginning of the fourth century. (2) The inscription from the portrait of Aristion (Part II. § 2. 1 ad fin.) (Löwy 92) dates from the first half of the fourth century. Another inscription (Löwy 93) from Thebes is inscribed on the same block and in the same characters as an inscription of Lysippos. It belonged to a portrait of Timokles, victorious in the chariot-race at the Herakleia, and also at the Βασίλεια of Lebadeia (instituted 371 B. C.), while that of Lysippos belonged to a portrait of Konidas, victorious in the pankration at the Pythia. Dittenberger (*I. G. S.* 2532, 2533) pronounces both posterior to 316 B. C., and the inscriptions are therefore probably restorations ; the portraits may have had no original connexion. (3) Antipatros (Part II. § 2. 1 ad fin.) was probably victorious in Ol. 98 = 388 B. C. ; No. 240 is posterior to 371 B. C. ; and No. 165, if a work of the younger P., is posterior to 370 B. C.

240. Paus. viii. 31. 4 τοῦ περιβόλου δέ ἐστιν ἐντὸς Φιλίου Διὸς ναός, Πολυκλείτου μὲν τοῦ Ἀργείου τὸ ἄγαλμα, Διονύσῳ δὲ ἐμφερές· κόθορνοί τε γὰρ τὰ ὑποδήματά ἐστιν αὐτῷ, καὶ ἔχει τῇ χειρὶ ἔκπωμα, τῇ δὲ ἑτέρᾳ θύρσον· κάθηται δὲ ἀετὸς ἐπὶ τῷ θύρσῳ.

Within the enclosure is a temple of Zeus, the God of Friendship. The image is the work of Polykleitos of Argos and resembles Dionysos in type ; for it is shod with buskins, and holds in one hand a cup and in the other a thyrsus, upon which is perched an eagle.

τοῦ περιβόλου] That of Demeter and Kore at Megalopolis.

Other works :—See Nos. 165, 166, to which may be added :—
HEKATE at Argos (No. 171).
Athlete-statue at Olympia :—
AGENOR of Thebes, victorious in the boys' wrestling-match (Paus. vi. 6. 2). Dedicated by the Phokians, since A.'s father was πρόξενος of Phokis at Thebes.

2. LYSIPPOS.

Date.—The inscription (Löwy 94) from the portrait of Troilos (v. infr.) mentions his second victory (probably 368 B. C.), and the statue may not have been erected immediately. On the inscription

from Thebes (Löwy 93) see under Polykleitos the younger (1 (b)).
Athenaios tells an anecdote of Lysippos connected with the
foundation of Kassandreia (316 B.C.). An inscription (Löwy 487)
copied from an older original reads Σέλευκος βασιλεύς. Λύσιππος
ἐποίει : but the portrait may have been executed before Seleukos
assumed the royal title in 312 B.C. Pliny's date is Ol. 113 = 328
B.C., determined by that of Alexander.

241. Plin. *N. H.* xxxiv.
61 Lysippum Sicyonium
Duris negat ullius fuisse
discipulum, sed primo ae-
rarium fabrum audendi
rationem cepisse Eupompi
responso. Eum enim in-
terrogatum, quem sequere-
tur antecedentium, dixisse
monstrata hominum mul-
titudine, naturam ipsam
imitandam esse, non arti-
ficem. Plurima ex omnibus
signa fecit, ut diximus,
fecundissimae artis, inter
quae destringentem se,
quem Marcus Agrippa ante
Thermas suas dicauit mire
gratum Tiberio principi.
Non quiuit temperare sibi
in eo, quanquam imperiosus
sui inter initia principatus,
transtulitque in cubiculum
alio signo substituto, cum
quidem tanta populi
Romani contumacia fuit ut
theatri clamoribus reponi

Duris asserts that Lysip-
pos of Sikyon had no master,
but originally worked as a
bronze-caster, and was in-
spired to attempt higher
things by an answer of
Eupompos. That artist,
when asked which of his
predecessors he followed,
pointed to a crowd of men,
and replied that Nature
herself and no artist was
the true model. Lysippos
produced more works than
any other artist, being, as
was mentioned above,
extraordinarily prolific.
Among them is the youth
scraping himself, which
M. Agrippa dedicated in
front of his baths. The
Emperor Tiberius conceived
a wonderful passion for this
statue, and was unable to
restrain his desire, although
in the early years of his
reign he practised self-

apoxyomenon flagitauerit princepsque quanquam adamatum reposuerit. Nobilitatur Lysippus et temulenta tibicina, et canibus ac uenatione, in primis uero quadriga cum Sole Rhodiorum ; fecit et Alexandrum Magnum multis operibus, a pueritia eius orsus. Quam statuam inaurari iussit Nero princeps delectatus admodum illa, dein, cum pretio perisset gratia artis, detractum est aurum pretiosiorque talis existimabatur etiam cicatricibus operis atque concisuris in quibus aurum fuerat remanentibus. Idem fecit Hephaestionem Alexandri Magni amicum, quem quidam Polyclito adscribunt, cum is centum prope annis ante fuerit, item Alexandri uenationem, quae Delphis sacrata est, Athenis satyrum, turmam Alexandri, in qua amicorum eius imagines summa omnium similitudine expressit ; hanc Metellus Macedonia subacta transtu-

control. He transferred it to his bedchamber and set another statue in its place, but the populace of Rome showed such displeasure that the Emperor restored it in response to the clamour of the theatre in spite of his passion for it. The fame of Lysippos rests also on his drunken flute-player and on his dogs and hunters, but especially on the four-horse chariot, with the Sun executed for Rhodes. He also made many portraits of Alexander the Great, beginning from his boyhood. The last-named statue the Emperor Nero, who admired it extremely, ordered to be gilded. Afterwards, since the charm of the work had vanished, though its value had increased, the gold was removed, and it was esteemed more valuable in this state even though scars and incisions which had contained the gold still remained. Lysippos also made a portrait of Hephaistion, the friend of Alex-

lit Romam. Fecit et quadrigas multorum generum. Statuariae arti plurimum traditur contulisse capillum exprimendo, capita minora faciendo quam antiqui, corpora graciliora siccioraque, per quae proceritas signorum maior uideretur. Non habet Latinum nomen symmetria quam diligentissime custodiuit noua intactaque ratione quadratas ueterum Staturas permutando, uolgoque dicebat ab illis factos quales essent homines, a se quales uiderentur esse. Propriae huius uidentur esse argutiae operum custoditae in minimis quoque rebus.

ander the Great, which some ascribe to Polykleitos, although he lived about a century earlier, also Alexander's hunt, dedicated at Delphi, a satyr at Athens, a troop of Alexander's horse, in which he introduced portraits of his friends which displayed a marvellous likeness : this work was removed to Rome by Metellus after the conquest of Macedonia. He also represented four - horse chariots of several kinds. He is said to have done much to advance the art of sculpture in bronze by his careful treatment of the hair, and by making the head smaller and the body more slender and firmly knit than earlier sculptors, thus imparting to his figures an appearance of greater height. There is no Latin name for the 'canon of proportions' which he carefully observed, exchanging the squarely-built figure of the older artists for a new and untried system. He was in the habit of saying that they had represented men as they were, while he represented them as they appeared to the eye. The extreme delicacy of his work even in the smallest details, would seem to be its most individual feature.

Duris] V. Introduction, § 1.

Eupompi responso] E. was a painter of Sikyon, whose date appears to fall at the close of the fifth and beginning of the fourth century (Plin. *N. H.* xxxv. 64, 75), so that if the saying is rightly ascribed to him, it cannot have been addressed directly to Lysippos.

ut diximus] V. No. 242.

destringentem se] Reproduced by the Apoxyomenos in the Vatican, *F. W.* 1264.

Alexandrum Magnum] V. No. 243.

quam statuam] Almost certainly to be taken, with Urlichs, of a statue of Alexander as a boy. Others suppose the words ' fecit ... orsus' to be misplaced, and refer ' quam statuam' to the chariot of the Sun ; but though there is some probability that this was removed to Rome, Pliny would scarcely describe it by the term ' statua,' which is properly applicable to a portrait in bronze.

Alexandri uenationem] V. No. 244.

turmam Alexandri] V. No. 245.

Metellus] Q. Caecilius Metellus subdued the pretender Andriskos in Macedonia (146 B. C.), and hence received the name Macedonicus.

Statuariae arti] Clearly used in the narrow sense of ' sculpture *in bronze*,' exclusively practised by Lysippos. In this use the term is opposed to ' sculptura ' = sculpture in marble. Cp. xxxv. 156 plasticen matrem . . . statuariae sculpturaeque dixit Pasiteles. xxxvi. 15 non omittendum hanc artem (marmoris sculpendi) tanto uetustiorem fuisse quam picturam aut statuariam.

sicciora] The word is used of the trained athlete, whose body is free from unhealthy humours and superfluous fat. Cp. Varr.

Logist. Fr. 27 R. Persae propter exercitationes puerilis modicas eam sunt consecuti corporis siccitatem ut neque spuerent neque emungerentur sufflatoue corpore essent.

quadratas ueterum staturas] With special reference to the canon of Polykleitos. Cf. No. 160 ad fin.

quales essent . . . quales uiderentur esse] Assuming that the natural sense of the words is the true one, we must interpret them to mean that while Polykleitos and his school had represented the human body in its actual proportions, Lysippos employed such proportions as to produce the impression received by the eye (quales esse uiderentur = οἷοι ὁρῶνται). Many authorities, however, (after Otfried Müller) suppose 'quales uiderentur esse' to be a mistranslation by Pliny of οἷους ἔοικεν εἶναι = as they ought to be; the meaning will then be that Polykleitos was a realist, Lysippos an idealist. The conception was familiar in art-criticism. Cp. Arist. *Poet.* 1448 a 5 Πολύγνωτος μὲν κρείττους, Παύσων δὲ χείρους, Διονύσιος δὲ ὁμοίους εἴκαζεν.

argutiae] Cf. xxxv. 37 Parrhasius . . . picturae dedit primus argutias uultus, elegantiam capilli. argutus = clear to the senses, and so clearly defined, clearly cut. Cp. Verg. *G.* iii. 80 argutum caput (of a horse). Hence 'argutiae operum' here refers to clearly cut, delicate outlines.

242. Plin. *N. H.* xxxiv. 37 Insignia maxime et aliqua de causa notata uoluptarium sit attigisse artificesque celebratos nominauisse singulorum quoque inexplicabili multitudine, cum Lysippus MD opera fecisse prodatur, tantae omnia artis, ut claritatem possent dare uel singula, numerum apparuisse defuncto eo, cum thesaurum effregisset heres, solitum enim ex manipretio cuius-

Let it be our pleasure to touch on works of special excellence or with special cause for remark and to record the names of famous artists, since the multitude of single works is innumerable. Lysippos alone is said to have produced 1500 works, all of such artistic value that each would have sufficed by itself to make him famous. The number became known

que signi denarios seponere aureos singulos.

after his death, when his heir broke open his strong-box, since it had been his custom to set aside a piece of gold from the price of each statue.

From the preface to Pliny's account of sculpture in bronze.

denarios] Pliny no doubt refers to the gold stater, worth twenty drachmae. The Roman gold denarius (xxxiii. 47) was worth twenty-five silver denarii, the silver denarius being considered equivalent to an Attic drachma.

243. Plut. de Alex. Magno ii. 2 Λυσίππου δὲ τὸ πρῶτον 'Αλέξανδρον πλάσαντος ἀνα-βλέποντα τῷ προσώπῳ πρὸς τὸν οὐρανόν, ὥσπερ αὐτὸς εἰώθει βλέπειν 'Αλέξανδρος, ἡσυχῇ παρεγκλίνων τὸν τρά-χηλον, ἐπέγραψέ τις οὐκ ἀπι-θάνως·

αὐδασοῦντι δ' ἔοικεν ὁ χάλ-κεος εἰς Δία λεύσσων,
γᾶν ὑπ' ἐμοὶ τίθεμαι, Ζεῦ,
σὺ δ' Ὄλυμπον ἔχε.
διὸ καὶ μόνον 'Αλέξανδρος ἐκέ-λευε Λύσιππον εἰκόνας αὐτοῦ δημιουργεῖν· μόνος γὰρ οὗτος, ὡς ἔοικε, κατεμήνυε τῷ χαλκῷ τὸ ἦθος αὐτοῦ καὶ συνεξέφερε τῇ μορφῇ τὴν ἀρετήν· οἱ δὲ ἄλλοι τὴν ἀποστροφὴν τοῦ τραχήλου καὶ τῶν ὀμμάτων τὴν

When Lysippos first made a portrait of Alex-ander with his countenance uplifted to heaven, just as Alexander was wont to gaze with his neck gently inclined to one side, some one wrote the following not inappro-priate epigram :—

The man of bronze is as one that looks on Zeus and will address him thus: O Zeus, I place earth beneath my feet, do thou rule Olym-pos.

For this reason Alexander gave orders that Lysippos only should make portraits of him; since Lysippos only, as it would seem, truly revealed his nature in

διάχυσιν καὶ ὑγρότητα μιμεῖσθαι θέλοντες οὐ διεφύλαττον
αὐτοῦ τὸ ἀρρενωπὸν καὶ λεον-
τῶδες.

bronze, and portrayed his courage in visible form, while others in their anxiety to reproduce the bend of the neck and the melting look of the eyes failed to preserve his masculine and leonine aspect.

On the portraits of Alexander, see *F. W.* 1318 and Köpp, 52. *Winckelmannsprogramm* (1892). From Plut. *de Is. et Osir.* 24 we learn that the statue here referred to held a spear.

244. Plut. Alex. 40 τοῦτο
τὸ κυνήγιον Κρατερὸς εἰς Δελφοὺς ἀνέθηκεν, εἰκόνας χαλκᾶς
ποιησάμενος τοῦ λέοντος καὶ
τῶν κυνῶν, καὶ τοῦ βασιλέως
τῷ λέοντι συνεστῶτος, καὶ
αὐτοῦ προσβοηθοῦντος· ὧν
τὰ μὲν Λύσιππος ἔπλασε, τὰ
δὲ Λεωχάρης.

Krateros erected a memorial of this hunt at Delphi. He caused figures of bronze to be made, representing the lion, the dogs, the king in combat with the lion, and himself coming to the rescue; some of these were made by Lysippos, the rest by Leochares.

Κρατερός] A general of Alexander, afterwards allied with Antipater, killed in battle 321 B.C.
Λεωχάρης] V. § 1. 2 (b).

245. Arrian, Anab. i. 16. 7
Μακεδόνων δὲ τῶν μὲν ἑταί-
ρων ἀμφὶ τοὺς εἴκοσι καὶ πέντε
ἐν τῇ πρώτῃ προσβολῇ ἀπέ-
θανον, καὶ τούτων χαλκαῖ
εἰκόνες ἐν Δίῳ ἑστᾶσιν,
'Αλεξάνδρου κελεύσαντος Λύσιππον ποιῆσαι.

Of the Macedonians there fell about twenty-five of the king's guard in the first onslaught. Bronze portraits of these stood at Dion, made by Lysippos by order of Alexander.

ἐν τῇ πρώτῃ προσβολῇ] At the battle of Granikos (334 B.C.). Since the dead were buried on the field of battle (Arr. i. 16. 5) Pliny's story as to the resemblances can hardly be correct. According to Vell. Pat. i. 11. 3 a portrait of Alexander himself formed part of the group.

246. Plin. *N. H.* xxxiv. 40 Talis et Tarenti (Iuppiter) factus a Lysippo XL cubitorum. Mirum in eo, quod manu, ut ferunt, mobilis—ea ratio libramenti est—nullis conuellatur procellis. Id quidem prouidisse et artifex dicitur modico interuallo, unde maxime flatum opus erat frangi, opposita columna. Itaque magnitudinem propter difficultatemque moliendi non attigit cum Fabius Verrucosus, cum Herculem, qui est in Capitolio, inde transferret.

Such too is the Zeus of Tarentum made by Lysippos, which is forty cubits in height. It is remarkable from the fact that although, it is said, a touch of the hand will turn it—so cunningly is it balanced—no storm can overturn it. The artist is said to have provided against this by interposing a pillar at a short distance on the side from which it was most necessary to break the force of the wind. And so on account of the huge size of the figure and the difficulty of attacking it, Fabius Verrucosus did not lay hands on it when he removed from Tarentum the Herakles which stands on the Capitol.

Talis] Colossal in size.
Fabius Verrucosus] Q. Fabius Maximus, the opponent of Hannibal, took Tarentum 209 B.C.

247. Anth. Pal. App. 66
Ποσειδίππου.

τίς πόθεν ὁ πλάστης ; Σικνώ-
νιος. οὔνομα δὴ τίς ;
Λύσιππος. σὺ δὲ τίς ; Και-
ρὸς ὁ πανδαμάτωρ.
τίπτε δ' ἐπ' ἄκρα βέβηκας ; ἀεὶ
τροχάω. τί δὲ ταρσοὺς
ποσσὶν ἔχεις διφυεῖς ; ἵπ-
ταμ' ὑπηνέμιος.
χειρὶ δὲ δεξιτερῇ τί φέρεις
ξυρόν ; ἀνδράσι δεῖγμα
ὡς ἀκμῆς πάσης ὀξύτερος
τελέθω.

ἡ δὲ κόμη, τί κατ' ὄψιν ; ὑπαν-
τιάσαντι λαβέσθαι,

νὴ Δία. τἀξόπιθεν δ' εἰς τί
φαλακρὰ πέλει ;
τὸν γὰρ ἅπαξ πτηνοῖσι παρα-
θρέξαντά με ποσσὶν
οὔτις ἔθ' ἱμείρων δράξεται
ἐξόπιθεν.
τοὔνεχ' ὁ τεχνίτας σε διέπλα-
σεν ; εἵνεκα ὑμέων
ξεῖνε, καὶ ἐν προθύροις θῆκε
διδασκαλίην.

POSEIDIPPOS.
Who and whence was thy sculptor? From Sikyon. His name? Lysippos. And who art thou? Occasion, the all-subduer. Why dost thou tread on tiptoe? I am ever running. Why hast thou wings twy-natured on thy feet? I fleet on the wings of the wind. Why dost thou bear a razor in thy right hand? To show to men that I am keener than the keenest edge. And thy hair, why grows it in front? For him that meets me to seize, by Zeus. And why is the back of thy head bald? Because none may clutch me from behind, howsoe'er he desire it, when once my winged feet have darted past him. Why did the sculptor fashion thee? For thy sake, stranger, and set me up for a warning in the entry.

From Kallistr. *Stat.* 3, who describes the statue at length, we learn that it originally stood at Sikyon (whence it was afterwards removed to Constantinople). K. also states that it stood on a globe, as do Ausonius and Tzetzes. Himerios (*Ecl.* xiv. 1) mentions that in the left hand it held a balance. But these late authorities seem to have added characteristics and attributes to the original type. See the monuments published by Curtius, *A. Z.* 1875, Pl. i, ii, who shows that the personified Καιρός was a figure specially connected with athletic contests.

248. Strab. vi. 278 (At Tarentum) τὰ μὲν κατέφθειραν Καρχηδόνιοι λαβόντες τὴν πόλιν, τὰ δ' ἐλαφυραγώγησαν Ῥωμαῖοι κρατήσαντες βιαίως· ὧν ἐστὶ καὶ ὁ Ἡρακλῆς ἐν τῷ Καπετωλίῳ χαλκοῦς κολοσσικός, Λυσίππου ἔργον, ἀνάθημα Μαξίμου Φαβίου τοῦ ἑλόντος τὴν πόλιν.

(At Tarentum) Some works were destroyed by the Carthaginians when they captured the city, and others carried away as spoils by the Romans, who took forcible possession of them ; among the latter was the colossal bronze Herakles on the Capitol, the work of Lysippos, dedicated by Fabius Maximus, who captured the city.

Μαξίμου Φαβίου] V. No. 246 note. The statue was removed to Constantinople 'in the consulship of Julian,' probably 322 A. D. (Suid.), and placed in the Hippodrome. It is described in the following No.

249. Niket. Chon. de Sign. Constant. 5 κατήρειπτο τοίνυν Ἡρακλῆς ὁ τριέσπερος μέγας μεγαλωστὶ κοφίνῳ ἐνιδρυμένος, τῆς λεοντῆς ὑπεστρωμένης ἄνωθεν. . . ἐκάθητο δὲ μὴ γωρυτὸν ἐξημμένος, μὴ τόξον ταῖν χεροῖν φέρων, μὴ τὸ ῥόπαλον προβαλλόμενος, ἀλλὰ τὴν μὲν δεξιὰν βάσιν ἐκτείνων ὥσπερ καὶ τὴν αὐτὴν χεῖρα εἰς ὅσον ἐξῆν, τὸν δὲ

The great Herakles then begotten of three nights lies mighty and mightily fallen, he who was seated on a basket, whereon was strewn the lion's skin. There he sat with no quiver hung about him, with no bow in his hand and no club to defend him, but extending his right leg and right arm as far as he

εὐώνυμον πόδα κάμπτων εἰς τὸ
γόνυ καὶ τὴν λαιὰν χεῖρα ἐπ'
ἀγκῶνος ἐρείδων, εἶτα τὸ λοιπὸν τῆς χειρὸς ἀνατείνων, καὶ
τῷ πλάτει ταύτης ἀθυμίας
πλήρης καθυποκλίνων ἠρέμα
τὴν κεφαλὴν . . . ἦν δὲ τὸ
στέρνον εὐρύς, τοὺς ὤμους πλα-
τύς, τὴν τρίχα οὖλος, τὰς
πυγὰς πίων, βριαρὸς τοὺς
βραχίονας καὶ εἰς τόσον προ-
έχων μέγεθος εἰς ὅσον, οἶμαι,
καὶ τὸν ἀρχέτυπον Ἡρακλῆν
εἴκασεν ἂν ἀναδραμεῖν ὁ Λυσί-
μαχος ὁ πρῶτον ἅμα καὶ
ὕστατον τῶν ἑαυτοῦ χειρῶν
πανάριστον φιλοτέχνημα του-
τονὶ χαλκουργήσας, καὶ οὕτω
μέγιστον ὡς τὴν περιελοῦσαν
τὸν αὐτοῦ ἀντίχειρα μήρινθον
εἰς ἀνδρεῖον ζωστῆρα ἐκτεί-
νεσθαι, καὶ τὴν κνήμην τοῦ
ποδὸς εἰς ἀνδρόμηκες.

could, and with his left leg
bent at the knee. His left
arm was supported at the
elbow and the forearm
raised, and on the palm of
the left hand he was resting his head gently, full of
despondency. His breast
and shoulders were broad,
his hair thick, his buttocks
fat, and his arms brawny,
and his height was such
as Lysimachos might have
supposed the original He-
rakles to reach, when he
fashioned of bronze this,
the choicest jewel of his
art, first and last, of such
colossal bulk that the string
which enclosed its thumb
might serve as a man's
girdle and the shin of its
leg was tall as a man.

κατήρειπτο τοίνυν] In the sack of Constantinople by the Franks
in 1202 A. D.
Λυσίμαχος] A mistake of Niketas for Λύσιππος.

250. Mart. ix. 44
Hic, qui dura sedens por-
recto saxa leone
mitigat exiguo magnus
in aere deus,
quaeque tulit spectat resu-
pino sidera uultu

He who sits here temper-
ing the hardness of the rock
with the outstretched lion's
skin, a mighty god im-
prisoned in the tiny bronze,
and gazes with upturned
eyes at the stars which once

cuius laeua calet robore,	he bore, whose left hand is
dextra mero,	hot with the club, and his
non est fama recens, nec	right with the wine-cup,
nostri gloria caeli :	enjoys no upstart fame, nor
nobile Lysippi munus	is his fame that of a Roman
opusque uides.	chisel. 'Tis a famous work
	and offering of Lysippos
	which thou seest.

This statue was known as 'Herakles Epitrapezios,' i. e. it served as a table-decoration. According to Stat. *Silv.* iv. 2. 35, 6 it was less than a foot in height. Martial states that it belonged successively to Alexander, Hannibal, Sulla and Novius Vindex. It appears to be more or less faithfully reproduced in various works enumerated by Weizsäcker, *Jahrb.* 1889, p. 109.

tulit] While Atlas fetched the apples of the Hesperides, Herakles supported the heavens.

251. Strab. x. 459 ἡ Ἀλυζία . . . καθ᾽ ἥν ἐστι λιμὴν Ἡρακλέους ἱερὸς καὶ τέμενος ἐξ οὗ τοὺς Ἡρακλέους ἄθλους, ἔργα Λυσίππου, μετήνεγκεν εἰς Ῥώμην τῶν ἡγεμόνων τις, παρὰ τόπον κειμένους διὰ τὴν ἐρημίαν.

Alyzia, in whose territory is a harbour sacred to Herakles and a precinct from which a Roman commander removed to Rome the labours of Herakles, the work of Lysippos, which had become displaced through the desolation of the district.

Ἀλυζία] In Akarnania.

On monuments which appear to reproduce these groups see *Ov.* II⁴. 144 and references.

Other works :—
ZEUS at Sikyon (Paus. ii. 9. 6).
ZEUS Nemeios at Argos (Paus. ii. 20. 3).

ZEUS and the MUSES at Megara (Paus. i. 43. 6). The inscription
from Megara published in *Ath. Mitth.* 1885, p. 150, may have belonged to this work.

POSEIDON at Corinth (Lucian, *Jup. Trag.* 9).

DIONYSOS on Mount Helikon (Paus. ix. 30. 1).

EROS at Thespiai (Paus. ix. 27. 3).

HERAKLES at Sikyon (Paus. ii. 9. 8).

SOKRATES (Diog. Laert. ii. 43).

PRAXILLA (Tatian, *c. Graec.* 52).

AESOP and the Seven Sages (*Anth. Plan.* iv. 332).

PYTHES of Abdera (Paus. vi. 14. 12).

Athlete-statues at Olympia :—

POLYDAMAS at Skotussa, victorious in the pankration, Ol. 93 =
408 B.C. (Paus. vi. 5. 1).

TROILOS of Elis, victorious with the two-horse chariot, and with
a team of four colts, Ol. 102 = 372 B.C. (Paus. vii. 4. 1). Inscription Löwy 94.

CHEILON of Patrai, twice victorious in wrestling (Paus. vi. 4. 6).

KALLLIKRATES of Magnesia, twice victorious in the race in
armour (Paus. vi. 17. 3).

XENARKES of Stratos, victoricus in the pankration (Paus. vi. 2. 1).

3. LYSISTRATOS.

252. Plin. *N. H.* xxxv.
153 Hominis autem ima-
ginem gypso e facie ipsa
primus omnium expressit
ceraque in eam formam
gypsi infusa emendare instituit Lysistratos Sicyonius
frater Lysippi, de quo diximus. Hic et similitudines
reddere instituit ; ante eum
quam pulcherrimas facere
studebant. Idem et de

The first artist who took
plaster casts of the human
face from the original, and
introduced the practice of
working over a wax model
taken from the plaster, was
Lysistratos of Sikyon, the
brother of Lysippos, who
has already been mentioned.
He also instituted the
practice of rendering portraits with lifelike precision,

signis effigies exprimere
inuenit.

while previous artists had
striven to make them as
beautiful as possible. He
also discovered how to take
casts of statues.

4. THE FAMILY AND SCHOOL OF LYSIPPOS.

(a) DAIPPOS, BOEDAS, EUTHYKRATES, TISIKRATES.

253. Plin. *N. H.* xxxiv.
66 Filios et discipulos
reliquit (Lysippus) laudatos
artifices Daippum et Boe-
dan, sed ante omnis Euthycraten, quanquam is con-
stantiam potius imitatus
patris quam elegantiam
austero maluit genere quam
iucundo placere. Itaque
optime expressit Herculem
Delphis et Alexandrum
Thespiis uenatorem, et
proelium equestre, simulacrum ipsum Trophonii ad·
oraculum, quadrigas com-
pluris, equum cum fuscinis,
canes uenantium. Huius
porro discipulus fuit Tisicrates et ipse Sicyonius, sed
Lysippi sectae propior, ut
uix decernantur complura
signa ceu senex Thebanus
et Demetrius Rex, Peuces-

The sons and pupils (of
Lysippos) who survived
him were Daippos and
Boedas, artists of recog-
nized merit, but above all
Euthykrates, although he
followed his father's un-
flinching conscientiousness
rather than his refinement
of taste and rested his claim
to popular favour on a
severe rather than an effec-
tive style. He was thus
eminently successful in
representing Herakles (at
Delphi) and Alexander as
a hunter (at Thespiai), and
a cavalry engagement, and
the image of Trophonios
which adorns his own ora-
cular seat, many four-horse
chariots, a horse with forked
poles, and a group of
hounds. His pupil again

tes Alexandri Magni serua- | was Tisikrates also a native
tor, dignus tanta gloria.

was Tisikrates also a native of Sikyon, but in closer contact with the school of Lysippos, so much so, that many of his works can barely be distinguished from those of that artist. Such are the sage of Thebes, King Demetrios, and Peukestes, who saved the life of Alexander the Great, and richly deserved to be immortalized.

Daippum] Dated by Pliny Ol. 121 = 296 B.C. Works :—

'Perixyomenos,' i.e. an athlete scraping himself (= apoxyomenos), Plin. *N. H.* xxxiv. 87.

Athlete-statues at Olympia :—

Kallon of Elis, victorious in the boys' boxing-match (Paus. vi. 12.6).

Nikandros of Elis, twice victorious in the double foot-race (Paus. vi. 16. 5).

Boedan] Pliny, *N. H.* xxxiv. 73, attributes to him a 'praying figure' (adorans). The so-called 'Praying Boy' at Berlin (Brunn-Bruckmann 283), if it is not a reproduction of this work, may serve as an illustration of the type.

Euthycraten] Besides the works here mentioned, Tatian (*c. Graec.* 52, 53) mentions four female subjects—Anyte of Tegea (floruit circ. 300 B.C.), Mnesarchis of Ephesos, Thaliarchis of Argos, and Παννυχίς (so Jahn for Παντευχίς, an impossible name).

constantiam] Urlichs and Brunn translate 'boldness,' an idea hardly conveyed by the word and inappropriate to the 'austerum genus.' Blümner translates 'perseverance,' i.e. in details. Cp. No. 241 (of Lysippos) argutiae . . . custoditae in minimis quoque rebus, and this is probably nearly right, though the paraphrase given in the text may represent the meaning more exactly.

uenatorem] Kekulé would place a comma before this word, and seek the original in that of the Meleager of the Vatican. But it is more probable that it should be taken closely with 'Alexandrum.' In this case we may interpret (1) a single figure in hunting costume, or (2) a group of hunters. Urlichs, taking the latter interpretation, connects with this 'equum cum fuscinis,' a horse carrying either (1) forked sticks for the support of the hunting-nets, or (2) three-pronged hunting-spears—the word is applied to Poseidon's trident —and 'canes uenantium.'

proelium equestre] No doubt from the wars of Alexander. The mounted Alexander in bronze from Herculaneum (*Ov.* II⁴, Fig. 183) has been referred to this group.

equum cum fuscinis] See above note on 'uenatorem.' Jahn corrects 'coquum cum fiscinis,' a cook with baskets. 'Genre' figures of this nature exist (Clarac, 879, 2244, 2245).

Tisicrates] Pliny, *N. H.* xxxiv. 89 attributes to him a chariot and pair, to which another sculptor, Piston, added a female driver.

senex Thebanus] Possibly Pindar.

Demetrius Rex] Demetrios Poliorketes became king 307 B. C., and died 283 B. C.

Peucestes] A member of Alexander's body-guard, who saved his life in the attack on the city of the Malli.

(b) EUTYCHIDES.

Date.—Antioch (v. No. 254) was founded by Seleukos Nikator in 300 B. C.

254. Paus. vi. 2. 6 Εὐτυ-
χίδης Σικυώνιος παρὰ Λυσίπ-
πῳ δεδιδαγμένος . . . Σύροις
τοῖς ἐπὶ 'Ορόντῃ Τύχης ἐποίησεν ἄγαλμα, μεγάλας παρὰ
τῶν ἐπιχωρίων ἔχον τιμάς.

Eutychides of Sikyon, a pupil of Lysippos, made a statue of Fortune for the Syrians who live on the Orontes, at whose hands it receives great honour.

From John Malalas, pp. 201 and 276 Bonn, we learn that the figure (representing the Fortune of Antioch) was seated 'above the river Orontes' (ἐπάνω τοῦ 'Ορόντου ποταμοῦ). It is reproduced by the statuette in the Vatican, *F. W.* 1396.

255. Plin. *N. H.* xxxiv.
78 Eutychides (fecit) Eu-

Eutychides represented the river Eurotas. Of this

P

rotam, in quo artem ipso amne liquidiorem plurimi dixere.

figure it has often been said that art has made it more liquid than the river itself.

An epigram of Philippos (*Anth. Pal.* ix. 709) on this statue speaks of the bronze as ὕδατος ὑγρότερον—more liquid than water. Pliny seems to derive his notice from a similar epigram—probably terminating with the phrase ὢ τέχνην ὕδατος ὑγροτέραν (cp. No. 92 *b*).

Other works :—
DIONYSOS in the collection of Asinius Pollio (Pliny, *N. H.* xxxvi. 34).
Athlete-statue at Olympia :—
TIMOSTHENES of Elis, victorious in the boys' foot-race (Paus. vi. 2. 6).

(c) CHARES OF LINDOS.

256. Plin. *N. H.* xxxiv. 41 Ante omnes autem in admiratione fuit Solis colossus Rhodi, quem fecerat Chares Lindius Lysippi supra dicti discipulus; LXX cubitorum altitudinis fuit. hoc simulacrum, LVI post annum terrae motu prostratum, sed iacens quoque miraculo est. Pauci pollicen eius amplectuntur, maiores sunt digiti quam pleraeque statuae, uasti specus hiant defractis membris, spectantur intus magnae molis

The greatest marvel of all. however, was the colossal figure of the Sun at Rhodes, made by Chares of Lindos, a pupil of Lysippos mentioned above. This figure was 70 cubits in height. and after standing 56 years was overthrown by an earthquake; but even as it lies prostrate it is a marvel. Few men can embrace its thumb: its fingers are larger than most statues, there are huge yawning caverns where the

saxa, quorum pondere sta-biliuerat eum constituens. Duodecim annos tradunt effectum MCCC talentis, quae contigerant ex ap-paratu regis Demetrii relicto morae taedio ob-sessae Rhodo.

limbs have been broken, and within them may be seen great masses of rock, by whose weight the artist gave it a firm footing when he erected it. The story runs that twelve years were occupied in its construction, for which the artist received 1,300 talents, produced by the sale of Demetrios' siege-train, which the king aban-doned when he raised the siege of Rhodes through disgust at its protraction.

The siege of Rhodes was raised by Demetrios Poliorketes in 303 B.C., while the recorded dates of the earthquake range from 227 B.C. to 222 B.C. The colossus was therefore erected circ. 280 B.C. There is no foundation for the common belief that it bestrode the entrance to the harbour of Rhodes.

Pliny, *N. H.* xxxiv. 44 also mentions a colossal head by Chares, dedicated by P. Lentulus Spinther cos. 57 B.C. on the Capitol.

Other members of the school of Lysippos were :—

PHANIS, a pupil of Lysippos, to whom Pliny, *N. H.* xxxiv. 80 attri-butes one work—'epithyusan' = ἐπιθύουσαν, a woman sacrificing.

XENOKRATES, pupil of Tisikrates, or, according to other accounts, of Euthykrates. See Introduction, § 1.

KANTHAROS of Sikyon, pupil of Eutychides and father of Alexis, enumerated by Pliny, *N. H.* xxxiv. 50 amongst the pupils of Poly-kleitos, by whom we must in this case understand the younger. According to Pliny (*N. H.* xxxiv. 85) he was an artist of merit, but not of special distinction.

Athlete-statues at Olympia :—

Kratinos of Aigeira, victorious in the boys' wrestling-match (Paus. vi. 3. 6).

Alexinikos of Elis, victorious in the boys' wrestling-match (Paus. vi. 17. 7).

§ 3. OTHER ARTISTS.

1. HYPATODOROS AND ARISTOGEITON OF THEBES.

Date.—Pliny's date (Ol. 102 = 372 B.C.) is probably somewhat late, since an inscription from Delphi (Löwy 101) uses the Boeotian alphabet, and must therefore be dated early in the fourth century, and this is confirmed by the probable date of No. 257 (v. note).

257. Paus. x. 10. 3 πλησίον δὲ τοῦ ἵππου καὶ ἄλλα ἀναθήματά ἐστιν Ἀργείων, οἱ ἡγέμονες τῶν ἐς Θήβας ὁμοῦ Πολυνείκει στρατευόντων, Ἄδραστός τε Ταλαοῦ καὶ Τυδεὺς Οἰνέως καὶ οἱ ἀπόγονοι Προίτου Καπανεὺς Ἱππόνου καὶ Ἐτέοκλος ὁ Ἴφιος, Πολυνείκης τε καὶ Ἱππομέδων ἀδελφῆς Ἀδράστου παῖς· Ἀμφιαράου δὲ καὶ ἅρμα ἐγγὺς πεποίηται καὶ ἐφεστηκὼς Βάτων ἐπὶ τῷ ἅρματι ἡνίοχός τε τῶν ἵππων καὶ τῷ Ἀμφιαράῳ καὶ ἄλλως προσήκων κατὰ οἰκειότητα· τελευταῖος δὲ Ἀλιθέρσης ἐστὶν αὐτῶν. 4. οὗτοι μὲν δὴ Ὑπατοδώρου καὶ Ἀριστογείτονός εἰσιν ἔργα, καὶ ἐποίησαν σφᾶς, ὡς αὐτοὶ Ἀργεῖοι λέγουσιν, ἀπὸ τῆς

Near to the horse are other offerings of the Argives, consisting in statues of the leaders of the expedition which accompanied Polyneikes to Thebes, Adrastos the son of Talaos, and Tydeus the son of Oineus, and the descendants of Proitos, Kapaneus the son of Hipponous and Eteoklos the son of Iphis, and Polyneikes and Hippomedon, Adrastos' sister's son ; and hard by is represented the chariot of Amphiaraos and Baton, who has mounted the chariot and drives the horses, besides being otherwise intimately associated with Amphiaraos ; last of all comes

νίκης, ἥντινα ἐν Οἰνόῃ τῇ
'Αργείᾳ αὐτοί τε καὶ 'Αθηναίων
ἐπίκουροι Λακεδαιμονίους ἐνί-
κησαν· ἀπὸ δὲ τοῦ αὐτοῦ, ἐμοὶ
δοκεῖν, ἔργου καὶ τοὺς 'Επιγό-
νους ὑπὸ 'Ελλήνων καλουμέ-
νους ἀνέθεσαν οἱ 'Αργεῖοι·
κεῖνται γὰρ δὴ εἰκόνες καὶ
τούτων, Σθένελος καὶ 'Αλκ-
μαίων, ... ἐπὶ δὲ αὐτοῖς Πρό-
μαχος καὶ Θέρσανδρος καὶ
Αἰγιαλεύς τε καὶ Διομήδης· ἐν
μέσῳ δὲ Διομήδους καὶ τοῦ
Αἰγιαλέως ἐστὶν Εὐρύαλος.

Alitherses. These are works of Hypatodoros and Aristogeiton, and were made, according to the Argives, from the spoils of the victory which they and their Athenian allies gained at Oinoe over the Spartans. It was, in my opinion, in memory of the same victory that the Argives dedicated statues of the chieftains whom the Greeks call the Epigonoi. For their statues too stand there. Sthenelos and Alkmaion and after them Promachos and Thersandros and Aigialeus and Diomedes ; and between Diomedes and Aigialeus stands Euryalos.

At Delphi. τοῦ ἵππου refers to the 'wooden horse' of Antiphanes, No. 173. The victory referred to is obscure, but must have been gained in the course of the 'Corinthian war' of 392–387 B. C.

Paus. (viii. 26. 7) attributes to Hypatodoros a colossal bronze Athena at Aliphera in Arkadia. Polyb. iv. 78 couples with the name of H. that of Sostratos, whom Pliny in the chronological table dates Ol. 113 = 328 B. C.

2. BOETHOS OF CARTHAGE.

Date.—The original of the group representing a boy strangling a goose (No. 258) appears to date from the *early* Hellenistic period.

258. Plin. *N. H.* xxxiv. 84 Boethi quanquam ar-

Though Boethos is more famous for his work in silver,

gento melioris infans *ui
summa*anserem strangulat.

he is the artist of the boy strangling a goose with all his might.

argento] Boethos was a 'caelator' or τορευτής in the narrow sense of the word, a worker in repoussé in precious metal.

infans ... anserem strangulat] On copies of this group see *F. W.* 1587, who places it in the Hellenistic period.

ui summa] The best MS. has sex anno (corr. annis), inferior MSS. eximiae. Bücheler detected the fact that ' sex' concealed 'ui.'

259. Paus. v. 17. 4 Παιδίον δὲ ἐπίχρυσον κάθηται
γυμνὸν πρὸ τῆς 'Αφροδίτης·
Βοηθὸς δὲ ἐτόρευσεν αὐτό.

A gilt figure of a nude boy is seated before the Aphrodite ; it is the work of Boethos' chisel.

Wieseler corr. ἐπίκυρτον 'bent,' and brought this work into connexion with the existing figures of a boy removing a thorn from his foot. See reff. given by *Ov.* II⁴. 184. But the evidence for the change is slender.

A statue of Asklepios as a child is ascribed to Boethos in two epigrams (*Anth. Pal. App.* 55, 56).

3. ARISTODEMOS.

260. Plin. *N. H.* xxxiv.
86 Aristodemus (fecit) et
luctatores bigasque cum
auriga, anus, Seleucum
regem, habet gratiam suam
huius quoque doryphorus.

The works of Aristodemos are : wrestlers, a two-horse chariot with its driver, old women, king Seleukos ; his warrior with the spear too has a charm of its own.

anus] Since the best MS. spells the word 'annus,' Urlichs wishes to construct another artist's name, but without much probability.

Seleucum regem] Seleukos Nikator, king of Syria 312–281. Tatian, *c. Graec.* 55 attributes to A. a portrait of Aesop, to which original Brunn would trace the existing portraits. See *F. W.* 1324.

APPENDICES

Nos. 261–271.

APPENDIX I.

THE SCHOOLS OF PERGAMON
AND RHODES.

1. THE SCHOOL OF PERGAMON.

Date.—The following table shows the succession in the Pergamene dynasty:—

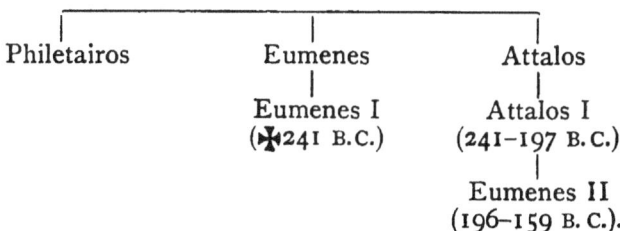

Of the four artists mentioned by Pliny in No. 261, (1) Phyromachos was the maker of a statue taken by Prusias of Bithynia in a war with Attalos I; (2) Antigonos was the object of a controversial work of Polemon (v. Introduction, § 1), who flourished 220–170 B.C.; (3) the name of ... γονος (whether Antigonos or Isigonos [Epigonos] is uncertain) appears on inscriptions from monuments commemorating the victory of Attalos I over the Gauls (Fränkel, *Inschriften von Pergamon* 22ᵇ, 29). Hence the group of artists named by Pliny evidently belongs to the reign of Attalos I. The same is true of Epigonos (Fränkel, Nos. 19, [22ᵇ ? 29 ?] 31, 32) if indeed he is to be distinguished from 'Isigonos.'

261. Plin. *N. H.* xxxiv. 84 Plures artifices fecere Attali et Eumenis adversus

The battles of Attalos and Eumenes with the Gauls were represented by

Gallos proelia, Isigonus, Phyromachus, Stratonicus, Antigonus qui uolumina condidit de sua arte.	a group of artists—Isigonos, Phyromachos, Stratonikos and Antigonos (who was the author of works treating of his art).

Attali et Eumenis] A. is certainly Attalos I, but it is disputed whether E. is the first or second of that name. It seems clear that the latter must be meant, although his successes in war do not appear to have been important, and the inscriptions (Löwy 154) of Pergamon all refer to the victories of Attalos I over the Gauls and Antiochos Hierax (the first apparently 241 B.C.; the chronology is obscure).

Isigonus] As this name is not otherwise known, and Pergamene inscriptions (v. supr.) mention Ἐπίγονος (No. 263), it is possible that this name should be here restored. See note on No. 263.

Phyromachus] Plin. *N. H.* xxxiv. 80 mentions a four-horse chariot driven by Alkibiades as the work of Phyromachos; while in xxxiv. 88 he states that one Nikeratos represented 'Alkibiades and his mother Demarate sacrificing at the kindling of the lamps.' It was formerly supposed that these artists worked in the fifth century; but

(1) Phyromachos is shown to have worked at Pergamon by No. 261, and by Polyb. xxxvii. 27, Diod. xxxi. 46, who mention an Asklepios taken from the Nikephorion at Pergamon by Prusias I of Bithynia.

(2) Nikeratos made a statue dedicated at Delos by one Sosikrates to commemorate the victories of Philetairos, brother of Eumenes II (Löwy 147), and a Pergamene inscription (Fränkel 132) of the reign of Eumenes II is restored [Νικήρατος] Εὐκτήμονος Ἀθ[ην]αῖος ἐποίησεν, on the authority of Tatian, *c. Graec.* 53, while in a collection of inscriptions published in 1543 is one from a portrait of Eumenes at Pergamon by N. (Löwy 496).

(3) An inscription from Delos (Löwy 118) reads Νικήρατος Φυρόμ[αχος Ἀθηνα]ῖοι ἐποίησαν.

It is therefore quite possible that the two works mentioned above are to be attributed to these artists, and had reference to Alkibiades' victory at Olympia. (See Bursian, *Sitzungsberichte der bayr. Akad.* 1874, 139 ff.) Other works of Nikeratos were:—Portraits of the Argive poetess Telesilla and of Glaukippe (Tatian, *loc. cit.*),

Asklepios and Hygieia in the temple of Concord at Rome (Plin. *N. H.* xxxiv. 80), portraits of athletes, &c. (id. *ib.* xxxiv. 88).

Stratonicus] Probably to be identified with a famous silver-smith (caelator) mentioned by Plin. *N. H.* xxxiii. 156, and stated by the same author (xxxiv. 90) to have represented 'philosophers' and 'scopas' – apparently = σκῶπας, satyrs or 'grotesques.'

Antigonus] Identified by v. Wilamowitz with A. of Karystos (Introduction, § 1).

262. Paus. i. 25. 2 πρὸς δὲ τῷ τείχει τῷ νοτίῳ Γιγάν-των οἳ περὶ Θρᾴκην ποτὲ καὶ τὸν Ἰσθμὸν τῆς Παλλήνης ᾤκησαν, τούτων τὸν λεγόμενον πόλεμον, καὶ μάχην πρὸς Ἀμαζόνας Ἀθηναίων, καὶ τὸ Μαραθῶνι πρὸς Μήδους ἔργον, καὶ Γαλατῶν τὴν ἐν Μυσίᾳ φθορὰν ἀνέθηκεν Ἄτταλος, ὅσον γε δύο πηχῶν ἕκαστον.

Close to the southern wall is to be seen the 'war of the Giants,' as it is called (they at one time inhabited Thrace and the isthmus of Pallene), and the battle of the Athenians against the Amazons, and the battle with the Persians at Marathon, and the destruction of the Gauls in Mysia. All these were dedicated by Attalos, and each figure is about two cubits in height.

τῷ τείχει] Of the Akropolis at Athens.

On existing figures from these groups see *Ov.* II⁴. 234 ff., *F. W.* 1403-1411. The question whether these are originals (so the authorities quoted above) or copies from bronze (so Milchhöfer and S. Reinach (*Rev. Arch.* 1889, 18) is a very doubtful one. Plutarch (*Anton.* 60) records that a figure of Dionysos from the Gigantomachia was blown down by a storm and fell over the south wall of the Akropolis. This seems more likely in the case of a bronze.

263. Plin. *N. H.* xxxiv. 88 Epigonus omnia fere praedicta imitatus praecessit in tubicine et matri inter-

Epigonos followed his predecessors in most of the subjects which I have named, and surpassed them with

fectae infante miserabiliter blandiente.

his trumpeter and his infant pitiably engaged in caressing its murdered mother.

praedicta] The passage comes from the list of those 'qui eiusdem generis opera fecerunt'—usually portraits of athletes, 'philosophers,' &c.

tubicine ... blandiente] Ulrichs conjectured that 'tubicine' referred to the Dying Gaul of the Capitol (*F. W.* 1412), beside whom lies a horn ('liticen' would have been a more correct translation of σαλπιγκτής (Urlichs) or κεραυλής (Reinach)). Michaelis (*Jahrb.* 1893, p. 119 ff.) identified the group of mother and child with the Amazon (from the group described in No. 262) at Naples (*F. W.* 1411), which is grouped with an infant in early descriptions and a sixteenth-century drawing. Petersen has shown, however (*Röm. Mitth.* 1893, p. 261 ff.), that the child was the work of an early restorer, afterwards removed. Moreover, Amazons are never represented as mothers. S. Reinach (*Revue des Études Grecques*, 1894, p. 37 ff.) suggests that a group of a *Gaulish* mother and child formed part of the series represented by the Dying Gaul and the so-called 'Arria and Paetus' (*F. W.* 1413).

The inscriptions of Epigonos (v. supr.) all point to the reign of Attalos I.

264. Ampel. Lib. Memor. viii. 14 Pergamo ara marmorea magna, alta pedes quadraginta cum maximis sculpturis ; continet autem gigantomachiam.

At Pergamon there is a great altar of marble 40 ft. in height, with colossal sculptures ; it contains the battle of the Giants.

Discovered by the German excavators 1878-1883. The inscriptions (Fränkel 70-84) give the artists' names Θεόρρητος ['Ορ]έστης [Διο]νυσι[άδης] (?) [Μενεκρ]άτης (?), and point to the reign of Eumenes II, the greatest builder among the kings of Pergamon. On the reliefs, (1) Gigantomachy, on the outer face of the substructure, (2) story of Telephos, inside the colonnade, the fragments of which are now at Berlin, see *Ov.* II¹. 261 ff. and references (especially Brunn, *Jahrbuch der preuss. Kunstsammlungen*, 1884).

2. THE SCHOOL OF RHODES.

A number of artists' signatures (Löwy 159-205) have been found on the island of Rhodes. Hiller v. Gärtringen (*Jahrb.* 1894, p. 23 ff.) has shown that these fall into two groups, (1) belonging to the latter part of the third and earlier part of the second century B. C. This period closes with the political decline of Rhodes after 168 B. C. ; (2) belonging to the first quarter of the first century B. C. The literary notices of Rhodian art are scanty.

(a) THE SCULPTORS OF THE LAOKOON.

265. Plin. *N. H.* xxxvi. 37 Nec deinde multo plurium fama est, quorundam claritati in operibus eximiis obstante numero artificum, quoniam nec unus occupat gloriam nec plures pariter nuncupari possunt, sicut in Laocoonte qui est in Titi imperatoris domo, opus omnibus et picturae et statuariae artis praeferendum. Ex uno lapide eum ac liberos draconumque mirabiles nexus de consilii sententia fecere summi artifices Agesander et Polydorus et Athenodorus Rhodii.

There are many more whose fame is not preserved. In some cases the glory of the finest works is obscured by the number of the artists, since no one of them can monopolise the credit nor can the names of more than one be handed down. This is the case with the Laokoon, which stands in the palace of the Imperator Titus, a work to be preferred to all that the arts of painting and sculpture have produced. Out of one block of stone the consummate artists Hagesandros, Polydoros and Athenodoros of Rhodes fashioned Laokoon, his sons, and snakes marvellously entwined about them, after deliberation among themselves.

On the Laokoon v. *Ov.* II⁴. 296 ff. and reff., *F. W.* 1422.

in Titi imperatoris ... domo] The Laokoon was discovered in 1506 A.D., *not* in the spot which tradition points out (in the Thermae of Titus), but in the 'Sette Sale,' corresponding to the Palace of Titus.

ex uno lapide] The Laokoon is constructed of six blocks, but the joins are so carefully concealed that even Michael Angelo could only detect three, and Pliny's account was no doubt popularly current in his time. Cp. No. 266.

de consilii sententia] Those who uphold a late date for the Laokoon maintain that these words mean 'by a decree of the Emperor's cabinet,' although no historical ground or occasion can be alleged. The phrase is however a common one, especially with writers of the Silver Age, in applied uses (cp. Sen. *Ep.* vii. 5. 11 quidquid honeste fit, una uirtus facit, sed ex consilii sententia; quod autem ab omnibus uirtutibus comprobatur ... optabile est) and would be quite appropriate in a rhetorical passage such as the present. There is therefore no necessity to seek an explanation in 'the βουλή of Rhodes' (Jahn) or 'the friends of the artists' (Mommsen).

Agesander et Polydorus et Athenodorus] The inscriptions of Athenodoros are published in facsimile by Förster, *Jahrb.* 1891, p. 191 ff., and treated by Hiller v. Gärtringen (*loc. cit.*), who shows that they are contemporaneous with an inscription in which L. Licinius Murena Imp. (82 B.C.) and (possibly) Sulla are mentioned. They therefore belong to group (2). The three artists may have been brothers, or Hagesandros may be the father of the others. Plin. *N. H.* xxxiv. 86 attributes to him portraits of 'feminae nobiles.'

(b) The Sculptors of the Farnese Bull.

Date.—Hiller v. Gärtringen (*Ath. Mitth.* 1894, 37 ff.) publishes an inscription from Magnesia on the Maeander which reads Ἀπολλώνιος | Ταυρίσκου | Τραλλιανὸς | ἐποίει, and dates from the early imperial period. If the father of the artist be identified with the sculptor of the bull, that work must be dated somewhat later than the Laokoon.

266. Plin. *N. H.* xxxii. 33 Pollio Asinius, ut fuit acris uehementiae, sic quo- Asinius Pollio with characteristic keenness and determination resolved that his

que spectari monumenta sua uoluit. In his sunt ... Hermerotes Taurisci, non caelatoris illius sed Tralliani ... 34 Zethus et Amphion ac Dirce et taurus uinculumque ex eodem lapide, a Rhodo aduecta opera Apollonii et Taurisci. Parentum hi certamen de se fecere, Menecraten uideri professi, sed esse naturalem Artemidorum.

gallery should be an object of general interest. In it stand the Hermerotes of Tauriskos, not the silversmith but the sculptor of Tralles, also Zethos, Amphion, Dirke, the bull and the rope —all made from one block of marble. and transported from Rhodes, the work of Apollonios and Tauriskos. These artists occasioned a rivalry of parents, for they declared that Menekrates was nominally, but Artemidoros really, their father.

On this group, discovered in 1456 in the Thermae of Caracalla see *Ov.* II[4]. Bk. v. c. 3 and reff., *F. W.* 1402.

Hermerotes] Busts with double heads—Hermes on the one face, Eros on the other. Cp. Hermathena.

Taurisci] On Tauriskos as a painter v. Brunn, *K. G.* II[2] 193, I[2] 330.

parentum hi certamen] This is merely a rhetorical way of expressing the fact that their adoptive father's name was Menekrates. The signature would run :—'Απολλώνιος καὶ Ταυρίσκος 'Αρτεμιδώρου, καθ' ὑοθεσίαν δὲ Μενεκράτους, Τραλλιανοὶ ἐποίησαν.

(c) ARISTONIDAS.

Date.—The inscription of his son Mnasitimos (Löwy 197) belongs to the earlier group mentioned above.

267. Plin. *N. H.* xxxiv. 140 Aristonidas artifex cum exprimere uellet Atha-

The artist Aristonidas, desiring to represent the madness of Athamas giving

mantis furorem Learcho filio praecipitato residentem paenitentia, aes ferrumque miscuit ut robigine eius per nitorem aeris relucente exprimeretur uerecundiae rubor. Hoc signum exstat hodie Rhodi.

way to remorse after he had hurled his son Learchos from the rocks, mixed iron with copper, in order that the iron rust might suffuse the brightness of the copper and portray the blush of shame. This statue is still to be seen at Rhodes.

Athamantis furorem] A. was visited by Hera with madness and murdered his son Learchos.

aes ferrumque miscuit] The story can scarcely be true, as the amalgamation of the metals would be a matter of great difficulty, nor would it produce the desired effect. Cp. No. 225 for a similar story.

APPENDIX II.

DAMOPHON OF MESSENE.

Date.—Since D. worked mainly at Messene and Megalopolis, it was formerly supposed that he lived in the fourth century B.C., when the first-named city was restored and the second founded by Epameinondas (371 B.C.). Fragments of the works described in No. 271 were, however, discovered at Lykosura in Arkadia in 1889 (see Kavvadias, *Fouilles de Lycosura*, 1893, Part I). Dörpfeld (*Ath. Mitth.*, 1893, 219 ff.) considers that the temple to which they belonged was erected not earlier than cent. II–I B.C., and others (especially Robert) attribute the sculptures on grounds of style to the Roman period. Kavvadias defends the earlier date.

268. Paus. iv. 31. 6 Μεσσηνίοις δὲ ἐν τῇ ἀγορᾷ . . . ἐστὶν . . . οὗ μάλιστα ἄξιον ποιήσασθαι μνήμην, ἄγαλμα Μητρὸς θεῶν, λίθου Παρίου, Δαμοφῶντος δὲ ἔργον, ὃς καὶ τὸν Δία ἐν Ὀλυμπίᾳ, διεστηκότος ἤδη τοῦ ἐλέφαντος, συνήρμοσεν ἐς τὸ ἀκριβέστατον . . . 7. Δαμοφῶντος δέ ἐστι τούτου καὶ ἡ Λαφρία καλουμένη παρὰ Μεσσηνίοις . . . 10. πλεῖστα δέ σφισι καὶ θέας μάλιστα ἄξια τοῦ Ἀσκληπιοῦ

The most remarkable work in the market-place of Messene is an image of the Mother of the Gods, of Parian marble, the work of Damophon, who restored the Zeus at Olympia with the greatest possible precision when the seams of the ivory opened. This Damophon also made the statue of Artemis, called Laphria, for the Messenians. The most numerous

παρέχεται τὸ ἱερόν. χωρὶς μὲν γὰρ τοῦ θεοῦ καὶ τῶν παίδων ἐστὶν ἀγάλματα, χωρὶς δὲ Ἀπόλλωνος καὶ Μουσῶν καὶ Ἡρακλέους, Πόλις τε ἡ Θηβαίων καὶ Ἐπαμεινώνδας ὁ Πολύμνιδος, Τύχη τε καὶ Ἄρτεμις Φωσφόρος. τὰ μὲν δὴ τοῦ λίθου Δαμοφῶντος ὃς εἰργάσατο· Μεσσηνίων δὲ ὅτι μὴ τοῦτον ἄλλον γε οὐδένα λόγου ποιήσαντα ἀξίως οἶδα ἀγάλματα· ἡ δὲ εἰκὼν τοῦ Ἐπαμεινώνδου ἐκ σιδήρου τέ ἐστι, καὶ ἔργον ἄλλου, οὐ τούτου.

and remarkable of their works of art are to be found in the Sanctuary of Asklepios. In one part stand images of the god and his children, in another those of Apollo, the Muses, and Herakles, the city of Thebes, and Epameinondas, the son of Polymnis, besides Fortune and Artemis of the Dawn. The marble statues are the work of Damophon —who, so far as I know, was the only Messenian sculptor of repute—while the portrait of Epameinondas is of iron, and is the work of a different artist.

ἡ Λαφρία καλουμένη] Probably represented on coins of Messene, *Num. Comm. P.* iii. For the scheme associated with this title cp. No. 71.

269. Paus. vii. 23. 5 Αἰγιεῦσι δὲ Εἰλειθυίας ἱερόν ἐστιν ἀρχαῖον, καὶ ἡ Εἰλειθυία ἐς ἄκρους ἐκ κεφαλῆς τοὺς πόδας ὑφάσματι κεκάλυπται λεπτῷ, ξόανον πλὴν προσώπου τε καὶ χειρῶν ἄκρων καὶ ποδῶν· 6. ταῦτα δὲ τοῦ Πεντελησίου λίθου πεποίηται· καὶ ταῖς χερσὶ τῇ μὲν ἐς εὐθὺ ἐκ-

At Aigion there is an ancient precinct of Eileithuia; the image of the goddess is clothed from head to foot in a fine woven garment, and is made of wood, except the face, hands, and feet, which are of Pentelic marble; one hand is extended, while the

τέταται, τῇ δὲ ἀνέχει δᾷδας... | other holds torches. The
ἔργον δὲ τοῦ Μεσσηνίου Δα- | image is the work of Damo-
μοφῶντός ἐστι τὸ ἄγαλμα | phon of Messene. Not far
7. τῆς Εἰλειθυίας οὐ μακρὰν | from this Eileithuia is a
Ἀσκληπιοῦ τέ ἐστι τέμενος | precinct of Asklepios, con-
καὶ ἀγάλματα Ὑγιείας καὶ | taining images of Hygieia
Ἀσκληπιοῦ. ἰαμβεῖον δὲ ἐπὶ | and Asklepios. On the
τῷ βάθρῳ τὸν Μεσσήνιον Δα- | base is inscribed an iambic
μοφῶντα εἶναι τὸν εἰργασμένον | verse, which states that
φησίν. | Damophon of Messene
wrought them.

δᾷδας] MSS. read δᾷδα, but the plural is used in the mythological explanation which follows in the text of Paus., and on the coins of Aigion, which seem to reproduce this work (*Num. Comm. R.* vi, vii), the goddess holds *two* torches.

Ὑγιείας καὶ Ἀσκληπιοῦ] Perhaps represented on the coins of Aigion, *Num. Comm. R.* ix–xi.

270. Paus. viii. 31. 1 τὸ | At the opposite or west-
δὲ ἕτερον πέρας τῆς στοᾶς | ern end of the colonnade is
παρέχεται τὸ πρὸς ἡλίου δυσ- | an enclosure sacred to the
μῶν περίβολον Θεῶν ἱερὸν | great Goddesses. Before
τῶν μεγάλων... ἐπειργασμένοι | the entry are represented
δὲ ἐπὶ τύπων πρὸ τῆς ἐσόδου | in relief on the one side
τῇ μὲν Ἄρτεμις, τῇ δὲ Ἀσκλη- | Artemis, on the other As-
πιός ἐστι καὶ Ὑγιεία. 2. Θεαὶ | klepios and Hygieia. Of
δὲ αἱ μεγάλαι Δημήτηρ μὲν | the great Goddesses, De-
λίθου διὰ πάσης, ἡ δὲ Σώτειρα | meter is made entirely of
τὰ ἐσθῆτος ἐχόμενα ξύλου | marble, while the Saviour,
πεποίηται· μέγεθος δὲ ἑκα- | so far as her garments are
τέρας πέντε που καὶ δέκα εἰσὶ | concerned, is of wood; each
πόδες. τὰ δὲ ἀγάλματα ⟨ Δαμο- | figure is, I suppose, about
φῶν ὁ Μεσσήνιος ⟩ καὶ πρὸ | fifteen feet in height. Da-
αὐτῶν κόρας ἐποίησεν οὐ με- | mophon of Messene made

γάλας, ἐν χιτῶσί τε καθήκουσιν
ἐς σφυρά, καὶ ἀνθῶν ἀνάπλεων
ἑκατέρα τάλαρον ἐπὶ τῇ κεφαλῇ
φέρει· εἶναι δὲ θυγατέρες τοῦ
Δαμοφῶντος λέγονται· τοῖς
δὲ ἐπανάγουσιν ἐς τὸ θειότερον
δοκεῖ σφᾶς Ἀθηνᾶν τε εἶναι
καὶ Ἄρτεμιν τὰ ἄνθη μετὰ
τῆς Περσεφόνης συλλεγούσας.
3. ἔστι δὲ καὶ Ἡρακλῆς παρὰ
τῇ Δήμητρι μέγεθος μάλιστα
πῆχυν· τοῦτον τὸν Ἡρακλῆν
εἶναι τῶν Ἰδαίων καλουμένων
Δακτύλων Ὀνομάκριτός φησιν
ἐν τοῖς ἔπεσι· κεῖται δὲ τράπεζα ἔμπροσθεν, ἐπειργασμέναι
τε ἐπ᾽ αὐτῇ δύο τε εἰσὶν Ὧραι,
καὶ ἔχων Πᾶν σύριγγα καὶ
Ἀπόλλων κιθαρίζων. ἔστι δὲ
καὶ ἐπίγραμμα ἐπ᾽ αὐτοῖς, εἶναι
σφᾶς θεῶν τῶν πρώτων. 4.
πεποίηνται δὲ ἐπὶ τῇ τραπέζῃ
καὶ Νύμφαι· Νέδα μὲν Δία
φέρουσα ἔτι νήπιον παῖδα, Ἀν-
θρακία δὲ νύμφη τῶν Ἀρκα-
δικῶν καὶ αὕτη δᾷδα ἔχουσά
ἐστιν, Ἀγνὼ δὲ τῇ μὲν ὑδρίαν,
ἐν δὲ τῇ ἑτέρᾳ χειρὶ φιάλην·
Ἀρχιρρόης δὲ καὶ Μυρτωέσσης
εἰσὶν ὑδρίαι τὰ φορήματα, καὶ
ὕδωρ δῆθεν ἀπ᾽ αὐτῶν κάτεισιν. . . 5. ἔστι δὲ ἐντὸς τοῦ
περιβόλου τῶν μεγάλων Θεῶν

the statues, as well as the
small female figures which
stand before them, clothed
in tunics reaching to the
ankles, and bear each a
basket full of flowers on
her head. They are said
to be the daughters of Damophon; but those who
refer them to a divine origin
believe that they repre-
sent Athena and Artemis
gathering flowers with Persephone. Beside Demeter
stands Herakles, about a
cubit in height; this He-
rakles is stated by Onoma-
kritos, in his poems, to be
one of the so-called Idaian
Daktyloi. Before them
stands a table, on which
are wrought in relief two
Seasons, Pan holding a pipe,
and Apollo playing the
lyre. There is an inscription relating to them, which
states that they are amongst
the first of the gods.
Nymphs are also repre-
sented on the table; there
is Neda carrying the infant
Zeus, and Anthrakia, also
an Arkadian nymph, hold-

καὶ Ἀφροδίτης ἱερόν· . . 6.
ἀγάλματα δὲ ἐν τῷ ναῷ Δαμο-
φῶν ἐποίησεν, Ἑρμῆν ξύλου
καὶ Ἀφροδίτης ξόανον· καὶ
ταύτης χεῖρές εἰσι λίθου καὶ
πρόσωπόν τε καὶ ἄκροι πόδες.
τὴν δὲ ἐπίκλησιν τῇ θεῷ
Μαχανῖτιν . . . ἔθεντο.

ing a torch, and Hagno
with a pitcher in one hand
and a bowl in the other ;
there is Archirroe, too, and
Myrtoessa, each of whom
bears a pitcher, from which
water, no doubt, is supposed
to be flowing. There is
also a sanctuary of Aphrodite within the precinct of
the great Goddesses. Da-
mophon made the images
in the temple ; there is a
Hermes of wood, and a
wooden image of Aphro-
dite, which also has hands,
face, and feet of marble.
The goddess received the
surname of Machanitis.

At Megalopolis. For akrolithic sculpture in the fourth century,
cp. No. 216.

Σώτειρα] The Arkadian appellation of Persephone.

271. Paus. viii. 37. 1 ἀπὸ
δὲ Ἀκακησίου τέσσαρας σταδίους ἀπέχει τὸ ἱερὸν τῆς
Δεσποίνης . . . 3. θεῶν δὲ
αὐτὰ τὰ ἀγάλματα, Δέσποινα
καὶ ἡ Δημήτηρ τε καὶ ὁ θρόνος
ἐν ᾧ καθέζονται, καὶ τὸ ὑπόθημα τὸ ὑπὸ τοῖς ποσίν ἐστιν
ἑνὸς ὁμοίως λίθου· καὶ οὔτε
τῶν ἐπὶ τῇ ἐσθῆτι οὔτε ὁπόσα

The sanctuary of De-
spoina is four stades distant
from Akakesion. The
images of the goddesses
themselves, Despoina and
Demeter, and the throne
whereon they are seated,
and the footstool beneath
their feet, are all of one
block ; and no part of the

εἴργασται περὶ τὸν θρόνον οὐδέν ἐστιν ἑτέρου λίθου προσ-
εχὲς σιδήρῳ καὶ κόλλῃ, ἀλλὰ
τὰ πάντα ἐστὶν εἷς λίθος.
οὗτος οὐκ ἐσεκομίσθη σφίσιν
ὁ λίθος, ἀλλὰ κατὰ ὄψιν ὀνεί-
ρατος λέγουσιν αὐτὸν ἐξευρεῖν
ἐντὸς τοῦ περιβόλου τὴν γῆν
ὀρύξαντες. τῶν δὲ ἀγαλμάτων
ἐστὶν ἑκατέρου μέγεθος κατὰ
τὸ Ἀθήνησιν ἄγαλμα μάλιστα
τῆς Μητρός· 4. Δαμοφῶντος
δὲ καὶ ταῦτα ἔργα. ἡ μὲν οὖν
Δημήτηρ δᾷδα ἐν δεξιᾷ φέρει,
τὴν δὲ ἑτέραν χεῖρα ἐπιβέβλη-
κεν ἐπὶ τὴν Δέσποιναν· ἡ δὲ
Δέσποινα σκῆπτρόν τε καὶ
καλουμένην κίστην ἐπὶ τοῖς
γόνασιν ἔχει· τῇ δὲ ἔχεται τῇ
δεξιᾷ κίστης. τοῦ θρόνου δὲ
ἑκατέρωθεν Ἄρτεμις μὲν παρὰ
τὴν Δήμητρα ἔστηκεν ἀμπε-
χομένη δέρμα ἐλάφου καὶ ἐπὶ
τῶν ὤμων φαρέτραν ἔχουσα,
ἐν δὲ ταῖς χερσὶ τῇ μὲν λαμ-
πάδα ἔχει, τῇ δὲ δράκοντας
δύο· παρὰ δὲ τὴν Ἄρτεμιν
κατάκειται κύων, οἷαι θηρεύειν
εἰσὶν ἐπιτήδειοι. 5. πρὸς δὲ
τῆς Δεσποίνης τῷ ἀγάλματι
ἔστηκεν Ἄνυτος, σχῆμα ὡπλισ-
μένου παρεχόμενος. φασὶ δὲ
οἱ περὶ τὸ ἱερὸν τραφῆναι τὴν

decoration, either of their
garments, or of the throne
itself, is made of a separate
block, or fastened with
clamp or solder, but the
whole is one block. This
block was not imported,
but (as they say) they found
it by digging a hole within
the precinct at a spot indicated by a vision. Each of
the images is about equal in
size to that of the Great
Mother at Athens; they
also are the work of Damophon. Demeter bears a
torch in her right hand,
while she has laid the left on
Despoina; Despoina bears
a sceptre and ' cista,' as it is
called, in her lap; with one
hand—the right—she holds
the ' cista.' On each side
of the throne is a figure;
beside Demeter stands Ar-
temis, clad in a deer-skin,
with a quiver on her
shoulder; in one hand she
holds a torch, in the other
two snakes; beside Artemis
lies a bitch, like those used
in hunting. Close to the
image of Despoina stands